CW00542670

DAVID HILLYARD.
YACHT. LAUNCH & BOAT BUILDER.

HILLYARD

Often when I see a boat I admire, it turns out to be a Hillyard

Clare Allcard, author and sailor, wife of the late Edward Allcard
(lone circumnavigator and long-term cruising yachtsman,
who died aged 102 in 2017)

We who adventure upon the sea, however humbly, cannot but
feel that we are more fortunate than ordinary people and that
we have something which we could not tell nor they understand

Claud Worth, well-known yachtsman, ophthalmologist
and writer of sailing books in Victorian Britain

To the memory of

Michael and Nicky Joyce

HILLYARD

The Man, His Boats, and Their Sailors

Nicholas Gray

Lodestar Books

Published 2021 by
Lodestar Books
71 Boveney Road, London, SE23 3NL, United Kingdom

lodestarbooks.com

A CIP catalogue record for this book
is available from the British Library

ISBN 978-1-907206-54-2

The author and publisher would like to thank all those who gave permission
for their photographs to be reproduced, and apologise to those we were
unable to locate. Any errors or omissions notified to the publisher in the
attribution of photographs will be corrected in future editions of this book

Typeset by Lodestar Books in Adobe Jenson Pro and Gill Sans Std

Printed in Wales by Gomer Press

All papers used by Lodestar Books are sourced responsibly

CONTENTS

PLATES

Between pages 96 and 97:

1. The High Street, Rowhedge, c1900
2. The Ferry, Rowhedge
3. Rowhedge Regatta
4. Congregation of the Mariners Chapel, Rowhedge
5. Hillyard, aged 16, sailing his home built 16ft sharpie
6. Forrestts' Shipyard, Wivenhoe c1902
7. Littlehampton c1906, as Hillyard would have found it
8. The chain ferry crossing the river Arun at Littlehampton
9. The swing bridge, which replaced the chain ferry in 1908
10. Littlehampton lifeboat, *The Brothers Freeman*, being launched
11. The Shipyard c1960
12. Views of the Shipyard
13. Hillyard's stand at an early Earl's Court Boat Show
14. Hillyard with Reginald Moody at an Earl's Court Boat Show c1960
15. David Hillyard at the Shipyard
16. The Shipyard's wartime fire float – a converted ship's lifeboat
17. Women employed at the yard during World War II
18. The workforce expanded to some 150 during World War II
19. Harbour Defence Motor Launch (no. 1458)
20. Workers on their HDML
21. Probably the first yacht built by Hillyard in Littehampton, in 1906
22. Hillyard motor cruiser the 40-ft *Iorana*

Between pages 160 and 161:

FOREWORD

David Hillyard, founder of the famous firm of boatbuilders in Little-hampton, was born in the late nineteenth century, at the height of the Big Boat era. His family were stalwarts of Rowhedge, where the aristocratic owners of the enormous cutters dicing in the Solent sent their skippers to pick their racing crews of hard-bitten fishermen. Yachts, in those days, were for the very rich, but the men who sailed them were often the reverse. It is tempting to think that it was a consciousness of this divide that led Hillyard—a devout Christian, descended from a long line of fishermen—and his successors to build boats that were robust, practical, and within the means of owners who did not have the advantage of dukedoms or armaments factories.

Nobody has ever accused Hillyards of being ocean greyhounds, and that was never their builders' intention. They have always been practical cruising boats, their sail plans divided into easily-handled areas, their family-friendly accommodation the prototype for many of their successors to this day. Hillyards brought cruising under sail within the reach of thousands, and many of the owners they served remained loyal to the yard's designs throughout their cruising lives.

This account of David Hillyard's voyage from apprentice boatbuilder to founder of a boatbuilding dynasty will be deeply interesting not only to owners of his boats and enthusiasts of traditional boatbuilding, but to anyone interested in the story of messing about in boats as practised in Britain. It also provides fascinating insights into the development of a small but significant corner of the relationship between the people of these islands and the seas that surround us.

Sam Llewellyn
April 2021

PROLOGUE

When Vice-Admiral Sir Lancelot Bell Davies, KBE was a boy of thirteen, he went along to the Hillyard shipyard in Littlehampton with his seventeen-year-old sister to buy a boat. It was 1939.

David Hillyard met them with great courtesy and led them out into the yard. 'Yes,' he said, 'I do have a craft for sale at £100, but I will not sell her to you two. She would be too much for you to handle. However, I have *Lindy* here—she won me the 1927 Estuary Cruiser design competition—and you can have her for £150.' The young man said he did not have £150, but if Hillyard would accept £15 as a deposit for first refusal, he would go home and see if he could raise the balance. David Hillyard agreed, and the boy handed over the £15.

Then war broke out and it was not until many years later that Bell Davies, now a Sub-Lieutenant, could think again about sailing. As the war neared its end, he went back to Littlehampton to find the shipyard in full production building coastal craft for the Navy. The Sub-Lieutenant saw David Hillyard and asked him if *Lindy* was still available. He was delighted to be told 'Yes'. Realising that prices today would be quite different from pre-war days, he asked Hillyard how much he wanted for her. Hillyard looked at him in faint surprise and said, 'You trusted me with your £15 in 1939, so the price is the same as it was then. £150.'

'Is it surprising,' Sir Lancelot said many years later, 'that David Hillyard became a legend?'

INTRODUCTION

Around the shores of the United Kingdom and many other European countries and, indeed, the rest of the world, you will find in many harbours, rivers or creeks examples of a rounded, sensible looking, often double ended, seamanlike wooden sailing yacht, usually with a mast which at first sight looks too small for the boat. These vessels are universally recognized the world over as being a 'Hillyard'. Indeed, the word has become almost a generic term for a small wooden cruising yacht. The question 'is she a Hillyard?' is asked over and over again all over the world.

Often ignored, sometimes ridiculed, occasionally laughed at and derided, this fleet of similar looking boats, which engender huge affection amongst its owners and crews, is the result of the inspiration, ingenuity, hard work, cussedness and stubbornness of just one man and a small team of shipwrights. The man was David Hillyard.

Working in the periods before and after the Second World War, from ramshackle and run-down sheds in Littlehampton on the banks of the river Arun in West Sussex, Hillyard produced in his yard a unique collection of over eight hundred small innovative wooden yachts, all built to a similar concept and to his own designs. Today they are recognized by many as being something rather special.

Coming from a humble background, David Hillyard recognized in the 1930s, and more particularly in the post war boom years of wooden boat building during the 1950s and 1960s, that boating was for all the people and not merely for the wealthy who had made sailing headlines in the pre-war years. Hillyard recognized before anyone else that post-war yachting was not going to be about paid-hands, or hardy young men roughing it in damp cramped leaking cabins, but about families, often in straitened circumstances, who would sail together at weekends and on longer summer holidays, whilst barely being able to afford to buy, let alone maintain, their vessels.

As a canny observer of life, Hillyard began to realise that women would come to take a larger and larger part in the sport and that they would be looking for some of the comforts of home in their husband's choice of vessel. Thus he began to put curtains over portholes, carpets or lino on cabin soles, and single-handedly invented the 'three cabin layout' which has today become associated with his vessels and adopted by many family cruising yachts built from then on. Today this provides an aft cabin for the owner and his wife, separated from the rest of the boat by a safe deep cockpit, a midships saloon/galley and a separate forecabin for the children. Originally, he sold the idea to a sceptical public as an arrangement whereby the ubiquitous paid hand or hands of those days could have their own space aft away from the owner's party.

Hillyard's other innovation was to introduce, albeit in a somewhat haphazard way, a system of production and series building offering customers an ever-changing range of standard boats (all to Hillyard's own designs) which could be varied according to customers' wishes. Many were built by the yard 'on spec', hoping for a buyer on or before completion. This 'production line' method of building allowed the yard to keep costs to a minimum, something Hillyard put at the forefront of his thinking throughout his life. It also meant he was often able to offer 'immediate delivery' of a completed boat.

As a result of this approach, it is believed that in total some eight hundred boats came out of the yard. Hillyard was never good at record keeping and the yard lost all its pre-Second World War records in a major fire which occurred soon after this war ended. Thus, it is impossible to know exactly how many vessels were actually built. An estimated four hundred are still afloat today. Wooden boat building at the yard ceased in the 1970s, after which there was a failed attempt at producing a glass reinforced plastic 'Hillyard' (this one designed by Laurent Giles) which for various reasons never took off. After that the yard staggered on for several years undertaking repairs and maintenance until it finally closed, insolvent and in ignominious circumstances, in 2009.

There is no doubt that Hillyards are considered by many, in the words of Peter Gregson of the brokerage Wooden Ships, as being 'like Marmite—you either love 'em or you hate 'em'. They are among the most maligned of all classic wooden yachts and are perhaps the only class of yacht that carries the cultural baggage of an 'official' sailors' joke. In the same way people would crack jokes about Skoda motor cars in the 1980s (filling one up with petrol doubles its value, etc.), there is a joke about Hillyards that you 'won't drown in one but you might starve'*. In reality the joke is actually a backhanded compliment.

It is correct to say that the boats David Hillyard designed and built are neither the quickest nor the most heart-stoppingly elegant, but they absolutely will get you there. 'Heavy, workmanlike build, sensibly judged sail area (some will say under canvassed), the double ended hull form, good freeboard and wide side decks all mean that they are boats which will get a family safely, comfortably and cheaply wherever their hearts desire.' †

And as we shall see in this book, such desires have taken Hillyards safely, competently and quietly to almost all corners of the Earth, where many remain in commission, well loved, maintained and cared for by owners who will hear nothing bad said about their boats.

Whatever view you may have of the Hillyard fleet, there is no doubt it is something unique. Other yards and designers may, in the heyday of wooden boat building, have produced more beautiful, more elegant, more racy or faster vessels, but no other company had at that time designed and built so many vessels, producing a distinctive 'house style' recognized the world over. An analysis of Lloyd's Register of Yachts for the year 1965 discloses that at that time there were three hundred and twenty-four yachts listed as having been built by Hillyard's. No other boatbuilder came close to that number, the nearest being Thorneycrofts with one hundred and fifty-four vessels, many built for the Navy. James Silver built one hundred and thirty-nine and the Berthon Boat Company one hundred and seventeen.

In the days before modern mass production of GRP boats there was no other boatbuilder in the world of whom one could safely say of their boats words like 'that's a Moody' or 'that's a Nicholson'. These yards all built yachts to different designers' shapes, sizes and designs.

---

*   Steffan Meyric-Hughes, 'Affordable Classics 13: Little Hillyards', *Classic Boat*

†   Ibid.

Only David Hillyard built his own instantly recognizable fleet of which almost anyone in the world can say 'that's a Hillyard'.*

*   *   *

David Hillyard was a man of rare integrity who never went back on his word and who became respected and trusted by his customers, many of whom went back to the yard for new boats, year after year. He trusted them and they trusted him for their quality of workmanship, for their low cost and because he built sensible seaworthy boats.

Stories of Hillyard's honesty and trustworthiness abound and, unlike some of today's boatbuilding businesses, which seem to bounce from one bankruptcy to another with customer's deposits disappearing along the way, Hillyard himself never did anyone out of a penny and would never have got involved in any sort of financial misdealing. Indeed, it was not uncommon for customers to hand over signed blank cheques to be filled in on completion of the job, based purely on a verbal quote from the old man. Who would do that in today's climate? Invoices were simple, often not arriving until six months after the new owner had taken delivery and saying no more than 'to supply one 12-ton yacht' and a price. There were never any written contracts.

Hillyard was a deeply religious man and his Christian faith was important to him throughout his life. He was invariably kind and thoughtful to all those with whom he dealt, whether customer or work hand.

In the 1960s, prompted by Hillyard's nephew Dennis Cullingford, the yard adopted the practice of putting on board all newly built boats, as they slid down the slipway for the first time, a Bible inscribed with the yacht's name. They wanted each boat to have and leave the yard with something which embodied the two men's spiritual beliefs, which both David Hillyard and Dennis Cullingford valued and held dearly. Over one hundred and forty- five yachts completed by the yard had one of these bibles on board. They have become collectors' items

---

*   A few years ago I was sitting at lunch at a farm deep in the heart of the French countryside many hundreds of miles from the sea when I was asked to describe my boat. I said it was a heavily built solid 42-foot wooden ketch with a centre cockpit. A man sitting opposite me, who so far as I knew was a local farmer, asked me 'Est-ce un Hillyard?'

and many subsequent owners would return to the yard requesting replacements for damaged or lost copies.

David Hillyard was born in 1883 in Rowhedge in Essex and died childless in 1963, aged eighty, attending the yard daily up to three months before his death. On his death, he left the business to his nephew, Dennis Cullingford, who had been brought up in Littlehampton and who started working at the yard in 1941 when he was sixteen.

Dennis kept the yard going through the 1960s and the early 1970s by which time the fibreglass revolution was sounding the knell for traditional wooden boat building. During the 1970s the yard undertook a great deal of maintenance and repair work but from 1975 to 1977 they built only one new boat a year. Then nothing until 1982 when the last new build wooden yacht was launched—a 34ft gaff cutter.

In 1979 Dennis Cullingford was joined by his son, Simon, who had previously worked in another yard. The Cullingfords hatched a plan to produce a 36ft GRP 'modern' Hillyard, the plans for which were drawn up by Laurent Giles & Partners. Although a few were built, their plan never came off and was abandoned after the moulds for the hull mysteriously caught fire and were destroyed.

An attempt was made to set up branches in Gosport near Portsmouth, and in Chichester, but nothing came of this. The yard staggered on looking after customers' yachts until it closed for good in 2009, under somewhat confusing circumstances as we shall see.

*   *   *

This book looks at the life and times of David Hillyard, what made him the man he was, how he developed his own distinctive designs and concepts for his boats, and how he kept these ideas alive for nearly a century. It looks at the boats themselves, how they were built, at the people who built, bought and sailed them and who have kept the Hillyard fleet alive and relatively intact. It looks at the voyages undertaken by these boats, many crossing oceans and even circling the world. It looks at many of the people who over the years have owned Hillyards and those who have done so much to keep the fleet intact. Finally, it describes what happened to the yard after David Hillyard's death in 1963 and how his closest descendant kept his philosophy and ideas alive until modern materials and cultural changes made the continuation of the dream impossible and no longer financially viable.

Whilst David Hillyard commenced building small boats well over a century ago, originally small fishing boats and then vessels for the Navy during World War One, he did not start to build yachts until 1922. It therefore seems appropriate to publish, in time for this Centenary year of David Hillyard's first yacht, a revised, lengthened, and updated version of a book originally written and published by Dr John Balchin in 2004 titled 'The David Hillyard Story'. The original has long been out of print and today copies are difficult to come by.

In 2019 The Hillyard Owners Association asked me if I would undertake this work, which invitation I was pleased to accept. I am an ex-Hillyard owner with a long association with the boats and many of their owners.

I am pleased to have been able to resurrect and expand this work, which I have done with the full approval of the original author, making it once more available to all those interested in this small, but important, part of Britain's maritime heritage.

Part I

THE MAN AND HIS LIFE

Chapter 1

EARLY DAYS

'Hillyard's of Littlehampton'—the two names run together so easily for those of us who know about the boatyard, that it's something of a surprise to discover that the man who founded it was originally a foreigner to the Sussex coast. However, David Hillyard's marine pedigree was without question. He was born in 1883 in the little Essex village of Rowhedge, a community married to the sea and sailing if ever one was. There he spent his childhood years.

Lying on the banks of the River Colne, upstream of the somewhat larger Wivenhoe, and about four miles downstream from Colchester, Rowhedge was at the turn of the century a self-contained settlement of about twelve hundred souls with an influence on yachting out of all proportion to its size. This was because, in the heyday of large racing and cruising yachts, many Rowhedge men, along with men from neighbouring Wivenhoe, Brightlingsea and Tollesbury, served as captains and crews on the big boats during the British summer sailing season.

These were the days of the 'big boats', when a yacht was a social acquisition and when yachting really was the sport of queens and kings. An enormous amount of aristocratic money was invested annually in the game. But for many owners, as became their wealth and station in life, it was sailing at second hand. Although many did go aboard their expensive creations, and some became accomplished helmsmen, the real work of sailing these craft and winning races was left to hired crews and skippers without whom the whole exercise would have been impossible. Handling many tons of boat, driven along at high speed by towering rigs, took immense skill and muscle power and this is where the inhabitants of these Essex villages came into their own.

During the late Victorian period, many of these villagers worked on the big boats as professional skippers or 'hands', spending the summer months moving with their yachts from regatta to regatta around the British Isles, or taking their owners cruising to the Mediterranean or places further afield. And they were good at it. By the end of the nineteenth century most of the big names in yachting employed Colneside crews, and the Rowhedgers were amongst the best.

Captain John Carter and most of the thirty hands on King Edward VII's famous cutter *Britannia* were all Rowhedge men. The 129ft *Valkyrie III*, unsuccessful challenger for the ninth America's Cup, was crewed from this forgotten little Essex village. So famous was the skill of these Essex professionals that not only were they in demand in the Solent and on the Clyde, but several were hired by Americans and shipped over to the United States of America to crew on some of the yachts sailing in the first defence of the America's Cup held in 1870[*]. Even the German ultra-nationalistic Kaiser Willhelm II filled his racing yachts *Iduna* and the 161ft *Meteor III* with Rowhedge crews in his bids to attempt to dominate the yacht racing scene in the period running up to the start of the Great War.

Smartly kitted out each year by the owners and sharing prize money at the end of the season, these men of Rowhedge shared a far from plebeian although somewhat insecure life, while their spouses kept house and reared their children at home. Some of the Rowhedge dwellings, built with their earnings and their share in the prize money, were named after the yachts which gave their owners employment, as were many of their fishing boats. Out of season, many turned from the glamour of the big boats to the mundane business of earning their keep by fishing. There was a sizeable smack fleet based at Rowhedge which ranged around the coast chasing winter catches of sprats or dredging for oysters, dangerous work from which some did not return.

For all its glitz, professional yachting was an uncertain way of life. Whilst employment on the yachts was steadier than that offered on the local farms or in the numerous shipyards, wages were lower than on land. But there was always prize money for the crews on successful yachts. Some crews did end the season relatively well-off, but the

---

[*]   In 1870 a single British yacht, the Schooner *Cambria*, owned by railway tycoon James Lloyd Ashbury, challenged a fleet of seventeen American schooners in the first challenge to attempt to win back the America's Cup. *Cambria* was unsuccessful and the challenge was won by the American yacht *Magic*.

vagaries of winter fishing could leave them hard-up by the following spring. At least their children would enjoy one perk, however; this was to wear their fathers' cast-off last season's gear. Many a Rowhedge child was known to turn up at school in a guernsey with the name of a famous yacht emblazoned across the front.

For some, but only the best, there was the opportunity to become a yacht's captain. If one had the necessary ability (and luck) it was possible to rise through the ranks to become skipper and sailing master of one of those magnificent yachts. This would lead to more pay and the chance to get on familiar terms with the great and wealthy owners, but within the constraints of the social stratification of the day.

Such class structure as there was in Rowhedge society was along the lines of 'captains' and 'hands'. They tended to live in different streets, and even to walk on different sections of the quay, but even acclaimed captains of these big racing yachts could rapidly fall from grace in the event that they and their yachts stopped winning.

David Hillyard's father, also David, worked on the big yachts, although there is doubt as to which ones. There is mention of a Captain Hillyard of the yawl *Edwina*, but this might refer to a relative living in Rowhedge. On the other hand, *Edwina* was a recurring Hillyard name. In later years, when David Hillyard made his nephew Dennis his first model yacht, he called it *Edwina*. Certainly, David Sr was always known in later life as a former yacht 'hand'. Another hint of David Sr's life as a yacht hand/captain is that in later years he named one of his son's boats *Ailsa*, after a yacht on which he had once crewed. *Ailsa* was a 283-ton racing cutter, skippered by Rowhedge Captain Tom Jay, which raced against the royal yacht *Britannia* both around British coasts and in the Mediterranean. David Sr was no doubt one of the large crew employed to get such a vast yacht over the line first. No wonder that after a long life on board the yachts Davis Sr in his old age felt entitled to clump around his son's boatyard waving his stick, chaffing the men for not wearing the 'correct' gear whilst 'advising' them on matters like the right way to turn a dinghy over! It is also said that the reason why some of the earlier Hillyard yachts carry somewhat exotic names is that David Sr would suggest these, drawing on his fund of 'big yacht' names. In the Hillyard family the topic of conversation was not that of football teams or the like but of the skippers and crews of the big boats and the league tables of their races at the regattas held all around the coast during the summer months.

Out of season, the Colneside villages had an ongoing link with yachting, for the Essex creeks provided much sought-after soft mud berths during the winter months. Contemporary records estimate that about fifty large yachts laid up in Rowhedge each winter[*]. Margaret Leather, who wrote much detail about life in the village around the turn of the century[†], described rows of large yachts, both sail and steam, moored in the mud along the quays and riverbank throughout the winter. Photographs from around the same time tell the same story, although this is hard to believe when one sees the quays and banks deserted as they are today. Captains and hands were often paid retainers to look after these vessels during the laid-up season and the yachts' presence guaranteed a continuing source of work and employment for the local boatyards, of which there were several.

So when David Charles Gershom Hillyard was born to his mother Harriet in Rowhedge in 1883, there would have been three main career options open to him—sailing on yachts like his father, working on the fishing smacks, or working in the boat building and repair yards. When his time came, he chose the last one.

Like many boys reared on British rivers by the sea, David grew up with a natural love for boats and sailing. In later years he would translate this into a business which would set trends in yacht design and construction, but even as a young lad he was showing flair. His wood carving and sandpapering at his school were the inconspicuous beginnings of this. It was way back then that David Hillyard was seen to be making excellent model boats that actually sailed. A local trader in Colchester learnt of these models and bought some which, to the young schoolboy's delight, sold as well as they sailed. So began his boatbuilding career.

This skill with his hands dictated the predictable progression from school into a boatbuilding apprenticeship. For this he had a choice, as there were two yards in Rowhedge at that time and three in Wiven-

---

[*]   Compared with a fleet of some forty fishing smacks which were based in Rowhedge.

[†]   Leather, Margaret. *Saltwater Village*, Terence Dalton, 1977.

hoe. He chose Wivenhoe, where boats had been built for many years. David chose Forrestts to serve his apprenticeship. The largest Wivenhoe yard at the time, they were moving into steel construction, including pre-fabricating steamers and launches for the far-flung corners of the Empire. Many of these had to be constructed in bits and then crated up for export. Others were built for domestic destinations like Lake Windermere. The yard continued to build wooden boats and had a constant need for skilled shipwrights. David started with them when he was fourteen.

Wivenhoe is on the opposite bank, just downriver from Rowhedge. David would have had to leave his house early to catch the ferry across the river in time for a 6.30 am start at the yard. There was a half-hour break for breakfast at 8.00 am, and an hour for lunch at 12.30. They would then work on until 5.30 or 6.00 pm. He worked on Saturday mornings until 1.00 pm.

Apprentices were taken on by the yard manager and then assigned by a foreman to the care of a skilled shipwright. There was no formal training as such and the boy would have had to pick it up as he went along, usually beginning with the broom! Apprentices' first job was usually for them to be made to build their own wooden toolbox. At that time his apprenticeship would have been for a seven-year term. Over the years and with a better approach, the length of such apprenticeships was reduced from seven to four years, while currently it is claimed that shipwrights can be trained in basic skills in under a year.

It was hard work in those days, abysmally paid, and not always as secure as it seemed. Discipline was tight in the yard. At the end of the day, employees were frisked at the gate, and even if it was only the stub end of a candle (their main source of illumination) that was found in a pocket, they were out. If a boy did not show promise, he was summarily dismissed. On top of that, there were frequent bankruptcies amongst the yards, putting all hands out of work. Even Forrestts, despite its size and turnover, had a somewhat shaky financial history.

From 1897 until 1904, when he became twenty-one, David learned his trade and there was a good deal to learn. He had to develop his skills in handling and looking after his tools, particularly how to keep them sharp. He had to learn about different timbers and fastenings.

He had to learn to adze out keels, stems, deadwoods and stern posts from solid baulks of timber. He had to learn how to loft lines, produce moulds and set them up plumb, and then acquire the skills involved in cutting, scarphing, shaping and fastening planking, notching in deck beams and laying and paying decks. He would also have been initiated into the arcane worlds of masting and rigging and would have learnt the basics of mechanical and electrical engineering.

Early on this apprentice gained the reputation of being an incredibly fast worker and when he later became his own boss he expected his men to match his speed. As a shipwright he would have been engaged at a yard like Forrestts in building yachts and wooden craft up to a hundred feet long, as well as fitting wooden decking and upperworks to steel ships. The shipwrights were responsible for launching the boats when complete.

Even whilst working these long hours, David built small boats for himself. A photograph shows him sailing on the River Colne in a 16ft sharpie he had built himself at the age of sixteen, wearing the cap he was scarcely to be without for the rest of his life (it was said later that you could tell his mood by whether he was wearing it to port or to starboard!). For the men of Rowhedge and Wivenhoe, boating was not just a job to be done or a sport to be serviced, but something to be enjoyed. A highlight each year in those days was the combined Rowhedge and Wivenhoe regatta, run by each community in alternate years, and claimed to be under Royal patronage as the King was one of the yacht owners who contributed the prize money. Held at the end of the season when the crews on the big boats had returned home, the regattas included a variety of classes from small rowing boats to dinghies, yachts and fishing smacks. In these races David Hillyard would have found himself up against the crack skippers and crews of the day.

The Rowhedge involvement in the big boat scene of that day is a good illustration of just what yachting meant in the period up to the Great War. To be an accepted member of the yachting community you had to be wealthy, preferably aristocratic, and not involved in 'trade'*. There is a well-known story of a yacht broker of this period

---

* Sir Thomas Lipton, the grocer and tea baron, was never properly accepted into

who, when showing a potential buyer a 300-ton yacht floating in the fairway was asked, 'And how much to keep her serviced for a year?'

'Sir,' he replied, 'If that is your question, she is not the yacht for you!'

If, however, you did meet the criteria, you could belong to several exclusive clubs[*] and enjoy the kudos of seeing your heavy investment paying off in terms of racing wins. The yachting writer and sailor John Leather likened yachtsmen of the day to modern racehorse owners[†]. As has been said, most were often not even on board during races and would never have dreamt of sailing or helming their yachts themselves. That was left to their professional skipper and crews. The owners simply paid the bills and took the glory, a similar situation to that which pertains today with the corporate sponsors of yacht racing. These organisations, especially in France, have taken over from the no-longer-so-rich aristocrats. Today's equivalents are the huge yachts, often three-hulled trimarans, emblazoned with corporate logos, which race around the world at fantastic speeds, often singlehanded or with minimal professional crew[‡].

Because winning was everything, the important thing was to sail fast and this had detrimental effects on yacht design, something else which is as true today as it was then. Under the then current rating rules beam was heavily penalised and yachts tended to be long, of deep draught and narrow gutted. They were known as 'plank on edge' and nicknamed 'lead mines', owing to the mass of lead ballast required in their keels to keep them anything like upright.

Cruising yachts in those days aped the racing scene (history repeats itself today) and were consequently cramped in their accommodation, wet to sail and strictly limited by their draught as to where they could go. Yacht rating rules at the start of the twentieth century were changed so as not to penalize beam but instead they restrict-

---

yachting circles despite his several attempts to challenge for the America's Cup with the building of five very large yachts all called *Shamrock*.

[*]   It was only shortly before his death that Sir Thomas Lipton was admitted as a member of the ultra-exclusive Royal Yacht Squadron, a club based in the Castle in Cowes on the Isle of wight, then the mecca of yacht racing.

[†]   Leather, John. *The Northseamen*, Terence Dalton 1971.

[‡]   These yachts can now circumnavigate the globe non-stop in forty days.

ed waterline length. Therefore, yachts were built with long overhangs fore and aft to increase sailing length but doing nothing to produce more seaworthy cruising craft.

As with yacht racing, yacht cruising in those days was also essentially an upper-class pursuit. The provision of all the accessories considered necessary for cultured living by the average Victorian necessitated a yacht of such size and capacity that it needed a paid crew to run it. The principle then espoused was that you needed a foot of waterline length for every year of your life. The concept of the small sailing cruiser which could be handled by the owner was only just beginning to be accepted by the end of the nineteenth century. Books by people like John MacGregor, who sailed his canoe *Rob Roy* all over Europe with religious fervour[*], the eccentric E. E. Middleton who circumnavigated England in a three-ton yawl[†], and R. T. McMullen with his account of single-handed cruising (after he had lost his hired hands)[‡], were just beginning to fire the imaginations of others. It was these tales that drew middle-class young men to set out to emulate these pioneers. Some adopted the title 'Corinthian' from the other side of the Atlantic, where it was used to describe anyone who preferred to get involved in his sport rather than being a mere spectator. In the British Isles it tended to be applied most frequently to sailing. Around the turn of the century a number of Corinthian yacht clubs were set up based on this ideal[§]. These were paralleled by the production of several yachting magazines, most notably *The Yachtsman*, which started in 1892. These publications gave space to small boats and yachts, frequently stimulating interest by running design competitions.

At that time most small yachts were built on a one-off basis to a design produced by the actual boatbuilder himself, it being only the larger or more expensive yachts which would be built to a design produced by an outside designer or naval architect. Hilly-

[*]   MacGregor, John. *The Voyage Alone in the Yawl Rob Roy*. Grafton Books 1987

[†]   Middleton, E. E. *The Cruise of the Kate*, Grafton Books 1984

[‡]   McMullen, R. T. *Down Channel*. Grafton Books 1986

[§]   The best known of these clubs today is the Royal Corinthian Yacht Club with bases at Cowes on the Isle of Wight and Burnham-on-Crouch in Essex, although this club has moved far from the original Corinthian ideal.

ard from the outset would produce his own designs, a practice he continued all through his life. There were some notable amateur designers like Albert Strange, the Scarborough artist, whose work was in great demand, and who designed craft that were, at one and the same time, small, easily handled, seaworthy and pleasing to the eye. He and his fellow members in the Humber Yawl Club made some surprisingly adventurous passages for those days[*]. There were numerous other small boatbuilders around the country following the same track.

Such Corinthian pioneers were regarded—like the amateur aviators of that period—as being somewhat odd to say the least, typified by Davies in Erskine Childers' 1903 book *The Riddle of the Sands*[†]. Childers, of course, was writing from life. He was drawing on his own exploits in small cruising boats, and reflected the ways of a growing number who were acting, thinking and feeling the same. But there was a tendency among the 'professionals' to ignore the needs of this small but increasing band of amateur sailors. It is interesting that when Dixon Kemp produced the several editions of his famous Manual[‡], he wrote at length about the costs involved in running a steam yacht or building a racing yacht. He had some complimentary things to say about the seaworthiness of local fishing boats and a good deal to say about racing and cruising canoes. But, apart from an appreciation of Humber Yawls, he included few examples of small cruising yachts, thus overlooking what were the beginnings of the most significant development in yachting at that time, something which was to set a trend for the future. Overall what he did say gave the impression that sailing for pleasure was a very expensive sport, out of the reach of most people. All this would change after the Great War, but then the whole yachting scene and the fortunes of the village called Rowhedge would change too. For the time being, however, yachting in large and expensive vessels provided the Hillyard family with its bread and butter, as it did for most of those living there.

---

[*]   Leather, John. *Albert Strange*. Pentland Press 1990; Lodestar Books 2013

[†]   Childers, Erskine. *The Riddle of the Sands*. Penguin Classics 1995 (and many other reprints)

[‡]   Kemp, Dixon. *A Manual of Yacht and Boat Sailing*. Horace Cox 1904 (and many revised versions)

It was in that village that David Hillyard made a decision which was to affect the rest of his life. When he was in his late teenage years he discovered a deep, personal Christian faith which was to be of importance to him and to last throughout his life. He became a member of the local Mariners' Chapel, which had been founded some years before by John Martin, a Colchester boatyard owner. Martin had become so concerned about the spiritual state of the Rowhedge inhabitants that he had funded the building of a chapel because he wanted the locals to feel free to attend dressed just as they were, caps, jerseys, sea boots and all, without changing into their Sunday best—which many of them did not have anyway. He was a realistic man; he built the chapel so that it could be converted into cottages if his mission failed to take off. By the look of the roof timbers, he also seems to have economised in its building, with wood from his yard. As befitting a chapel for sailors, it was decorated with a painted hawser running round the walls, and an anchor over the pulpit. There is a story that, before David Hillyard's time, it was 'borrowed' by local smugglers to stash away their goods during a Customs raid on the village. This might have gone unnoticed except that the barrels had left damp rings on the chapel floor.

In David Hillyard's day the mission was run by Martin's nephew, George Scrutton, and then when he tragically died, by his son, Harold. They described themselves as 'yacht decorators' and ran a business which combined chandlery and yacht painting. David was christened at the Chapel, and by 1903 both he and his father were established members, as was Harold Scrutton's sister, Daisy Elizabeth, the girl Hillyard would eventually marry.

Martin's formula worked and the place became popular and well-attended, particularly when the men came home at the end of the sailing season. Many of them, as was the custom in those days, had their own seats in the Chapel. Its programmes were lively, as they had to be in a village where half-a-dozen pubs provided fierce competition. In fact, the Chapel rules tell us that not only was there just 'the one condition of membership...a desire to flee from the wrath to come and be saved from their sins,' but those joining must do their best to encourage temperance and to support measures for closing public houses on the Sabbath day! This may seem 'over the top' to us but it reflected the devastation which could be wrought by drink in working-class homes in those days.

Despite this tough stance on drink, the mission attracted a large crowd of young people and became well known for its choir, to which the young David contributed a fine tenor voice. In later years, he was known for being musical, playing several instruments including the cornet, trumpet, violin, harmonium and piano. He would have had plenty of scope for using his gifts at the Chapel in those days when everyone was expected to use the talents they had. He also attended and later taught in the big attached Sunday School, where on winter Sundays, whenever the sprat fleet docked, the youngsters were made to turn out their pockets before they were allowed in. This was because, when the smacks unloaded their catches on to the quay, the kids would help themselves on the way to church!

Though life was hard, there could also be happy days. Rowhedge at that time was akin to a large family where everybody was 'aunt' or 'uncle'. Although not wealthy by any means, the inhabitants were proud of their work and content with their lot. David would live the rest of his life by the values he learned there.

It was the custom of that time, when a young man's apprenticeship ended, for him to find work elsewhere before returning to join the permanent workforce of his original firm, if he wished it and if the company wanted him back. Thus in 1904 David began to look around for a new employer. He was taken on at the newly founded Rowhedge Iron Works, a yard he would later always look in on during his infrequent return visits to his birthplace. This yard was in business from 1904 to 1964 and built several coastal vessels including Clyde 'puffers' and ferries, some for the Hythe to Southampton ferry. They built several vessels in kit form to be assembled later for use on Lake Titicaca in South America and on the River Nile. At its peak the firm employed more than three hundred men and built some nine hundred ships in all. Whilst they were no longer built in iron it was thought that the inclusion of the word in the name would reflect solidity and reliability. It was a good training ground for the young Hillyard. After a couple of years there, in 1906, he moved away from the east coast once and for all.

Chapter 2

LITTLEHAMPTON

David Hillyard arrived at Littlehampton on the Sussex Coast in 1906 when he was in his early twenties, through one of those strange combinations of circumstance that make up life. Call it serendipity. Fred Raven, a friend and contemporary apprentice-shipwright at Forrestts, had become involved in building lifeboats for the Thames Ironworks Company in London, a location which did not suit his health. Raven discovered, however, that when he was sent away to the coast on repair jobs, he came back fighting fit. His doctor suggested a permanent move and this became possible when a colleague, a draughtsman in the Thames Ironworks office called Humphries-Brown, came into some cash and decided to set up on his own. He invited Raven to join him and work for his newly formed Littlehampton Motor Boat Company. As trade increased it became apparent that the pair needed another shipwright. Fred remembered his old friend and invited Hillyard to move South to join him in Littlehampton. So that is how this young man, taking with him the attractive Essex lilt which he never lost throughout his life, turned up in a strange town on the South Coast with a bag of tools and little else, and went on to fame if not fortune.

The Littlehampton to which Hillyard arrived had developed in the mid to late Nineteenth Century from a small fishing village into a prosperous tourist town. Originally an exclusive resort had been planned on a stretch of land owned by the Duke of Norfolk[*], fronting a fine beach to the east of the mouth of the River Arun which runs through the town. But the coming of the railway in 1863, which was built right through this land, put paid to that. However, the town developed its tourist business apace without the new resort and by the

---

[*]   The Dukes of Norfolk live in the nearby Arundel Castle and the family owns
       much land in this area of West Sussex.

1880s it was invaded annually by thousands of holiday makers, many of whom were day-trippers. This burgeoning holiday trade brought to Littlehampton hotels, guest houses, landladies, shops and prosperity.

Later, in the 1930s, Billy Butlin got in on the act, buying up and destroying a picturesque windmill at the harbour mouth in order to replace it with the funfair which still greets you on the starboard side when you arrive in the town by sea. Other more respectable pastimes flourished, including a golf course, which was laid out on fields behind the dunes of the West Beach. The old oyster pond was converted into the model boating lake it is today.

But it is the river which interests us. After the mouth had been stabilised in the previous century with new piers and jetties, the river and its harbour provided a welcome refuge for shipping, though with a somewhat tricky entrance across a shallow bar with strong tidal streams. For a while the local railway company ran a steam packet service across the Channel to Honfleur in Normandy, but abandoned it because an irregular lack of water over the bar disrupted schedules. Wharves and boatbuilding sheds were constructed on both banks and photographs from around the time of David Hillyard's arrival show a wide variety of craft, mostly sail, tied up there. Baltic timber came in, and coal from the north of England for the gasworks and for domestic use. The harbour was also home port for ships owned by the Robinsons of Littlehampton, whose vessels in their heyday sailed all over the world (some members of this family would later work for David Hillyard). Littlehampton was never a major trading port but, within its limitations, was a busy one; it was a development on the west bank opposite the town which gave Hillyard his opportunity in the years to come.

In 1837 a Stephen Diddlesford Olliver decided to invest in a new shipyard on this west bank, south of the chain ferry which used to operate before a swing bridge was built. At great expense he had a patent slipway built, along with all the accessories of a boatyard used primarily for repairing craft and sawing timber. You can still see that date along with the initials SDO on a building in what was the old Hillyard yard. Then in 1846 a master shipwright, Henry Harvey, arrived from Rye and took over part of the Olliver yard and devoted this to shipbuilding. He founded the firm known as Harveys which would make his name, and would last some seventy years through his hard work and the help of two of his sons, John and William. Between them they built some notable vessels up to about 600 tons. When the demand for wooden merchantmen declined they concentrated on smaller coastal traders. Around the time of Hillyard's arrival in the town they even built a steam-powered vessel, the *Prince Eddie*. This was employed in the day-tripper trade out of Littlehampton but was not a great success. They also ventured into the yachting scene, at one time converting an old east coast trawler into a yacht for the composer Sir Hubert Parry. We shall see more of Harveys yard later.

When David Hillyard came to Littlehampton, you still crossed the river by the chain ferry or by rowing ferry, if you wanted a short cut to the golf course where an old windmill was still grinding corn. It was there that fishermen hauled up their boats along the shoreline. There was at that time a sail-assisted rowing lifeboat based in the town, called *The Brothers Freeman*, which continued in use until 1922. Trading ketches, schooners, brigs and the like were frequently towed out of the harbour by the paddle-tug, the *Jumna*. In the summer months paddle steamers took day trippers out to sea and fishermen were still making a respectable contribution to the local economy with their catches.

From the point of view of the ordinary working man, Littlehampton at that time had little more to offer in terms of prospects than Rowhedge. Apart from the holiday trade and its associated service industry, the locals would find employment in the shipyards, the gas works, the railways or on one of the local farms. Or they fished.

In spite of its somewhat pretentious name, David Hillyard's new employer, the Littlehampton Motor Boat Company, offered only basic shipwright work, largely confined to repairing fishing boats as they lay in the open on the beach. Before long it became evident that the business was in bad shape. It was rumoured, and was probably obvious to David, that the proprietor, Humphries-Brown, was more skilled with handling the bottle than handling cash. Soon bankruptcy loomed, which left David and Fred having to search for alternative employment. Fred Ravens found another niche in Lancing, while David looked further afield.

Chapter 3

A NEW BUSINESS

It was at this point that the landlady of the house where David Hillyard lodged altered the course of history. Mrs Batchelor of Lyndon Road in Littlehampton was not just a devout Methodist, she was also a superb cook. After the demise of the Littlehampton Motor Boat Company, Hillyard found a new job in Portsmouth Dockyard, which of course involved a move and a change of lodgings. On the Saturday he was due to leave, 'Mrs B' excelled herself with a farewell meal for him and on the spur of the moment David said to her, 'You know I will never get lodgings like these again, so I've decided to stay here with you and start up on my own in Littlehampton.' That is what he did. In later years his loyalty and generosity never ceased towards Mrs B, who he came to regard as his second mother. He supported her right up to her death.

Naturally, David not having much in the way of money, his business career had very modest beginnings. He managed to find a place he could afford in River Road, which backed onto the East Bank wharves. This street was home to boatbuilders, chandlers, and engineering workshops. It had six pubs and some picturesque houses belonging to shipowners. The premises he found were just across the river from where he later moved. They comprised nothing more than an upper story loft, and this meant the boats he built had to be launched by being swung out on a hoist and lowered into the river below. He employed a boy and paid himself a penny over the going port rate[*]. There is some evidence that for a short time he had a partner who soon opted for farming, leaving him on his own again. However, it was not long before David Hillyard began to build his reputation for good work, and this led to him winning his first real contract.

---

[*]   The hourly rate for shipwrights and the like which varied from port to port around the coast.

The famous London department store of Gamages, then in Holborn, decided to sell an eight-foot wooden clinker pulling dinghy. At the start of the twentieth century Gamages' ethos was to focus on fine British craftmanship and they set about finding a boatbuilder to produce these dinghies. It is not known how Hillyard came to be awarded the contract, but his name must have begun to be bandied about. He agreed to build these little boats for £5 a time, a transaction on which he made a ten-shilling profit. They were transported to London by rail but, unfortunately, it is not known how many he built. In spite of his later success with the building of larger yachts, dinghies would always remain his great love. Once he even conceived the idea of setting up a 'dinghy factory' and he converted part of the yard for that purpose, but this scheme never really took off. The cost of building them only too often far exceeded the price at which he could sell them.

At this early stage in his career, however, he was still finding his feet and, along with the dinghy building, he was open to any work he could pick up. This included fishing-boat repair work, in which he had been engaged with his first firm.

The new business thrived and Hillyard felt able to return home to Rowhedge to marry his childhood sweetheart and fellow-chapel member, Daisy Scrutton. This he did in the summer of 1908. He was twenty-five and she was eighteen months older. Daisy proved to be a loving and supportive wife through all the years which lay ahead. Tom Jeffers, Hillyard's foreman in later years, remembered her as 'a charming, quiet person', who not only set up a home for her husband but also took in and looked after David's father, David Sr, who lived out his old age with them at Littlehampton.

One of the couple's common interests was their garden and later on, when David had become established, he saw to it that his wife always had a good-sized plot, buying extra land for them to cultivate. Daisy, however, became physically weak in later life and David, who enjoyed the 'looking' rather than the 'doing', solved the problem in characteristic manner by finding a suitable boatyard hand who could double as gardener in his spare evenings. George, a committed Methodist and six foot in his boots, performed the duty for many years. Hillyard's nephew, Dennis Cullingford, who would later inherit the business, remembered the acquisition of an orchard, a vegetable garden and several greenhouses as a result of which Dennis' mother was inundated with vegetables and fruit.

By the outbreak of the Great War in 1914, Hillyard was thirty-one and an established small boatbuilder. His adopted town of Littlehampton, being so near to France, rapidly changed roles from a holiday resort to a place of embarkation for goods and troops leaving for the Western front. Activity greatly increased along the river and in the harbour. Wartime photographs show the wharves lined with steamers given over to carrying men and materials to France. Frustrated by the shallow bar, the military decided to move it in their own inimitable way by blowing it up with high explosives; needless to say, it was not long before nature took over once again and the bar returned.

Hillyard's skills were desperately in demand for the war effort. Boatbuilding being a reserved occupation, he not only avoided the trenches but, like many other boatbuilders, soon had no shortage of work. He was engaged by the Admiralty to produce lighters and 27ft Montagu Whalers, a commission that continued for some time after the war ended in 1918. This all prevented him from embarking on his long-held scheme to enter the world of designing and building small sailing yachts. That would have to wait until the war was over.

Chapter 4

THE BIRTH OF A LEGEND

During the Great War, with the volume of Admiralty work coming his way, Hillyard had to find larger premises. These he found further downriver on the eastern bank at Fisherman's Quay, where there were some large sheds used originally for drying timber. He acquired one of these, which was then a two-storey warehouse.

The other sheds were occupied by Hubert Williams, another boat-builder, who was turning out seaplane hulls for the Norman Thompson Flight Company, which were taken away for completion at nearby Middleton. Incredible though it may seem to anyone who knows Littlehampton, this aircraft company used the river Arun at its widest point opposite Fisherman's Quay as a runway and landing strip for their seaplanes. Life must have been quite exciting then.

There was in those days a great deal in common between building yachts and building flying-boat hulls. Norman Thompson's aircraft were constructed out of wood under the direction of a yacht designer and built in a similar fashion to a yacht's hull. Sad to say, like many pioneer ventures in aviation, the firm became bankrupt at the end of the Great War. They say it's an ill wind that blows nobody any good, and for Hillyard this was a stroke of luck. The demise of his neighbour's business meant that he was able to take over the whole of the premises at Fisherman's Quay and to inherit some of its staff. Amongst these was Harry Todman, the man in charge of building the flying-boat hulls. Before working for Norman Thompson, Todman had been a boatbuilder himself and had been in the habit of relaxing from his work by wandering into the Hillyard shed and watching their work.

So when Norman Thompson's finally folded at the end of 1918, Todman joined Hillyard's operation as foreman. It turned out to be a productive and long-lasting relationship. Harry Todman, as might be expected having worked on aircraft, was a superb craftsman as well as being an accomplished draughtsman. It was he who became responsible for turning many of Hillyard's dreams into reality. In fact, the relationship worked so well that the boss might say 'man wants a boat of such and such dimensions,' outlining his ideas. Harry would go away and get to work. The problem was that Hillyard never knew when to expect him back. His disappearances could be of several days' duration but when he did return it would be with working drawings. Unusually, these were always drawn to inside plank measurements from which the moulds could be directly lifted, the plans being intended for the shipwrights and not for customers[*]. Those were the days when boatbuilders were expected to be able to both read and produce drawings, and Todman's work was always of the highest quality.

As well as relying on Todman's draughtsmanship, Hillyard's favourite design method was to make up a half-model, altering the shape until he was satisfied. The lines would then be taken off the half-model to make the working drawings. Dennis Cullingford recalled many frustrating occasions when, having worked hard to produce neat and precise drawings, his uncle would energetically 'improve' on them with a thick carpenter's pencil. It was then back to the drawing board. As an aside, although, when it came to yacht design Hillyard had some strikingly original ideas, sometimes his sudden inspirations were not always practical. Dennis remembered the time when his uncle decided that a certain 30ft sloop, being somewhat beamy, only needed inside ballast with a timber keel. Dennis and another yard employee were elected to take her for a trial sail out of the harbour—which they did, perched out over the windward rail like dinghy sailors, praying that when they reached the open sea the wind would not increase. It did and they quickly turned and fled for home before disaster struck.

It was said that Harry Todman saved Hillyard from some of his wilder propositions. Although the boss liked to control ideas in the firm and took personal responsibility for everything it produced, Hillyard needed people like Todman and the rest of his team around him to achieve what he did. But at the same time, these men would never have fulfilled their potential without Hillyard driving them

---

[*]   These plans were frequently drawn on waxed linen paper and consequently made excellent trophies for a young Dennis Cullingford to take home for the ladyfolk of the town during the years of rationing in World War II, when a three-foot by two-foot piece of boiled linen was a prize not to be sneezed at.

on. Whilst Todman could be an exceedingly difficult person to work with, he was meticulous in his approach to a job, though not as fast as Hillyard would have liked. Todman could be aloof and distant and he later left the firm in Littlehampton to join another busines in East Anglia, feeling he could better himself elsewhere. He would often be heard to say to Hillyard things like: 'Alright, we'll do it your way if you insist, but otherwise I'll do it the right way.' He was usually right. Unfortunately, he could be equally brusque with customers and it was a tribute to Hillyard's patience that their efficient working relationship lasted as long as it did.

Another acquisition from the flying-boat firm was Tom Jeffers who was then on the bottom rung of the ladder but later served Hillyard faithfully as one of his foremen. They became firm friends. One of the striking aspects of the Hillyard story is that Hillyard kept the core of his workforce almost from apprenticeship to retirement. Although there were the inevitable conflicts of personality within the firm, in general terms the employees were intensely loyal. Attitudes to employment were different then and the men found real satisfaction in seeing the work of their hands shaping up and then being launched to become part of the growing Hillyard fleet.

This is not to say that all was sweetness and light among the work force. As in any multi-faceted operation, individuals could get very jealous about their contribution and there was, at times, real rivalry between different sections. It tells us something about Hillyard as a man that he was able to hold them all together to produce the results that they did. They worked hard in those days and enjoyed it. Tom Jeffers remembered that when two men had to cut a plank with hand saws, they would begin at each end, putting a sixpenny piece in the middle. The first one there pocketed it. Or two pairs, working each side of a boat, would vie with one another as to how many planks they could fit in a day with the apprentices trying to run the skilled men into the ground. As Tom later recalled, 'we had a good team and felt we were building for something. The boats had an honourable name and were well built.'

Over the years there were three generations of Humphries employed at the yard and it was often difficult to get the oldest, Old Tom, to go home at night. Poor of eyesight, but aided by powerful glasses, in his heyday he would not leave the yard till eight o'clock in the evening. He always seemed to be there, doing whatever he could for customers at all times of the day. He was never put off by what were, at times, harsh or filthy conditions, and he was able to do anything with timber. He became the 'spar man', pushing a plane for miles slowly trudging his way up and down hollow spars, perhaps twenty feet, perhaps seventy feet long, trailing unbroken streamers of timber which paid tribute to the sharpness of his 'iron'. He was a heavy smoker of Woodbines in his young days until Hillyard told him, 'You know, you could buy several pairs of shoes for your youngsters if you gave up smoking for a year.' Old Tom never smoked again.

Behind him came 'Young Tom', still 'young' when he retired at sixty-five. Young Tom pushed his plane alongside Old Tom and learned it all from his dad, finally becoming 'spar-man' himself. He was never known as anything other than Young Tom. Boats were his love, and nothing delighted him more than crewing for customers, or crewing for Dennis every Saturday in the season, racing a lively little half-decker called *Diedre*.

Having established himself with new premises and a skilled workforce and with Admiralty work coming to an end, Hillyard now found himself able to do what he had wanted to do all along—build small yachts. There was no money to be made in building boats for the local fishermen[*] or repairing their old ones. As far as we can see[†], his first chance to design and build a yacht of any size was around 1920 by which time Hillyard was in his mid-thirties. He was commissioned by the local vicar of Angmering, a Reverend George Gordon, to build him a cruising boat. Gordon was already an experienced sailor, having made several cruises before the Great War, some of which he had written about to Maurice Griffiths, then editor of *Yachting Monthly*. During the War the Reverend had commanded a motor patrol boat out of Littlehampton, where he was renowned for once sailing it home, backwards under a makeshift jury rig, after engine failure.

David Hillyard designed a 34ft ketch, to be called *Jamaie*, of hard-

---

[*]   Fishermen habitually wanted something for nothing and wanted to finance their purchases by spreading the cost over a year or more.

[†]   As we shall see later Hillyard was notoriously bad at record keeping, and details of just what he built and when during the early years no longer exist.

chine construction*, which he built on the slip at Fisherman's Quay. Unusual for the time, she had a gaff wishbone rig†. Hillyard's liking for chine boats (which stayed with him throughout his life) stemmed not only from his childhood experience with his sharpie on the River Colne, but from his admiration for the barge yachts being built on the east coast. He recognised that hard-chine was not only a simpler construction than the traditional carvel or clinker builds, but that it built in strength and made for a larger interior volume. He was later to develop this form into a fine art, although his first attempt did not receive many accolades.

The boat itself was successful as a solid all-round cruiser and the Reverend Gordon wrote an account of a cruise in her for *Yachting Monthly*, including a rough sketch of her lines. Maurice Griffiths, the Editor, was not very complimentary about the boat, adding an editorial note to the effect that 'we have enjoyed the Reverend's cruises in the past, and appreciate his seamanship, but whatever persuaded him to go to sea in a box like this?'

David Hillyard was not impressed and it was some years later that he had his revenge. One day when Maurice Griffiths was visiting the yard, he noticed an ungainly looking craft lying in the river.

'What you got there?' Griffiths asked Hillyard pointing at the yacht, 'Is that one of your earlier ones?'

'Ah yes,' said Hillyard, 'It was designed by some chap… I can't remember his name…Oh yes! Maurice Griffiths! You sold the plans to somebody out Yapton way. They tried to build it themselves and then brought it here for us to finish.' As Hillyard later said to Tom Jeffers, 'The Lord delivered him into my hands!'

Jamaie survived for a good many years and Dennis Cullingford recalled family sailing holidays, when David would take the family away on a boat from the current yard 'stock'. Often this was one of his latest creations, but at first it was often old *Jamaie*.

Maurice Griffiths, a successful yacht designer as well as a well-known author and magazine editor, eventually became a great admir-

---

* Where the hull planks are broad and flat, and the sections are quadrilateral instead of being curved

† Where the mainsail resembles an inverted windsurfer sail, and the triangular space below is filled with a mizzen staysail

er of Hillyard's work. Griffiths remembered meeting up with him at many Boat Shows when they would discuss current trends in yacht design and construction. He had a great deal in common with Hillyard when it came to designing. He was very much an east coast man and therefore tended to think in terms of shallow draught for those shoal waters. In spite of his earlier criticism, he emulated Hillyard and moved into hard chine designs himself, though some might say that his tended to be more on the chunky side (particularly when compared with the fine lines of his round-bilge yachts). Griffiths designed many yachts for amateur self-builders for whom hard chine construction is considerably easier. Griffiths later had complementary things to say about Hillyard's work, particularly about the standard chine boats which he was to develop, where the chines were so fine that it was sometimes difficult to tell them from round bilge. As Tom Jeffers says, 'The standard chine Hillyards were too successful to be ignored.'*

One of the frustrating aspects of trying to tell the early years of the Hillyard story is that David Hillyard was exceedingly bad at record keeping. It was only the complications and procurement procedures involved in work for the Admiralty during World War II that forced him into proper procedure. For the first time he employed someone in the office to do this. Consequently, the official yard list maintained at the firm only commences in 1946 at boat number four hundred, probably a number taken at random and probably just a guess. Even tracing the history of individual craft through Lloyd's Register of Yachts is difficult as many boats which came out of the yard were never listed, whilst others only appear on it for the first time many years after the boat first hit the water. Add to this the fact that boats taken abroad drop out of the records completely. Therefore, what happened before 1946 is extremely uncertain. To date, around two hundred and fifty yachts have been identified as having gone down the Hillyard slipways before 1946 but it is certain there were many more, some no doubt still afloat, with others by now sunk or broken up. What we can say with some certainty is that we know of and can date only two sailing craft built before 1922, with three built in that year. Of these,

---

*   The author owned a 22-ton Hillyard for several years (called *Wendy Woo*)
     where the chine was cleverly designed so it was wholly underwater. It was im-
     possible to know the vessel had a chine until it was lifted out of the water.

the only one known to have survived to this day is *Twinkler*, of which more later. It was only in that year, four years after the end of the Great War and only a year or so after the world had recovered from the Spanish 'Flu pandemic which devastated the country in 1918[*], that people began thinking about leisure pursuits such as sailing.

It was in the 1920s and 1930s that a growing number of people began to discover the delights of cruising under sail in small boats. No longer the province of the crank and the maverick, the pursuit began to become socially acceptable among the middle classes, as well as bringing a satisfying challenge to an individual's skill and initiative. At the bottom end of the market there were at this time a large number of ex-Admiralty craft going at knock-down prices, as well as a ready supply of decommissioned commercial lifeboats, all of which could be bought for a song and then converted, with a modicum of skill, into basic yachts. Of course, they always looked like what they were and generally they sailed that way too, but they were the first rung of the ladder for many aspiring cruising men and women. To help such aspiring yachtsmen, Mr C.E.Tyrrell Lewis published in 1925 a book which became popular called '*Lifeboats and their Conversion*'[†], described by its publisher as 'a practical and uncomplicated treatise on how to convert ships' lifeboats to pleasure craft'.

The other route into cruising was by graduating from dinghy sailing, a slice of the market which Hillyard had been exploiting for years. The Walker and Blackett children in Arthur Ransome's *Swallows and Amazons* were not the only ones to work out their dreams afloat in the Lakes, on the Broads or around our rivers and estuaries. Some learned to sail dinghies with university sailing clubs and in sailing clubs run by the armed services. Having acquired a taste for it, they began to think bigger and better as their post-war incomes increased. These were the people who frequented the various boat shows which were beginning to pop up around the country. In this atmosphere, Hillyard was able to develop his idea of producing real seagoing craft for the ordinary man, at ordinary prices. But first he needed proper and larger premises.

---

[*]   There were further waves in 1919 and 1920, and the epidemic killed over 50
        million people worldwide with over 250,000 in Great Britain,

[†]   A revised version was published in 1958 when there was interest in converting
        surplus lifeboats after the Second World War (pub. H. F. & G. Witherby)

Chapter 5

A NEW HOME

By 1923 David Hillyard's reputation was spreading far and wide and orders were coming in from all quarters. It was Hillyard's keenness to fulfill one particular order that led to the yard making a move across the River Arun to the west bank, where it remained for the rest of its days.

Hillyard had already built one boat for one of his many military customers, a General Beal-Brown. This gentleman is reputed to have gone down in history as the last officer to have led a cavalry charge in battle during the Great War (and to have refused to lead another one the following day because he said that it was akin to murder). The General, with ambitions to join the exclusive Royal Yacht Squadron in Cowes, requested the building of a 22-tonner to be called *Daydream II*. Hillyard had Harry Todman draw out a lines plan, but on seeing it Hillyard realised that the craft would be too big for the slipway at Fisherman's Quay.

Casting around, Hillyard discovered that Harvey's yard across the river, which had recently gone into liquidation, was up for sale by auction. The entire premises, divided into various lots as set out in an auction catalogue dated April 1923, were on offer. Taking a huge risk and sinking everything he had into it, he put in a bid to buy the centre portion of the site, occupying nearly seventy yards of road frontage, with a depth of more than eighty yards leading down to the river-bank. It was a huge expansion for the business. His bid was accepted and Hillyard took possession toward the end of 1923. A further portion of the old yard, next door to Hillyard's acquisition, was bought by William Osborne's, who later became well known for building lifeboats and high-quality motor yachts.

Hillyard's first task was to build a shed in which he could build the General's yacht. During that cold winter he fixed a large sign to the front of the big building shed which faced the river and was clearly visible from the town on the east bank. The sign said:

DAVID HILLYARD
YACHT, LAUNCH & BOAT BUILDER

After the yard finally closed in 2009, this sign remained in place for many years.

Tom Jeffers remembered that first winter in the yard as being one of those bitter ones when conditions were so bad that the river froze. The men had to work hard to clear out the old sheds (including, curiously, a left-over dug-out canoe) before they could begin work on the General's boat. This yacht eventually turned out to be a disaster and cost Hillyard dear. The timber used in the construction of the transom contained fungal spores and, due to insufficient ventilation, the 1⅜-inch Columbian pine rotted through by the end of the first season. The General, understandably, was not amused, and threatened Hillyard with his solicitors. The yard put it right at its own expense, thereby eating up any profit there may have been in the project. It was all a trying time financially, but new orders followed and the yard survived.

Invoices from that time tell us that 'The Shipyard, Littlehampton (phone 327)' was all that you needed to find or contact Hillyard's. In years to come, so well-known did the whole operation become that letters from abroad with simply 'Hillyard's Shipyard', even without a town name, would get to them. From the same invoices we can see that Hillyard retained, for a while at least, an interest in his old premises at Fisherman's Wharf across the river. The move opened up considerably larger opportunities than Hillyard had ever had before and 'The Works', as he described them in a later Boat Show brochure, 'are well situated and equipped for carrying out... yacht building, with good laying up facilities, and a slipway capable of dealing with yachts up to 150 tons'.

If you had visited the yard at any time up until 2009, you would have found a conglomeration of buildings and covered spaces which had come together progressively (and haphazardly) over the years. These included some of the original 1837 buildings constructed by the local builder S. D. Olliver[*]. Fronting the road to the right was a

---

[*]   A plaque recording 'S.D.O. 1837' remains to this day in an end wall of one of these buildings, now used merely as a storeroom.

large shed where the 2½- and 9-tonners were built, while to the left, on the other side of a roadway running into the site, was another long shed which was used over the years variously as a spar-making shop, for the construction (during World War II) of 16ft launches for the Royal Navy and, post-war, for the 8-tonners. Joinery for the boats was put together in the upper story of this building.

Following the roadway into the yard, you would have passed under a large beam used for handling iron keels and then seen on your right a building holding the saw mill on the ground floor, a large room which was always in a haze of wood-dust particles, there being no dust extractors in those days. On the two floors above were individual yachts' stores, which were let out to owners, and right at the top you would for many years have discovered Alec Robinson, the rigger, plying his trade. A little further into the yard and to your left you would have seen an old air-raid shelter. This was built by the yard in World War II, with a thick concrete roof the weight of which was underestimated and inadequately supported. The result was beautifully concave. After the war the shelter became the staff canteen. Ahead you would have seen the doors of another large building, the outer half of which stretched out over the water creating, at high tide, a covered floating dock. The inner section housed the construction of the 12-, 18- and 22-tonners.

One great asset of the site was the old Harvey's slipway where the boats were launched. Getting some of the boats to the slipway, especially the 9-tonners, meant a hazardous journey from the front of the yard, where they had to be manhandled out into the main road, back into the yard and then round three or four ninety-degree turns across less than level concrete. An old, converted bomb carriage was used to move the boats. At the head of the slipway there was, at first, an old steam engine from Harvey's days to move the cradles and carriages on which the boats sat, moving on 'greasy ways' (wooden planks set athwartships, liberally coated with heavy thick grease). This engine was eventually sold on and replaced by a winch powered by a Ford Model T engine, the wire cables from which were directed around the yard by means of an array of snatch-blocks.

Perhaps, therefore, it was no accident that at the head of the slipway was situated the engineering shop, along with the paint shop and the blacksmiths (and in World War II the main pump for the fire hydrants). It was there that they cast lead and iron keels, while in the same vicinity sat the only steam box in the yard. To the right of the slipway was the conspicuously tall chimney of the yard incinerator. Over a covered area, also at the head of the slipway, was the yard office reached by a ladder. This was occupied over the years by David Hillyard, the clerk Hector Billings, and Tiddles the cat. Later this office was occupied by Dennis and Simon Cullingford. At the seaward end of the slipway there was a simple derrick, operated by a hand-winch, used for stepping masts, while in the river itself was a grid on which boats could be grounded and propped up for scrubbing or for work below the waterline when the tide receded.

On the face of it, this seemed an ideal spot for a boatyard but the River Arun was something of a liability. At the top of a high spring tide the whole yard would be flooded. This was particularly disastrous for the sawmill, which had an extremely low floor level. Also, the river is one of the fastest flowing tidal rivers in Britain with a strong current running past the yard on the ebb. Careful timing was needed when launching or slipping boats. Navigation in the river can be tricky for visitors and those with no local knowledge. But the premises were cheap and they suited Hillyard perfectly. In later years Hillyard's bought an area of the riverbank, together with mooring rights, downstream from the yard. This was used for mud berths for the laying-up and storage of boats.

Empty, and what must have seemed a pretty bleak place when he acquired it, this motley collection of buildings and land on the west bank of the River Arun soon became a hive of industry and the birthplace of many fine yachts, launches and dinghies. Winters would have seen every available space filled with laid-up craft. At the end, and before the yard closed-down for good, it became almost a place of pilgrimage for many Hillyard owners, ex-owners or crews, who were always welcome. The Cullingfords used to tell of the many people who called at the yard just to look round and see where their particular 'baby' was born.

When Hillyard first moved into the new yard there was, apart from the steam engine and hand winch, no machinery whatsoever. It was only later that he acquired a mechanical thicknesser and a circular saw. As a result, there was a great deal of hard physical work for the men, who prided themselves on their skill with tools like the adze and draw-knife. 'Handraulics' was how Tom Jeffers described cutting out a forty-foot plank of 1½-inch pitch pine with a hand saw. Keels would be adzed out of two wide slabs supplied rough cut from the timber supplier (keels for some of the larger boats could be 12in by 24in). The old tradesmen had immense skills, not only in working with wood, but in making their tools cut efficiently. Tom Jeffers even maintained that, because they knew how to look after and use their tools properly, he never saw planks fixed as quickly with an electric drill as they were by hand. Timber deliveries were equally labour intensive. In the early years, the wood came in great baulks from London by train. The men would haul an old boat carriage across to the station and drag it back to the yard over the swing bridge.

After Harry Todman left, the yard was split into two for administrative purposes. Tom Jeffers became responsible for the 'Nine Ton Shop', also known as the 'Bottom Shop', birthplace of the 9 tonners and smaller craft, while Harry Hicks superintended the 'Big Shop', also known as the 'Top Shop', where the larger boats were built. They were in effect two firms, with different practices and with clear lines of demarcation between them. However, each respected the other, and there were never any bad feelings. Hicks was a Brixham man of strong character and with demanding ways. He not only ruled supreme in his part of the yard but he also even summoned the boss to come to see him with an imperious beckoning of the finger when he felt like it. He became useful to the rest of the men, however, on those odd occasions when Hillyard got so wrapped up in his work that he forgot Friday was pay-day. It was then that Hicks, who was a law unto himself, and did not mind what he said or to whom, would come to the rescue. On one occasion he was working in a large yacht being built and fitted out for Major Younger, owner of the famous Scottish brewery of the same name, who had acquired his own special vitreous enameled stove for the galley. To reach his work better, Hicks dragged the stove to where he was working, and stood on it. Sometime later, the Major, who was a fiery-tempered man at the best of times, appeared and exploded, 'Get off my stove!'

Hicks said, 'What for?'

'You'll break it!' exclaimed the Major.

'No I won't,' said Hicks, 'I've been here all morning and it ain't broke yet.'

Hillyard heard the commotion and came running to see the Major about to hit Hicks.

'Get down, Harry,' he said, 'and get away from the Major.'

Hillyard knew that in such circumstances the customer was always right. However, Hicks had great boatbuilding skills. His background was in trawlers and he was supremely confident whether supervising the building of a 30-footer or a 70-footer.

Several members of a Littlehampton seafaring family, the Robinsons, worked for Hillyard's. Joe Robinson was Hillyard's chief engineer for many years, until he retired around 1958. His scope and abilities were enormous, covering engine installations, engine overhauls, tinsmithing, electrical work, machining, plumbing; you name it, he did it. It was all highly skilled work, but not highly paid. Like many others at that period, had he had the opportunity of a higher education he would have gone far. It says something for Joe's sense of job satisfaction that he stayed with the firm all his life. He not only fitted the engines on most of the boats but he also frequently took them out on sea trials. Like some others on Hillyard's staff, Joe was always made available to accompany owners who often had little idea of sailing or navigation. These trips were an interesting break from work at the yard. Joe recalled how on one long cruise, during a well-earned spell below, he felt something was wrong. He went on deck to discover the yacht was heading up the Bristol Channel, the owner having sailed right past his destination on the South Cornish coast, dutifully following the land round Land's End and onwards.

Joe's brother Alec was Hillyard's chief rigger, whose son also worked at the yard. Another Robinson who worked there was Gordon, also an engineer and another splendid yachtsman who would eventually die at sea on his own yacht. The Robinsons collectively lived ships and the sea, and even spent their week-ends visiting other boatyards.

'Big George' was the yard's factotum, always on duty behind the canteen table as thirty or forty men filed past with their tea mugs at the ready. His strength was immense as it had to be for manhandling slabs of iroko 25ft by 3ft by 5ft around the yard. He was utterly dependable and honest but was remembered for a certain lapse of concentration which resulted in one new boat being fuelled with 150 gallons of diesel in the water tank, and 150 gallons of water in the fuel tank. If he did feel it necessary to skive off, he always let it be known by whistling a hymn as he went. This was unfortunate because the painter Jack, who came every morning with his non-working shoes buffed in a way any guardsman would envy, could not abide whistlers. If any offender did not heed his request to desist, Jack would chuck in his hand, grab his cherished shoes, and head for home.

The painters knew their jobs well, having been properly trained by their forebears. But this was not a job always to the liking of the younger men. For a long time the latter would struggle with the final coat of enamel which was so stiff when cold that it demanded a two-handed approach. One exhausted youngster challenged a visiting paint sales representative.

'Why is your paint so stiff? It has been like this for years', he asked.

'Why?' the man replied, 'it's been specially mixed for your yard to your special requirements for the last ten years. Basil asked for it that way'.

Sadly, Basil had retired eight years previously and nobody had known of his little idiosyncrasy.

Generally, the men all got on well together, and the annual highlight was the summer coach outing when dads, mums and family all went out together. Life in the yard was not all work and no play.

The men, as well as the boss, used to sail. Hillyard, always a dinghy man, used to race in the Littlehampton handicap class for dinghies up to 18ft. For some reason he never joined the local sailing club, the Littlehampton Sailing and Motor Boat Club, who organized the races.

He did of course build his own dinghies but was always trying to improve on his workmanship. When afloat, he would take his tools along with him and his crew would have to put up with his making running adjustments as they sailed. If he felt that the angle of the foresheet could be improved, out would come the brace and bit and the race would proceed, with Hillyard leaning over the side completing the job. Lewis Raven, the son of an old friend of Hillyard's, found sailing with him a fascinating experience. He knew most of the boats on the river, having built a lot of them, and was an expert on the vagaries of the local tides and currents. Off the river, Hillyard and his men sailed model yachts on the town's boating pond. These were superb 36in long racing machines which they took around to model boat races in different parts of the country. They were highly competitive affairs. Dennis Cullingford retained for the whole of his life one of Hillyard's own model boats, which Hillyard gave him when he was twelve years old.

Hillyard also went cruising in the summer, initially taking along his brother-in-law, Clifford Cullingford, and an old Rowhedge friend, Fred Rose. Rose had helped to crew the America's Cup challenger, *Valkyrie II*, among other big boats. But as time went by the ladies in the family asked to come too, so Hillyard obliged by including all the Cullingfords as well as his own wife. A suitable craft from the Hillyard stock would be found (this was always a bit touch-and-go as the one they had decided on might well have been sold by the time they set out) and they would spend a happy summer month sailing together along the South Coast. In addition to friends and family, Hillyard always insisted on Ben Hodges joining the crew. Ben was one of the yard staff who had spent his life on the water. He not only accompanied the boss on his sailing exploits but was in great demand by customers as a paid hand. In the words of one, 'Ben was a wonderful fellow, a man of few words but absolutely reliable in all weathers.'

One customer recalled the occasion when Ben was rowing his skipper back to their boat (*Moonstone of Marlow*) late at night in a somewhat inadequate dinghy after an evening ashore in Lymington. The dinghy was a temporary replacement for their usual one and was home-built of plywood with very little freeboard. Ben insisted on rowing the skipper the short passage back to the piles off the railway station. It was blowing a near-gale and raining. Half-way across the skipper noticed that Ben's feet were awash. With water lapping over the gunwale the skipper shouted, 'Hey, Ben, are you okay—your feet are getting wet.'

'Don't worry about my feet, governor, what about your arse?' Ben called back.

The skipper, seeing water lapping over the gunwhale, set to with a rubber mug and started bailing calling to Ben, 'Can you swim?'

'I'm alright, Sir,' Ben said and carried on pulling. They did eventually make it to the boat, but it was a near thing and they were soaked. After a swallow of brandy, the skipper asked again,

'Now, tell me, can you swim?'

'No, Sir,' said Ben.

*   *   *

The depression of the 1930s savaged many businesses, including most yacht and boat building firms both here and abroad. At first Hillyard kept on his staff and continued to build for stock even though six months passed without even an enquiry. The yard began to fill up with unsold hulls and it became inevitable that something had to be done and that there would have to be lay-offs among the men. One Friday, Bert Austin was called to the office, but when Hillyard saw the look on his face he said, 'Well, perhaps you'd better stay for another week.'

That week-end providence intervened in the form of a man named W. J. L. Watts, who for those days was something of a pioneer. Having witnessed the success of yacht chartering on the Norfolk Broads, he decided to do the same on the east coast of England. For that he needed a fleet of boats. He visited Hillyard's that Saturday, saw the completed boats piling up in the yard and promptly bought the lot. Remarkably, his brochure for 1932 containing a description of his fleet complete with photographs and terms of hire, survives in hardback (they did things properly in those days) and it gives a very interesting insight into just how many Hillyards he took on. Out of the eight boats Watts bought, no less than five had been completed in 1931, and one in 1932, and all these were given names of birds. These six were *Heron* a 22ft 4-ton cutter, *Magpie* a 28ft 7-ton cutter, *Linnet* a 30ft 9-ton cutter (a boat exhibited at the Olympia Boat Show in 1931 and owned later, as *Penguin*, by the author Peter Heaton), *Plover* a 30ft 9-ton ketch, *Woodpecker*, a 30ft 9-ton cutter and *Missel Thrush*, a 35ft 12-ton ketch. The brochure gives the boats' specifications as 'all being carvel built of pitch pine on oak with Columbian pine decks and coamings, hatches and mouldings of Honduras mahogany'. The auxiliaries were either an Ailsa Craig 'Silent Seven' or the old faithful Thornycroft 'Handybilly' (*Missel Thrush* was apparently equipped with two of these). The 9-tonners and the 12-tonners had canoe sterns.

Operating out of Creeksea on the River Crouch in Essex, all were available for charter fully equipped with no apparent restrictions on cruising area. Mr Watts must have been a brave or a very trusting man. Among various hiccups, *Magpie* had to be brought in by the Lowestoft lifeboat on one occasion. All Mr Watts required from the charterer was a signed declaration as to how many years he had been sailing together with a £5 deposit to cover the excess on the yacht's insurance policy in the event of a claim. An extra five shillings would be charged if any boat were returned in a dirty condition. It is interesting to note that in those days you could charter one of his 9-tonners in the high season for £15 per week. Mr Watts even kept some of the boats in commission throughout the winter, having fitted them with coal stoves for which he provided coal and kindling.

Although Mr Watts did not pay for all his purchases immediately, the yard was able to continue building yachts all through the depression years. In 1932 they speculatively built at least a further nine boats without any buyers in sight and in the end did not have to lay off a single person; a tribute to Hillyard's sagacity and humanity. By December 1936 the magazine *Yachting World* was reporting increasing activity around the boatyards. They wrote that Hillyard's that winter would be building two 18-tonners, two 9-tonners, two 6-tonners, four 2½-tonners and ten 4-tonners; twenty boats in all. In addition, they were about to start on the first four 13-tonners, the lines of which they had earlier that year exhibited at Olympia. The yard also had in hand two clinker-built yachts, a 24-footer and a 30-footer.

The picture was the same right up to the outbreak of World War II, three years later. Whatever storm clouds might have been seen on the horizon, business for the yard was booming.

This was also a time of personal tragedy for Hillyard himself. His wife, Daisy, was as quiet and retiring as David was forthcoming. She was a charming person but had never enjoyed good health. In the summer of 1937 she fell sick and died. She was only fifty-six. 'I didn't realise how ill she was until she was dying', David, who was then fifty-five, is quoted as saying. With her death he lost a great deal as they never had any children and David was left on his own. However, his bereavement initiated a change in his domestic arrangements which had long-term repercussions for the yard.

Daisy's sister Nina had married a Clifford Cullingford and the couple were still living in Rowhedge, along with their two sons, Dennis and Eric. Clifford commuted every day to London, working as pharmacist for the Mildmay Mission to the Jews. He and Nina decided it would be just as easy for him to commute from Littlehampton. So, they moved south and into Hillyard's house, where they all lived together for many years. Hillyard soon became a second father to the two Cullingford boys. Dennis was introduced to the yard, which he would eventually inherit from his uncle. But that was a war and more away.

Chapter 6

INNOVATIONS AND DESIGNS

Before we go on to look at the boats that Hillyard designed and built in the inter-war period, 1918 to 1939, and how the Littlehampton yard built them, it is instructive to look at what lay behind these designs, how these and some of their unique characteristics developed, the innovations Hillyard introduced into small yacht building, and how he approached the marketing and selling of his boats.

The main characteristic of the Hillyard 'brand' (if we may use this modern term, a word Hillyard would no doubt have loathed) and something which really does make him and his yard unique is that in this period (and this continued after the war into the 1950s and 1960s) his was the only major boatbuilding yard in the country (and probably the world) which restricted itself to only building boats which were conceived and designed in-house. Virtually all other yacht and boat builders, however eminent, were merely 'jobbing' builders who would build to third parties' designs. Whilst many yards had their own in-house naval architects or design teams, these had no exclusivity and their designs were built by other yards. The result is the unique instantly recognizable fleet of 'Hillyards', some four hundred of which are thought to still exist. These can be found moored in harbours, rivers and creeks all over the world. Whilst many yachtsmen disparage these little ships, they engender in their owners a degree of affection and devotion hard to find elsewhere.

In the United Kingdom they are too often ignored when it comes to arcane discussion as to what is or is not a 'classic boat,' and they are rarely recognised for what they are. Everyone would concede that they don't have the 'pizzazz' of ,say, a Fife or Alfred Mylne metre-boat, a John Alden schooner, an Albert Strange yawl or one of Sparkman & Stevens' early yawls, but they have a rugged seamanlike presence which forms an important part of our maritime heritage. They should be better recognized for what they represent, as should the effort which their owners past and present put into ensuring their continued existence.

Hillyard was a self-taught designer and innovator, preferring to work by instinct and experience rather than by theory, although he had great respect for the designs of Dr T. Harrison Butler[*], a well-known amateur yacht designer, who attempted to work out the 'meta-centric shelf' formula for perfectly balanced hulls. They used to meet at boat shows, when Dr Harrison Butler would come on board and talk, although it is doubtful if Hillyard ever really took to his theories. At one Boat Show, a man named Daniels did persuade him that a lot of trouble might be avoided by tank testing models, rather than in building costly prototypes. At that time, the America's Cup boats were being tank tested before being built. Daniels got Hillyard to build him a hard-chine cat boat which he had designed and tested in this way. Not only was it expensive to construct but it was not a conspicuous success in any way. Hillyard thereafter never bothered with tank testing, which became widely used by many naval architects.

It was Hillyard's boast that all the boats that left his yard were built from in-house designs, which is why he said: 'you can always tell it's a Hillyard'. From the 1920s onwards, Hillyard fitted in the cockpit of every boat a bronze or brass oval builder's plate, about two inches by one-and-a-half inches, but there was really no need for these as he always said: 'You can tell by the look of them who designed and built them.'

In the light of this, it is all a bit puzzling that a quick look at Lloyd's Registers of Yachts will show a number of Hillyard-built craft credited with others as their designers. The explanation is not simple: in several cases Lloyd's are wrong; in other cases, the person credited merely assisted with the design or planned the interior; and only in a very few cases was another designer actually responsible for the hull shape. As this is a somewhat esoteric matter, and so as not to get in the way of the narrative, I have set out details of these vessels and what I believe actually happened in Appendix I. In the case of only three boats can we be one hundred percent certain that Hillyard was

---

[*]   Harrison Butler, T. *Cruising Yachts: Design and Performance.* Various re-prints, latest being Lodestar Books 2015.

not the designer, and in a handful of other cases he is credited as being a co-designer.

The feature which, almost more than anything else, has become the hallmark of a Hillyard is the centre cockpit, which anticipated modern yacht design by about fifty years. He was probably the first designer to adopt this feature, and for a reason which might seem odd to us today. Back in the 1920s, when Hillyard began building yachts, it was usual for owners to employ one or more paid hands to accompany the owner's party when cruising and who would undertake much of the work in sailing and maintaining the vessel. Traditionally, the paid hand or hands would occupy the forepeak of the vessel. Hillyard believed that the owner should be able to use what he considered to be the choice part of the accommodation and to enjoy some privacy besides. Why should the owner have the inconvenience of the hand making his way through the saloon whenever he wanted to get to the cockpit? Hence the stern cabin evolved in the early twenties. The locals used to joke, 'Here comes another Hillyard with the fo'c'sle aft'. But it was a feature which was to become immensely popular in future years for quite different reasons and has now been almost universally adopted on cruising yachts of all sizes. It turned out in the years after paid hands had all but disappeared that this arrangement was ideal for families or mixed parties. This meant that children could be separated and berthed in the forepeak, with their parents having the privacy of the aft cabin, leaving the main saloon for daytime use or for guests. In later years Hillyard promoted this as being the real purpose of the arrangement, as the idea of a paid crew was too elitist for most buyers of Hillyards.

Moving forward for a moment to the post-war years, Hillyard was also before his time in realising that sailing was no longer to be a predominantly all-male pursuit and that his yachts would principally be sailed by families. Therefore, he aimed a lot of his marketing efforts at the female sex by building in proper galleys, hanging curtains over the portholes, and laying carpets or linoleum on the cabin soles. Maybe the purists of the time objected but the popularity of his boats showed he was correct. Today, of course, no-one would attempt to sell a family cruising yacht which was anything other than a home from home with all 'mod cons'.

It is interesting to contrast Hillyard's achievements with those of his somewhat younger contemporary, Jack Laurent Giles, as their very different approaches illustrate for us the trends in yacht design in the inter-war years and those in the immediate post-war period. Laurent Giles' origins were as distinguished as Hillyard's were humble. A trained and qualified naval architect, his approach to hull design and performance was strictly scientific, whereas Hillyard's was more instinctive and based on long experience as a boatbuilder. Laurent Giles' brief was frequently to design for speed and racing; Hillyard was more concerned with comfort, low price and safety. The former pushed out the boundaries in a highly successful manner with regard to light displacement and a rigorous study of the race rating rules (and the loopholes in them) which gave his boats the edge and often novel appearance[*]; Hillyard concentrated on more traditional hull forms. Although a number of Laurent Giles' designs developed into well-known classes, most famously the Vertue class of small heavy displacement cruising yachts which, with their traditional hull form, could have come from Hillyard's drawing board, most were original bespoke yachts and expensive as a result. Hillyard's philosophy was that of a boatbuilder developing a range of standard boats with a view to the general market, and more particularly for the family man. Both were innovative, but in different ways. Both made their contribution to yacht design at a time when the sport was coming within the reach of an increasing number of people. When, toward the end of the life of the Hillyard yard, they did eventually foray into GRP, it was to the old firm of Laurent Giles that they went for a design.

There was no doubt a friendly rivalry between the two, and whilst Hillyard developed distinctive features like centre cockpits, canoe sterns, and shallow draught in the 1920s it was Laurent Giles who claimed to have introduced the first doghouse on his first commissioned design, *Etain* in 1930. Hillyard would have disputed this, claiming to have introduced such a feature on some of his earlier designs, although they somewhat lacked the elegance of the Giles doghouse.

---

[*]   Laurent Giles introduced to the world reverse sheer, cut off transoms and short overhangs leading to such 'monstrosities' (to some) as *Myth of Malham* and the aluminium *Gulvain*.

The author for many years owned Laurent Giles' second commission, the 31ft yawl *Argo* built in Shoreham in 1931. Like *Etain* she had the original elegant Giles doghouse (and very beneficial it was too) but the most distinctive feature of *Argo* was that she had a canoe stern—the only Giles design ever to have had one. In this case, was the great Laurent Giles actually following Hillyard?

Another of Hillyard's innovations was his approach to promoting his yard and his boats to the public. At that time (the 1920s) designers and boatbuilders were (and most still are) a conservative lot making little effort to promote their work other than through the excellence of their draughtsmanship or shipwright skills. Hillyard, who aimed the appeal of his boats at ordinary people and not the rich and famous (although as we shall see many of these were drawn to him), saw the potential of the then emerging number of public exhibitions and shows of consumer-orientated products. Motor shows and events like the Ideal Home Exhibition were the first to emerge, followed by boat and sports shows.

Hillyard's were certainly one of the first, if not the first, builders of small sailing cruisers to exhibit their boats at these shows. The first ever Boat Show, the *Marine and Small Craft Exhibition*, was held in 1922 at the Royal Agricultural Hall in Islington in London (affectionally known to one and all as 'the Aggie') from 14 to 24 November. Hillyard exhibited two boats there; these are believed to have been *Twinkler*, a 4-ton centreboard sloop[*] built in 1922, and an unidentified 5-tonner, possibly *Laranda*, which was built the same year.

A report on the show in the December 1922 edition of the magazine *Yachting Monthly* reads:

> Mr David Hillyard of Littlehampton had two boats on his stand which attracted a lot of attention. A 5-ton sloop-rigged keel cruiser and a 3-ton centreboard sloop for day work or cruising. The latter would be most suitable for Christchurch or Poole Harbours or similar waters. Both boats are of Oregon

---

[*] *Twinkler* is the same boat referred to earlier, built in 1922, and which the Hillyard Owners Association considers is the first real Hillyard which started the fleet. And, as we shall see later, she is still afloat and in commission 100 years later.

pine but could be built of pitch pine for the same price, which, by the way, is very moderate, the 3-tonner being priced at £145 and the 5-ton keel boat at £245. The show was visited on the 22nd by His Majesty the King, who showed his practical interest in yachting and all that appertains thereto by spending two hours in going from stand to stand examining, with the eye of an expert, all the most interesting exhibits and discussing their merits with those in charge of them.

The next year, 1923, the *Sports and Pastimes Exhibition* took over from the previous year's show, also held at the Aggie. Here Hillyard again exhibited two yachts, the same *Twinkler* and a 5-tonner *Beana*. Both were transom sterned and attracted a good deal of favourable comment. Although there were some fifty boats on show, they were mostly small, including half-deckers, dinghies and launches. The only other cruising yacht in the exhibition was a 7-tonner from Thorneycroft's yard on the Thames.

Tom Jeffers well remembered the effort involved in getting the boats to the shows. Hillyard employed a local firm, Thomas & Town, who had a flat-topped trailer with wooden wheels, which needed to be greased every so often and at regular intervals. The boats were slowly hauled in this way, with many stops for greasing, all the way from Littlehampton to the Aggie, where they were manhandled off the trailer. As Jeffers said, 'at the first show a through-deck mast was stepped by the grace of God and a few policemen!' On another occasion, the unloading team did not turn up as ordered and somehow Jeffers and the lorry driver unloaded a 5-tonner between them—health and safety and 'risk assessments' having not been thought of by then.

Later, these shows moved to Olympia and then Earl's Court. Some of these early shows combined a Boat Show with one of the regular Motor Shows. Hillyard's even exhibited on two occasions at the *British Industries Fair*, which was held annually at a purpose-built exhibition centre in Birmingham between 1920 and 1957[*]. It must have

---

[*]   These fairs, which lasted for two weeks each year, were at the time the most visited attractions in the country. The first diesel locomotive was exhibited there in 1933 and an air display was usually held at the associated airfield. The site has now become the National Exhibition Centre.

been quite an effort to get the boats from Littlehampton to Birmingham and back.

David Hillyard recalled the opening of one of the combined Boat/Motor Shows conducted by a member of the Royal Family, with the speeches being broadcast on the radio (using this medium for the very first time) and relayed to the exhibitors waiting in the hall over loudspeakers. The speeches seemed to take forever, and eventually one old boatbuilder shouted out, 'Doesn't anyone want to buy a boat?' King George V visited the Show and stopped at the Hillyard stand to ask Hillyard where his boats had been built.

'Littlehampton, Sir,' Hillyard said.

'And where it that?' asked the Monarch, displaying his royal ignorance before moving on to the next stand. A photograph of the encounter shows Hillyard with one trouser leg stuffed into his sock talking to the King. One wonders what his wife, Daisy, said to him when she saw it.

Over the years, these shows became a highly effective shop window for Hillyard's wares. In the early days, boatbuilding firms were smaller and the bosses used to man the stands themselves. Apart from the boat or boats being exhibited, Hillyard's stands would be empty but for a large box on which the boss used to sit and in which he kept brochures and boat plans, plus his customers' coats. He would take with him quarter-scale models of some of his larger boats. There were no desks or chairs. 'They come here to look at the boats,' he would contend, 'and if they sit down in a comfortable chair they'll only want to stay and talk and talk.' Unlike others who exhibited, he would never actually take an order at a show. The only time that he did, he sold the boat to someone else before the original buyer turned up at the yard! He believed the emotional pressure of a show meant that potential buyers might place an order only to think better of it. 'The bright lights and the atmosphere get hold of them,' he claimed. 'If I take an order and a deposit, it's as likely as not when they get home, they will have second thoughts or the wife begins to argue and then it's a cancelled order. I won't accept an order for a new boat until the customer has visited my yard and gone into all the details.' If anyone wanted a boat, Hillyard told them they had to go down to Littlehampton and negotiate with him there. However, many of his most faithful customers made their first contact with him and his work at the shows.

He took to producing brochures to illustrate his range, stating prices, and we have examples of these going back to the late 1920s. There is an assured self-confidence about the way in which he advertises his '2½-ton Sailing Yacht (price £100)' or his '4-tonner (price £150)' or his '9-tonner (price with Thornycroft DB2, £575)' as well as highlighting his sailing and rowing dinghies. The latter he marketed at £1 a foot, so that a nine-foot pulling dinghy would cost you £9. 'Enquiries and inspection at works invited', the brochures stated.

By the time the world moved into the 1930s, the Hillyard yard had become well established, productive, and profitable, with no shortage of customers. But then came the recessions and depressions which plagued the 1930s, when there were few if any orders, and certainly not enough to keep the yard busy. This is when Hillyard's last and probably greatest innovation came in. To keep the yard and its hands occupied during these periods, Hillyard's became probably the first boatyard in the country, and may be the world, to regularly and systematically built boats 'on spec.' or for stock with no buyer in sight. It needed a great deal of courage and money to finance such work. Whilst the yard never made great profits it had established a sufficient level of profitability to be able to fund the building of stock boats. This was principally because David, the sole proprietor, never paid himself very much and certainly never awarded himself big bonuses or dividends. Everything the business earned was ploughed straight back into it. There were no expense accounts, company cars, yachts or other perks provided to Hillyard or anyone else.

Costs at the yard were kept to the bare minimum, but sufficient funds were always made available to ensure quality did not suffer. Hillyard, despite owning a substantial business, was not interested in the trappings of success, and you will see this throughout his life. He was a simple man with a simple ethos who preferred looking after his men and his customers before himself. This is shown in such things like his never owning his own yacht (he preferred to 'borrow' a boat from the yard for his annual summer holiday cruise) and in never parting with his faithful motor cycle for an expensive motor car.

This decision to build for stock led him by degrees to establish his 'standard' range of boats and to adopt 'production line' boat building techniques, both novel concepts at the time. Apart from those specialist boatyards committed to building one-design racing classes, there were few if any yards which in the inter-war years undertook such yacht-building methods. Of those few that did try it in the United Kingdom, none attempted it on the same scale or with such a range of boats as Hillyard's. Just like the first production line set up by Henry Ford for his Model T, this led to a cheaper product which in turn attracted a larger market. Hillyard may perhaps have cut some corners (as mentioned later) but he never allowed this to cut or affect quality. As Maurice Griffiths commented, 'his instinct in selecting the best seasoned timber was the reason why Hillyard yachts usually passed stringent surveys even when already elderly.'

The building of wooden boats was and is a complicated and labour-intensive craft but there are ways of saving time and money. For example, the moulds, which determine the actual shape of the boat but which are removed once the planking and framing are complete, were used again and again (if you poked around the yard before it closed you would have found many of these lying around). Whilst It was common practice in most yards to keep the moulds of a 'one-off' boat for a while in the hope of a repeat order, at Hillyard's this was quite deliberate policy and boats of differing lengths were often designed with similar sections. Likewise, patterns were made for plank shapes on standard craft. Laid on the timber and scribed out with a pencil, they could be used repeatedly, saving time and money. Chined boats were considerably easier to plank than round bilge ones, where planks had to be shaped to fit their neighbours. Hillyard designed his chined ones so that only the two planks each side adjoining the chine needed shaping. You would not notice this when the vessel was complete.

Fittings such as hatches and companionways were standardised and prefabricated. Often the side decks of yachts were laid athwartships, using offcuts from the longer fore and aft runs, which reduced the need for half-beams or tie rods. This also saved a large amount of timber. The considerable amount of end-grain thus exposed was well painted and covered by deck canvas, but could lead to problems if not well maintained. The famous 'button' or truck at the masthead,

a feature of most Hillyards*, was designed to get the burgee clear of
all obstructions, there being no VHF aerials, wind instruments etc.
to worry about in those days. Simply, a hole was bored in the top of
the mast into which was inserted a pole to support the truck which
housed the burgee halyard sheeve. The end-grain of the mast was protected by a lead cap. Round scuttles were eventually abandoned for
square lights on a number of models, as they were cheaper to build,
less prone to leak and reduced the tendency for the cabin sides to split
in way of round or oval portlights. The whole philosophy was one of
simplification whilst retaining traditional quality.

Dinghies came in for the same treatment. A great deal of shaping is
needed in the planking of a clinker hull. To achieve the correct shape,
a four-inch-wide plank has to be scribed out of an eight-inch plank
with an attendant waste of timber. David Hillyard devised a method
of saving timber by putting most of the shape into the planks at the
turn of the bilge, angling them diagonally at the same time. This made
the rest of the hull considerably simpler and cheaper to build, with
little shaping of the remaining planks required.

Tom Jeffers, warming to the cause of simplicity, had the idea of
building, in his part of the yard, the decks, hatches and cabin tops
on a jig, and then lifting them complete onto the hull, anticipating
a method which is today commonplace with production-line GRP
boats. This method continued to be used at the yard to the very end.

There was a good deal of instinct in Hillyard's boatbuilding methods. Ballast keels always weighed around fifty percent of the ballast
required. The further ballast needed was in the form of iron pigs inside the boat and it was this fifty-fifty distribution which many gave as
the reason for the easy motion in a seaway which typifies all Hillyards.
The yard always made the bottom of an iron keel flat so that it would
take the ground easily. For a similar reason, Hillyard tended to build
in extra high cockpit coamings so that, if the boat did take the ground
and leant over, water would not flood inboard as the tide rose.

Another cost saver was the speed at which the loyal workforce produced a boat. As we have said, Hillyard himself was an extremely fast

---

*   This feature was incorporated into the house flag of the Hillyard Owners As-
        sociation.

worker and expected the same sort of commitment from his employees. Dennis Cullingford remembered one man working up the planks for a 2½-tonner with two apprentices each side fixing off his shaped and bevelled planks. They finished fourteen planks in a day. One Monday morning at the yard, Hillyard tripped over a piece of wood lying in the yard and said to Jeffers,'Ah, Tom, that will make me a nice stem for a dinghy.' By the end of the week it was a 16ft racing dinghy.

A typical season's production at that time might have been as many as half a dozen 2½-tonners, eight 9-tonners, four 12-tonners, as well as three or four 40ft craft. In his Boat Show brochures Hillyard was able to claim that there was 'generally one of each type' which could be inspected at the yard. The pace hotted up just before Easter when completing orders competed with fitting out. It was probably this rapid turnover which led to the men, whilst becoming absorbed in the construction, only maintaining a casual interest in the boats once they had left the yard. As Jeffers put it, 'In the early days there was a sense of urgency. The boats were turned out quickly and then there would be another one… a sense of urgency and satisfaction.'

For David Hillyard, who cared deeply for the welfare of his men, speculative building when there were no firm orders had another big advantage. It enabled him to keep his staff together and provide them with work however bad external circumstances were. He, in turn, could count on a workforce who became intensely loyal and did all they could to enhance and maintain the reputation of the yard. Hillyard and his men prided themselves on the seaworthiness of their craft, as well as the quality of their build.

They also valued their boats' reputation for ease of handling. This was true even of the larger boats like the 40ft schooners and later the 42ft ketches. Hillyard's argument was that, with the sail area well split up, a larger boat took no greater effort to control than a smaller one and they gave a steadier platform to work on. On one occasion a particular yachting magazine queried this, so Hillyard invited representatives from the magazine down for a trial sail. It turned out to be an exceedingly windy day and the arrivals were less than keen to embark. When the yard staff heard that the sail might be cancelled, they protested so much that the visitors had little option but to get on board and put to sea. One of the staff, Joe Robinson, from an old

Littlehampton sailing family, took them out and brought them back in with so little fuss that they acknowledged the truth of Hillyard's claim.

On another occasion, a very sceptical customer left all the handling of his intended purchase, one of Hillyard's 40ft schooners, to his twelve-year-old son who did all the letting go and raising and lowering the sails. They sailed to Brighton and on their return the customer admitted that Hillyard had proved his point.

It would have been interesting to see what Hillyard would have made of GRP and the methods of mass production with which we are now familiar. Perhaps it's an unfair comparison with the labour-intensive, highly skilled art form which is wooden boatbuilding, but certainly he would have shared the underlying motive. Hillyard's philosophy was 'boats for the people' and although his streamlining of production techniques could not produce boats for all the people, he did a great deal to popularise the pursuit. He enabled many for whom it would otherwise have been out of reach to buy one of his boats.

Whilst he was quite happy to build 'on spec', he was always keen to identify a suitable customer for an individual boat as soon as construction started. He encouraged and welcomed owners to visit the yard and take an interest in their boats all the way through the process, which most of them did. It has been said that if Hillyard did not like the look of you he would refuse to sell to you. This is not quite true. He built for a wide variety of customers and was quite ready to tell them what sort of boat would be suitable for their needs. He was particularly concerned that newcomers to sailing began with the sort of craft they could comfortably handle. Dennis Cullingford, however, remembered some occasions when Hillyard seemed to be over-anxious to meet his customers' demands about things like rig or deckhouses. 'If that is what he wants,' he would say, 'that is what he will get.' The results did not always work out well.

At other times, Hillyard was known to recommend a larger boat than what the customer had in mind. When Tom Southern[*] met David Hillyard at the 1954 London Boat Show, he was convinced that a 6-tonner would be ample for his family. Hillyard however persuaded

[*]   See Chapter 13.

him that he needed a 9-tonner. One spin-off from the development of a standard range of boats was that beginners let loose with his smaller models often came back when they felt it was time to graduate to something larger. In that way Hillyard not only sold them a new boat but would often be asked to sell the old one. The reverse also happened, of course. Some customers, after having gone through the range, opted for smaller models with advancing years and decline in strength.

At times, the demand for new boats was so great that customers might have to wait two or three years to see their order fulfilled. Hillyard would never, or hardly ever, give a definite delivery date. One customer, a Mr Latimer-Needham, an aero-engineer working for a local Littlehampton firm, kept on visiting the yard to look at the boats being built, trying to order a new one for himself. He reckoned that he had to ask Hillyard so many times to have his name put 'on the list', that when eventually he took delivery of his 2½-tonner, he christened her *Perseverance*!

Chapter 7

THE MAN AND HIS FAITH

The David Hillyard story is peppered with tales like that set out earlier in the Prologue, and throughout his life he dealt with all his customers much as he had dealt with the Admiralty during the war[*]. All this makes it hard to believe that his business was as successful as it was for so many years. But throughout Hillyard's life, his Christian faith was the driving motivation in his business as well as in his private life.

John Norbury, a frequent customer who bought several boats from Hillyard's and later became a firm friend, suspected that Hillyard tailored his bills to what he thought his customers could afford. Norbury, who was a poorly-paid teacher, wrote, 'with my profession and my scruffy 1935 Morgan 3-wheeler, I think I came near the bottom of the ladder. At the end of one bill was an entry, 'Extras—what did you have?' There was this perfect trust that neither side would try and do the other down.'

Norbury first met Hillyard sometime around 1932, when he persuaded his father to buy him one of Hillyard's standard 10ft lugsail dinghies. At that time they were selling complete for one pound ten shillings a foot. In this dinghy Norbury learned to sail off the beach at Selsey, 'rather to the Coastguards dismay', by watching and copying the fishermen.

In the 1930s his father bought a standard 2½-tonner which had been exhibited at the Boat Show that year. Hillyard marked it down in price 'because it was second-hand'. In those days there were no beginners' books on sailing and father and son were indebted to Hillyard for the advice he freely gave them. Hillyard took to the young Norbury, as he did to so many youngsters. 'Almost at once he began to call me "John" and I rapidly began to regard him as my

---

[*]   See Chapter 9.

"Sea-Daddy", although out of respect for his age I always called him "Mr Hillyard".

John Norbury testified to Hillyard's willingness to accommodate the wishes of his customers. When his father ordered a 5-tonner in 1938, he asked for considerable modifications which were gladly agreed to. 'So different,' John said, 'from my father's later experience with Westerlys in the 1980s when he tried to get his Konsort slightly modified, and was met with the attitude, 'If you don't want a standard boat, someone else will.'

When John designed his own gaff rig for his Hillyard and later, when he had to sell off his engine to raise some cash, Hillyard advised against it all but co-operated. After a scare off Land's End when John's boat was pooped and his cockpit and cabin were flooded, he asked Hillyard to build him a higher bridge deck. 'As usual he demurred, muttering that most people did not sail as stupidly as I did but once he saw I was determined he gave way. I shall always remember his closing comment, 'Well, alright, John, I'll do it for you, but it will cost you £15'. This to do a job which meant dismantling most of the cockpit, fitting two strong cross members, plus all the timber needed and the canvassing and painting to waterproof the top, as well as modifying the cockpit seats and lockers. I doubt if that £15 even covered the cost of the materials.'

There is no doubt that Hillyard was always choosy about his customers, but once you were accepted there was complete trust. The yard never entered into any form of written contract until the late 1980s, when it started building the Moonfleets. Up to that time it was all word of mouth, David Hillyard and then Dennis Cullingford relying on their own shrewd assessment of a customer's character as their guarantee that they would pay up when the boat was delivered. On occasion they would request a payment on account when the job was half done, but they would seldom quibble about the exact sum to be paid. Some customers habitually gave the yard blank cheques to settle their accounts, because they trusted them to fill in the correct figures. Simple invoices like 'to supply one 12-ton yacht' would often arrive up to six months after the new owner had taken delivery. Hillyard always wanted to be sure of complete customer satisfaction before he demanded payment. Dennis was to retain the same trust when he took over the running of the yard.

One of the reasons why new Hillyards were such good value for money was that the yard's profit margins were very modest. However, this worked in their favour, as it did with the Admiralty during wartime as we shall see later. Customers knew that they would always get a fair and honest deal and that, given the high level of inflation running throughout most of Hillyard's life, the value of their craft would appreciate. And they kept coming back. This, taken together with the well-proven reputation of his boats, produced a band of devoted followers, who would never contemplate going elsewhere or consider owning any other type of boat.

As a result of all this the yard prospered. As one enthusiast put it, 'David Hillyard was incapable of building a bad boat, because he understood what the ordinary, impecunious cruising yachtsman wanted, and he put that before profit.' Anthony Painter*, a yachting journalist, summed it up when he wrote 'in one respect David Hillyard was, perhaps, unique. He was the last yacht builder to be motivated by a love of the sea and little ships rather than the balance sheet.'

Although Hillyard was the proprietor of a successful business— and he was always pleased to point out that it was simply 'David Hillyard' and never, in his time at least, David Hillyard and Co. or Ltd., money never turned his head. To the end, he maintained the same, basic Christian values that he had learned as a youth. He had no desire to live it up. He was quite content with a simple life-style. One newly appointed manager of the Belgrave House Christian conference centre in Littlehampton, on being introduced to David Hillyard by one of the staff for the first time, actually thought he was the gardener. Later that summer, when running a young people's camp at Climping, the manager was faced with an overflowing sewage tank. An appeal went to the yard for a pump and who should arrive but Hillyard himself, this time dressed in a brand-new suit, which he appeared to disregard as he got down to the job of clearing the tank.

Quite a number of those who knew him speak about his quiet and kindly concern for other people. One day a young widow, left on her

---

* *Yachting World*, 1975 March issue.

own with a large family, was out with her youngsters for a winter walk in the snow and happened to meet him as they passed by the yard. 'Look in on your way back', Hillyard called out and when they did, they found that in their absence he had made them a sledge!

He was a man of simple tastes. 'You must be able to afford a decent car,' said a customer one day. 'Yes,' said David, 'come and look at it.' He took the customer around the corner of the shed to show him his old Francis Barnett motorcycle, with its wooden box on the back, leaning against the wall. He rode it for years becoming, it must be said, something of a risk to life and limb in his later years. He never wanted after anything different.

In his dealings with his customers, however well off they were, David was simply himself. Meeting them in cap and shirt-sleeves, he would talk to them, in the Essex accent he never lost, in exactly the same way he would talk to the men. It was said that he dealt with each client as a gentleman but ended up having a friend. Today, too often a boatbuilder's customer starts as a friend and ends up an enemy. Being born when he was, however, there was no such thing as being on first name terms. He was Mr Hillyard to all but a privileged few.

He was the sort of person who was absolutely above-board about everything. At one Boat Show he refused flowers on his stand because, he said, he had 'nothing to hide'. At the shows he was never a great publicity man, working on the principle that people interested in his stand would find their way to it. He would have nothing to do with trade unions in his yard because, as he maintained, 'if any man has a complaint, he can come to me.' This led to enormous mutual respect between boss and men and they knew he could do their jobs as well as they could. They knew where they stood with him and that, although they worked hard, he was always fair in the way he treated them.

He was always giving encouragement to young people and was prepared to take time to explain boats and their construction with them. Tom Jeffers told of how Hillyard taught his son to build a 10ft dinghy, using only manual tools. 'The boss was pleased to do this,' said Jeffers, 'and gave him every help and encouragement.' Denny Desoutter* remembered the time when, as a young man after the war with

---

*   Editor for many years of the magazine *Practical Boat Owner*.

no money to spare, he put his head into David's office at the yard and asked if he may look around but explaining there was no chance of him becoming a buyer. David merely said 'yes, please do, have a good rummage and enjoy yourself. If you want to know anything, come and ask me.' When David learned his name he said, 'Was your father the artificial leg chap? He used to come in and look around from time to time, just like you're doing...'

Many who knew him pay tribute to his engaging nature. One timber commercial traveler, who called on Hillyard at the yard for twenty-odd years or so, never actually received an order. When asked why he kept on coming to the yard said that he always felt good after a meeting with Mr Hillyard. 'It was as if I had been to church!' And in that is the clue to why this simple man made such an impression on everyone whom he met. Whereas many profess to be Christians, Hillyard was the genuine article. As we have seen, he became a committed Christian early in his life and thereafter lived out his faith so naturally that it was part of him. In fact, although he was not one to 'push religion down your throat', as Tom Jeffers put it, he was as ready to talk to his customers about his faith as he was about his boats.

After he arrived in Littlehampton, Hillyard was attracted to a group who had come together just a few years before and who stood outside the mainstream Christian denominations in those days. They met initially in homes in what they believed to be New Testament simplicity. They did not call themselves a church, but an assembly, with the emphasis on the people who attended rather than the building they met in. The name they preferred for themselves was 'brethren' and they were part of the movement which had begun in the nineteenth century in the West Country and had come to be known as the Plymouth Brethren. They had no paid ordained ministers, believing that ordinary members should be able to share their own understanding of scripture and to participate in worship. Every Sunday morning, they met to 'break bread', thus celebrating communion in a simple and unstructured way with members contributing a thought or a prayer or a meditation or a hymn.

As Evangelicals, they also went out of their way to share their faith. Every Sunday evening they would hold a 'Gospel Service' and during the summer they held open-air services in the surrounding villages.

The work prospered and the number of adults and children attending increased, particularly after the Great War, and it continues today as the Parkside Evangelical Church.

The assembly was run by a committee of 'elders'. These were men who were recognised as having leadership qualities and who demonstrated Christian integrity in their lives. It is not surprising that David Hillyard served the assembly as an elder in his time and took his share when it came to sorting out the problems and woes which form an inevitable part of the human condition. Being the intensely practical man that he was, he was often to be seen riding around on his motor-cycle, visiting people who were down on their luck and dispensing welcome gifts. But being the modest man that he was, it was the sort of charity he preferred not to have reported.

In anticipation of growing numbers, the group had first rented and then in 1924 bought a property in Littlehampton, Argyle Hall in River Road, not far from Hillyard's first premises and just around the corner from his second. On Sunday mornings he would always be seen performing his first duty—going to the yard to give Tiddles, the cat, his breakfast—before taking his place in the meeting. To sit near to David whilst the Bible was being read always meant hearing it twice! He was so well acquainted with it that he would often recite the passage *sotto voce* but just keeping one word in advance all the time. He was not so strictly devout, however, that he would not go to the aid of any yachtsman who got into distress on a Sunday.

Although committed to Argyle Hall until his death, David Hillyard had a broad grasp of the Christian faith. When the service times were adjusted to meet local and blackout needs during the Second World War, he would frequently visit the nearby Methodist church. Tom Jeffers, who was himself a Catholic, and David Hillyard both had pretty clear-cut convictions about morality. You can imagine his reaction when, at one of the Boat Shows, some brochures advertising a nightclub venue were delivered to his stand!

As we have already noted, he loved music, and would always sing his heart out. One of his self-appointed tasks was to pay a visit to the old folk in East Preston workhouse every fortnight to take a service. Dennis, taken along to support the programme, used to be told, 'Shout loud or they won't hear you.' Dennis Cullingford, who from the age of twelve played the piano at these events, said the shouting was actually to cover Hillyard's piano mistakes! The old folk certainly appreciated him, and he continued to serve them for many years until the workhouse was closed.

Of course, in those days, singing was not confined to church and many evenings at home were spent around the piano. In the early days at Littlehampton, when Hillyard was lodging with the Ravens, his old friend from Forrestts in Wivenhoe, Sunday afternoon might see his host, an ex-Salvation Army man, playing the cornet, while Hillyard wrestled with the harmonium. When his musical yearnings were aroused and unsatisfied, he would get on his motor bike and visit the Salvation Army citadel in nearby Worthing. It was quite in character that, when the BBC Home Service *Down Your Way* programme visited Littlehampton, Hillyard was coerced into taking part and chose for his favourite piece of music, 'The Lord's my Shepherd; I'll not want...' It summed up his life.

Part II

THE YARD AND THE BOATS

Chapter 8

THE BOATS THAT HILLYARD BUILT

So, what sort of boats did David Hillyard build in those early days, the boats that in turn built his reputation? Although he was disinclined to keep records before World War II[*], it is possible from exhibition brochures, Lloyd's Register of Yachts (which was published annually until 1980), the archives of the Hillyard Owners Association and direct from the many owners whose boats from this period are still alive and well, to build up a fair picture of what would have been offered had you presented yourself at the yard looking for a yacht, or enquired at the Hillyard stand at one of the many Boat Shows at which the firm exhibited.

The atmosphere you would have found in the yard would have been that of a world long gone, before the age of GRP, nylon and terylene, marine ply and laminates. Reading a pre-war specification for a Hillyard, one can almost smell the wood-shavings and the pot of glue on the stove. Keels would usually be of oak or elm, although Hillyard preferred the latter as the long line of fixings in the garboard could split oak keels. Stems, stern posts and deadwoods were of grown oak (that is, timbers sawn and shaped according to the flow of the grain in the selected branch of the tree) 'sided as required'. Timbers would also be of steam-bent oak, on most of the range at 6in centres, with every fourth timber doubled in the main part of the hull. On the larger vessels, sawn oak frames would alternate with the steam-bent timbers. Bilge stringers running the entire length of the ship were of a generous size. Planking was of pine (or pitch pine in the pre-World War II days, being virtually impossible to procure after that war), larch or mahogany, all copper fastened, with decks and cabin tops being of tongued and grooved pine, canvas covered and painted. Pitch pine or teak decks could be fitted as extras.

---

[*]   And any he did keep were destroyed in a fire in 1946.

Deck fittings, cabin coamings and cockpits were of mahogany, with a similar medley of pine and mahogany down below, although owners had a good deal of say as to what went into the cabin. A regular basic on all Hillyard boats was the 'brass bilge pump on bulkhead,' and the ballast was uniformly described as 'outside with a quantity inside for trimming.' The latter was always cemented in the bilge of hard-chine boats (though never in round-bilge boats), which made for a clean boat. Some later owners might express concern that they never knew what was going on under the cement, but the practice never seemed to cause trouble[*].

Painting was done in 'approved colours', although the brochures do not say who had to approve them. In fact, the standard colour in those days was always cream, white only being countenanced as 'standard' well after World War II. An anchor and warps were always included in the sail-away price. Metal fittings such as chainplates, stemheads and masthead fittings were typically on the heavy side, being fabricated at the smithy in the yard in mild steel then galvanised, but it all made for strength and peace of mind. Coming upon a Hillyard for the first time, particularly if you have been nurtured on stainless steel, the handrails and stanchions almost challenge you with their blunt ruggedness. After World War II, Tom Jeffers came up with the idea of having them constructed out of galvanized water pipe! It was sturdy, cheap and easily available through the local plumber and today these rails and stanchions make a Hillyard instantly recognizable.

Spars were of sitka spruce or pine, made in hollow glued box sections with solid inserts at the base, spreaders and truck. Masts were often mounted in tabernacles on deck which, of course, not only made them easier to step, but also left the cabin below unencumbered. Lucas of Portsmouth were the suppliers of sails in the early years. In fact, the relationship between the two firms became so close that the then young Peter Lucas always referred to Hillyard as 'Uncle David'.

---

[*]   The filling of bilges with concrete was standard practice in those pre-war days among many boat builders, a practice which originated with fishing boats. Provided the concrete was poured when the hull was new it rarely gave any problems and had several advantages. Beware however a boat whose bilges were filled with concrete later in its life. Invariably the reason for it was to hide some horrible defect from the prying eyes of subsequent owners and surveyors!

Over the years Hillyards have been powered by a wide range of auxiliary engines. They were classed as extras on some of the earlier boats but Hillyard, aware that any profit on a job often lay in supplying an engine, always tried to persuade owners to have one fitted. In the early years he adopted Kelvins, made by Burgess Marine of Glasgow. They were simple and reliable, used by the local fishermen and were extremely long-lasting and long-suffering. A Kelvin instruction book even advised the operator that if a gear lever stuck he should hit it with a hammer! The makers supplied a folding propeller, one of which caused a bit of excitement on one occasion. An engineer at the yard decided to test an engine in a boat whilst it was hauled out ashore under cover. In the process, one of the blades broke off the propeller and flew through the roof of the shed. The unbalanced prop then broke the shaft.

After trying Fortis and Watermota engines, Hillyard finally came to a good arrangement with Stuart-Turners—or 'Stupid-Turners' as the men called them. These engines could be highly temperamental. 'When you got to the narrows coming into the harbour,' claimed Jeffers, 'they stopped!'

The standard range of Hillyards gradually evolved over the years, although because of incomplete records, we do not know exactly when some of the models were introduced. We do know that the range varied from time to time as new craft were introduced and old designs were either not offered or were no longer ordered. By 1930 there was a comprehensive range to choose from, the 2½-tonner, a 4-tonner, a 5-tonner, a 7-tonner, a 9-tonner, a newly introduced 12-tonner and a 14-tonner. Most people would have been able to find a yacht of the size they wanted 'off the peg'. In 1933 an 18-tonner was introduced (which continued to be built until 1967). This model replaced the 14-tonner in popularity. It seems that the next year the 7-tonner was dropped and from 1937 no one bought the old 12-tonner.

Hillyard 'tonnage' requires a word of explanation. It did not always correspond to the Thames Measurement (TM)*, which was (and to

---

*   Thames Measurement is in fact nothing to do with tonnage although always
      called 'Thames Tonnage' . It was originally introduced in 1885 as a way of
      measuring a boat's size for the calculation of harbour dues. Later it became
      used as an early handicapping system for yacht racing. It is calculated as

some extent still is) the usually accepted measure of describing a boat's size. For example, a Hillyard 6-tonner might measure 5 tons TM, or a later 13-tonner, 12 tons TM. The reason for this is that, as seen in the footnote, Thames Measurement is based on beam and length between stem and sternpost or rudder stock. As many Hillyards had canoe counters, it meant that a considerable amount of hull aft of the rudder stock was never taken into account. Not unreasonably, Hillyard considered it right to measure from actual stem to actual stern. In transom sterned boats, as many of the pre-World War II boats were, the Thames Measurement and the 'Hillyard' Measurement would have been the same. Not so in the double ended boats.

Standard boats were advertised with a variety of extras. In fact, the canoe sterns, which are so distinctive of Hillyards, were optional extras on some of the earlier designs. At the same time, standard boats were frequently less than 'standard', in that Hillyard was quite prepared to modify his designs to suit a customer's individual requirements. If someone wanted a boat somewhat longer than the design, Hillyard saw no problem in spacing out the moulds on a longer keel. This was particularly easy to do with the chine designs. A 40ft schooner might become a 45ft schooner. Similarly, he would oblige by putting in an extra strake in the topsides if the customer wanted more headroom below. Another might want a bunk positioned athwartships, and so on.

Frequently alterations happened as construction went along, without anything being put on paper. It has been said that no two boats in the standard Hillyard range are exactly the same and there is something in this. To quote a brochure, 'Although these craft are standardised, it is recognised that in fittings there is much individual taste, and the purchaser's ideas are embodied to any extent, provided that they do not materially affect the cost.' Certainly, owners were given a say in the interior layout of their craft, although on one occasion Hillyard refused a request. This was when a customer wanted his cabins fitted out cabinet-maker style, in teak and bird's-eye maple, but he would not do it for him. In the event the man got in his own labour to do the

---

follows: (length minus beam) multiplied by beam multiplied by half beam, all divided by 94. Length being defined as that between the stem and the sternpost, or rudder post if shorter.

job but Hillyard was vindicated at the end of the season when, in spite of a beautiful appearance, the tolerances of the doors and shelves were so fine that nothing would open or close!

Although Hillyard was quite prepared to build motor cruisers for his customers, they were not a major part of his output other than his work for the Admiralty in World War II. He did advertise a 45ft motor-cruiser in the late twenties and early thirties (price—£1,200 less engines which were twin 36hp Kelvins) and the yard turned out several sizeable twin-screw motor-yachts around that time. For example, *Marguerite* (ex-*White Aster*), is a 35ft very traditional looking 12-ton twin screw motor yacht dating from 1926. Then there was *Iere* (22 tons) in 1929, *Five-O* (not the original name) (20 tons) in 1931, *Gay Adventure* and *Iorana* (both 14 tons) in 1932 and 1935. Around the same time, he was also offering a motorised version of his established 12-tonner and we have records of several smaller motor cruisers. One such was *Iceni*, the yard launch for many years, which was not built as a workboat but as a motor cruiser for a customer who later part-exchanged her for something larger. *Iceni* had the same 24ft hard chine hull as the gaff rigged sloop *Willing Boy*, which after several years as David's personal dayboat, was relegated to become the yard workboat. However, most of the craft produced were sailing cruisers.

In 1931, Hillyard's launched what was intended as a 50/50 motor sailor for a Mr A. A. Rowse, a director of Morris Motors Ltd, which received much publicity in the magazine *Motor Boat*. She was named *Cygnet* and was a 42ft 18-tonner with that distinctive 'Hillyard' double-ended look, although with an aft cockpit. She was ketch rigged with, not surprisingly, a 36hp Morris engine and a good deal of engineering gadgetry.

The smallest of what became the 'standard' range was the ever-popular and revered 2½-tonner which was hailed in the *Motor Boat Manual* as being 'the smallest practicable auxiliary yacht available in the country'. A 2½-tonner was offered from the early 1920s right through to the early 1960s, although in two successive versions. She was an 18ft sloop with a beam of 6ft 6in, drawing 3ft 6in with a slightly raked transom stern. A 1933 brochure offered a canoe stern for an extra £25. When launched she was offered at a price of £100 increasing to £149 with a 3hp Stuart Turner engine installed (£5 extra if a reverse gear was required). She was a proper little yacht with a pronounced wineglass section. She had an iron keel with extra ballast inside 'for trimming', which amounted to almost half the total ballast and took up all available space under the cabin sole. Even with this smallest of all standard Hillyards there was room for variation. *Bambi*, built in 1938, was slightly shorter than standard, being only sixteen feet long on the waterline and *Decibel* (ex-*Isobel*) was built in 1935 for a friend of Dr Harrison Butler who had Hillyard fit lead inside ballast (rather than iron), which made for a lower cabin sole.

The 2½-tonner came with either a gaff rig or a Bermudan mainsail (in the *Yachting Monthly* of December 1936, a D.H. Smith tells how he developed a 'boomless Balearic mainsail'—a sort of 'gunter-cum-sprit' loose footed main and topsail all in one piece but there is no evidence that anyone else travelled the same eccentric path). In her first version she had both a bumpkin and a bowsprit; the later version omitted the bowsprit*.

Mike Hill, who has both owned and researched the history of this amazingly popular little craft, believes that part of its secret was Hillyard's advertising. He offered a sailaway boat for £100, and thus did what Henry Ford did with his Model T, that is, he broke the psychological price barrier.

There is no doubt she hit the market at just the right time when there were no other 'pocket cruisers' at that sort of price. A high proportion of the early customers for the 2½-tonners were naval and military men, professionals, doctors and the like and Hillyard always made sure that people knew how many of them had come back asking for something bigger, a request he was always ready to oblige.

The 2½ was the sort of boat that could be built in an odd corner of the yard, often using offcuts from larger craft. She has beguiled plenty

---

* An uncle of mine, Richard Henty, who owned the brewery in Chichester, bought a new 2½-tonner in 1953, when I was ten. On her I experienced my first sails on a proper keel boat. He kept her on a mooring at Itchenor in Chichester Harbour and I have extremely fond memories of my times on her. She was probably the boat shown in the list of Hillyard boats at the end of this book as being named '*Miss Henty*', number 491. She was an absolute delight to sail and, to someone who had previously only sailed on a tiny lugsail scow, she seemed huge.

of post-war owners who often started their sailing exploits in one. One such was Ray Whitaker who chronicled the hilarious adventures that he and his wife had with *Puffin*, a 1936 2½ bought from an east coast yard in the 1950s. It was their very first yacht and the book they wrote, *Two-and-a-Half Ton Dream**, is described later in Chapter 16. The fact that *Puffin* brought them back alive, green though they were, is itself a tribute to the little ship's design and construction.

The 2½ was redesigned by Tom Jeffers after Harry Todman left the firm, because Hillyard wanted a boat with more generous accommodation than the earlier design. Constructional changes were also introduced which reduced costs. The beam shelf was replaced by a heavy sheer strake. Forward of the cabin top there was a fore-and-aft 'long knee' on which the deck beams rested, fitted inside the top strake and bolted to it. Side or half beams were replaced by athwartship deck planks. Fixed rectangular lights with rounded corners replaced portholes. The bilges were slacker and the underside of the keel was cut away in a curious bight aft of the external ballast. Hillyard considered this to be advantageous when coming about. Many thought that the second version was better looking than the first, although it sacrificed some sailing qualities for more cabin space. At least four were built with raised topsides from cockpit to stem, a device which was quite common in sailing cruisers in the 1930s. This made for increased internal volume, providing room for a marine toilet in the fo'c'sle.

Accommodation was, as to be expected in a boat of this size, limited but adequate for two. With one berth to port, a galley to starboard with a second berth ahead of it running into the fo'c'sle, she just about had sitting headroom. 'You have to stand up and put your head through the hatch to pull up your trousers' said the owner of the 1933 *May* (ex-*Kitty Rosa*), owned at one time by the family of Sir Hugh Casson, architect, artist and writer. 'The living accommodation is equivalent to a lightweight tent but everything is in reach when sitting down,' is how one owner described his 2½ *Margaret Ann*. Built in 1938, she had her cabin top widened which made her comfortable and spacious below. Her owner says that he has had six sat down for dinner; 'not bad in an 18-foot boat.' But then, as the skipper of *Grace*

---

*   Whitaker, Ray. *Two-and-a Half-Ton-Dream*, Herbert Jenkins 1959.

(1936) put it: 'sailing a pocket cruiser like her is all about quiet anchorages, cocoa, oil lamplight and too much reading of Maurice Griffiths'.

Despite its diminutive size, the 2½-tonner was a good sea boat. Owners report it to be remarkably dry, unless going to windward. The short waterline length could make progress in a seaway difficult and wet. Having a long keel, it could be slow in stays but its ability to carry way made up for that. With sheets trimmed correctly, it easily sailed itself on a reach. At least one owner added a bowsprit to the later stemhead version which improved performance and if nothing else, the owner reported: 'it made the boat seem bigger—a useful psychological effect when at sea'.

The hull of the original 2½-tonner was easily driven, finer in section and deeper in draught than many comparable yachts of the same period. Some surprisingly quick passages were made in it; in 1930, a Mrs Rickarson sailed her 2½ *Brat* all the way to the Kiel regatta in Germany, with a passage time from Littlehampton to Dover, some eighty-four miles, of twelve hours. Although many owners confined their sailing to local waters, some cruised extensively, endorsing Hillyard's oft repeated remark, 'The boat will take you anywhere your courage allows you to go.'

As we have seen, Hillyard began building sailing cruisers in earnest in 1922, starting with some 4-tonners. *Twinkler*, exhibited at a 1922 Boat Show, was one of the first, as was *Daisy* (ex-*Big Fizzer*). These were offered with either a transom or canoe stern and fitted with either a deep keel or a centreboard. They were 21ft long overall, with a beam of 7ft, the keel models drawing 3ft 6in. One example, *Fortuna II*, of which the lines plans still exist, was built in 1933 and is still sailing today. She has a solid looking profile; the sort of hull that inspires confidence. As her owner says, 'in the water she looks very purposeful'. *Talisman*, built around 1930, is an example of a 4-tonner with raised topsides, running from the stem back to the cockpit, a configuration often adopted by Hillyard in his early days.

The 4-tonners were stemhead sloops with a 250-square-foot sail area. They could be fitted with bowsprits and a larger sail-plan; something which would have added £7 10s on to a bill of £145 for the basic model. Like most Hillyards, they need plenty of wind to get going but were stiff and stable for their size. The gaff rigged versions were reported as sailing remarkably well and they were easily sailed single-handed. The interior arrangements, once again, were up to the individual owner, but the brochures offered two lockers, two seats with hinged pipe-cot berths over, and a patent W.C. forward. There was sitting headroom under the fo'c'sle hatch (presumably for the latter!) and under the cabin top. For an engine, Hillyard offered either a 4 or 8hp Stuart Turner (reverse gear £5 extra). They were fitted with roller reefing gear and the popular Wykeham-Martin furler on the foresail. They could easily be handled by one man (one current owner admitting that his 4-tonner sails best when it is allowed to dictate ninety per cent of the control!). They were capable of cruising during the summer months anywhere around the coast and were shallow enough for creek crawling. They were described as having a 'graceful' performance in winds Force 1 to 5, though Tom Jeffers remembered these early craft as being somewhat tender. However, they made some remarkable passages for their size as we shall see later.

Kit of Arun, a stemhead version from 1929, is another one still sailing today. She has been well looked after and, apart from some necessary repairs due to war damage, she has never needed a major refit in the years she has been afloat. Her owner sees no reason why she should not continue to sail well into the twenty-first century. *Arno* (ex-*Oran*), a 1938 bowsprit model, has also survived well. Like most boats of her age she has required a good deal of restoration. The original timbers and planking are still sound and are a tribute to the quality of boatbuilding in those days.

Lisa Jane (ex-*Vanette*), built in 1935, is an interesting variation on the 4-tonner standard model. She is unusual in that she not only has a canoe stern giving her that unmistakable Hillyard profile, but she was rigged as a ketch, quite something for a boat only 23ft long. The small mizzen mast was stepped in the cockpit, and the tiller had a built-in loop order to clear it.

Harry Todman also drew out the lines for a pre-war 5-tonner. Exhibited at some of the early shows, she was 24ft long, with a beam of 7ft 6in and a draught of just over 4ft. She was advertised in both transom and canoe-sterned versions, the canoe stern as usual being an extra. Standard accommodation included two settee berths with sitting headroom under the cabin top, plus a cot berth and W.C. forward. There was almost 6ft of standing headroom in the companionway and she was the first Hillyard to have a form of doghouse mounted on a sliding hatch over the companionway. She came with either gaff or Bermudan rig (roller reefing was an extra) and you could buy one for £250 plus £25 for a canoe stern. Jeffers recalled the design as being somewhat wet to sail but it was successful and sold well.

In 1925, Hillyard added a 7-tonner to his range. This had a transom stern, was 28ft long, with a beam of 8ft and a draught of 4ft 3in, and could be either gaff or Bermudan rigged. A later version was a motor-sailer with a flush deck, a reduced rig, and a draught of only 3ft 6in. *Whaup* (later to be known variously as *Fortuna III, Henty II, Patuna, Paulinski, Georgie Lass* and *Joanne!*), first registered in 1925, is a surviving much re-named example. Present owners of the standard 7-tonners speak highly of their construction. The planking was pitch pine with decks of Columbian pine, 'laid in narrow widths, caulked and payed with marine glue'. Unusually for a Hillyard, the cockpit was made in teak, as were all deck fittings, rails, covering boards and cabin coamings. As far as we know, six are still sailing, including *Moyune*, built in 1930, though now converted from her original gaff rig to Bermudan. Her owner describes her as a sturdy sea boat, and good under power.

These 7-tonners were immortalised by a well-known owner of one, the children's author Arthur Ransome, who used her as the fictional model for the boat in two of his children's best loved books, *We Didn't Mean to Go To Sea* and *Secret Water*. The boat was *Nancy Blackett*, whose exploits under Ransome are described in Chapter 15. She is still fully in commission, now owned by a charitable trust.

Her second owner, Mr Paget Bowyer, who was living in the Poole area in the early 1930s, stated that he understood from a friend that *Nancy Blackett* was in fact one of six part-completed hulls bought by Hillyard from Shutler's of Poole when they went bankrupt. Such evidence as we have, however, makes us wonder if his informant is correct. Lloyd's Register shows all the 7-tonners of which we are aware as having being designed and built by Hillyard's, and Shutler's, who were a small yard with a low output, would have been unlikely to have been mass-producing a yacht of such a size. Dennis Cullingford had never heard of this transaction and pointed out that the cost of transporting six 28ft hulls from Poole to Littlehampton would in those days have been prohibitive. But the design of these 7-tonners is somewhat non-Hillyard with a transom stern and a straight stem, more like many of the small boats being built at that time all over the country, especially along the South coast and in the West Country. Shutlers probably did built boats like this and they did go out of business around 1930. But most researchers into *Nancy's* provenance state that she was built by Hillyard's in 1931 for a retired solicitor called Seymour Tuely. In 1933 he sold her to Paget Bowyer who then sold her on to Ransome in 1935.

Next in size came the pre-war 9-tonners, 30ft long, with a 9ft beam and a 4ft draught. They had an aft cockpit and a canoe stern. Accommodation was originally for four, with upholstered settees in the main cabin and two bunks in the forecabin. In the 1920s and 1930s the general specification was the same as for the 7-tonners. They came with a variety of rigs—sloops, cutters and ketches. Peter Heaton, a well-known author and yacht deliverer, owned *Penguin* (ex-*Linnet*) and cruised extensively in her, described her as 'almost too comfortable to be a yacht' but he also thought she would have been much improved with finer lines and more sail area. Production of these pre-World War II 9-tonners continued right up to 1939 and a couple were built in the 1950s. Thereafter, Dennis Cullingford produced the lines for a new aft-cabin 9-tonner which became the best-selling Hillyard of them all.

The pre-war 12-tonner, another extremely popular design, first saw the light of day in 1930 and was readily identifiable as a member of the Hillyard family, albeit originally with an aft cockpit. In the Boat Show brochures of the time she was stated to be 35ft long, 9ft 6in beam and drawing 3ft 9in. Her standard rig was a ketch and, as we have noted, Hillyard also used the hull as the basis for a twin-screw motor cruiser.

In 1931 he launched an interesting variant of the 12-tonner for Dr Dudley Stone, at that time a well-known radiologist[*]. Although

---

[*]   The vessel was described in the 27 November 1931 edition of *Motor Boat* magazine.

the sail-plan was conventional, the power unit was innovative to say the least. *D'Sel* (later re-named *Dudley*) was a diesel-electric boat. A 110-volt generator was run off a two-cylinder high speed Gardner diesel, and powered an electric motor, which turned the propeller. In the event of a failure in the electrical system, the diesel could be connected to the shaft by means of a chain sprocket. It does not seem to have been successful. As can be imagined, the combined power plant took up a considerable amount of hull space, even though Dr Stone claimed that the electric motor under the saloon floor was useful as a footrest and 'for airing damp clothes'. The main problem, however, appears to have been that, despite a highly sophisticated control system, the electrics tended to over-heat. But as we shall see later, *D'Sel* lived to see another day.

Another pre-World War II design, which continued to be built after the war, was a 35ft 13-tonner. Double-ended with a beam of 10ft and a draught of 5ft 6in, she came with a variety of rig options. The standard was a Bermudan ketch, but equally you could order her with a gaff mainsail or with a wishbone main or as a Bermudan cutter. The ketch rig was particularly adaptable in heavy weather as she sailed well under mizzen and jib alone. The original design had a low flush deck, but this was later modified for more headroom by adding a raised foredeck and a coachroof. Normally, she was fitted with berths for six.

The 13-tonner was marketed after the war as a '13-ton Auxiliary with a BMC Commodore 50hp engine'. She was sold as being 'a sea-going boat to sail the family in safety, anywhere'. Considering her size and displacement she performed well in most conditions. Like many Hillyards, she often needed to be sailed round from tack to tack, helped by a backing of the jib, to blow her bows through the wind. Her long keel kept her steady, allowing the helmsman to steer with minimum effort. But in light airs the cry was 'switch the engine on!', which is how most people sail their boats today anyway.

The last standard design to appear before the war, and one which would continue to be built right through to the 1960s, was something different. All the previous models which we have been looking at were of carvel round bilge construction. This new 18-tonner had a beamy hard-chine shoal-draught hull and was designed to be cheap to build, without quality suffering. The boat was designed primarily to counter the then growing popularity of the 'Dutch barge' type yachts. It offered generous accommodation with an extreme shoal draught, but had only limited sailing ability. The 18-tonner would, Hillyard thought, correct that disadvantage. It had the familiar double-ended look which we now associate with Hillyard. Its schooner rig was particularly popular, having a gaff foresail and a Bermudan main. After the war it was offered in sloop, cutter and ketch versions. It was a large boat for the yard, 40ft long and 11ft wide, sleeping seven: four in the aft cabin, two in the saloon and one in the forecabin. Yet for all its size it could be purchased in those far-off days for only £800 all in. One example, built in 1939 just before the outbreak of war, was *Runagate*, for the author Nevil Shute, who incorporated sailing scenes in many of his books. He could have been describing *Runagate* as the yacht featured in his novel *What Happened to the Corbetts* published in the same year. We write more about Nevile Shute in Chapter 15.

As time went by the hull shape of the 18-tonner was modified. After the war, it had its sheerline raised to give more headroom below, and draught was increased. Brochures from that time showed the hull with a raised deck from bow to midships. Whilst it was double ended, the rudder was hung outboard from a raked sternpost, unlike the majority of Hillyard's hulls where the rudder was hung inboard. Some boats had external iron keels, the majority having only internal ballast, bedded in concrete, with the boat relying on its wide beam for stability, just like a barge yacht.

These boats attracted much favourable comment in the yachting press; 'a wholesome vessel, an offshore cruiser' said *Yachting Monthly* in January 1941 and Maurice Griffiths chose her as a good example of a shoal-draught cruising yacht in his 1937 book *Little Ships and Shoal Waters*[*]. He noted, as many have done since, that they (and many other of Hillyard's chined hulls) were designed so cleverly that the chines scarcely showed above the waterline at bow and stern when the vessel was afloat. 'Her good buoyant sections and nice flaring topsides give stability when pressed over,' Griffiths wrote. He also praised the cen-

---

[*] Griffiths, Maurice. *Little Ships and Shoal Waters: Designing, Building and Sailing Shoal Draught Cruising Yachts*, Kennedy Bros 1937 (many re-prints).

treboard arrangement, an optional extra, and in his book reproduced a drawing of this; the board slides down in a slot built through the hull just to one side of the keel rather than the traditional way of going straight through the middle of the keel. This method prevented any weakening of the wooden keel and strengthened the garboards. The board, which might be of oak or steel, was worked by a worm-driven winch in the cockpit. This feature, thought up by David Hillyard, puts paid to the commonly held belief that Hillyard merely repeated the same old design over and over again, just scaling it up or down for size. It demonstrates that he could be as clever and innovative as Jack Laurent Giles or other well-known designers working at that time.

Hillyard did not, as many people supposed, merely limit himself to turning out boats built to his stock designs but was always prepared to fulfil the needs of those who wanted something different. In 1928 the yard launched a 28-ton ketch called *Beaver* for Major C.A.H.Younger, the scion of the Scottish brewing family who we mentioned earlier. *Beaver* was written about and described in the *Yachting Monthly* of the time. Her sail and cabin plans indicate something different from the Hillyard norm, something more traditional, in fact. From the Major's previous experience in a barge yacht, he required light displacement, generous beam, and high freeboard, all of which earned a rather ungenerous comment from the magazine that she was 'not exactly a pretty ship owing chiefly to her rather heavy transom'. A photograph of her taken at anchor shows, to our modern eyes, a large well-proportioned very traditional looking ketch with a long bowsprit and a tall topmast of which anyone would be proud. However, despite the magazine's comment, she satisfied her experienced owner who stated she was 'a lively ship which sails well and which was always remarkably dry and easy on the helm'.

Apart from those mentioned, there are several other craft still afloat and sailing from these early days which do not fit any of Hillyard's standard specifications. One is *Winnie*, a large gaff rigged ketch (58ft long including a bowsprit) and there is more than one 8-tonner with different dimensions from the norm.

The largest ship to go down the yard's slipway, before World War II, was *Valmara*, a 28-ton gaff cutter which was launched in 1937. She was double ended and 55ft long, excluding bowsprit and bumpkin. Her owner, Mr W.W.Rowse, a consulting engineer, 'spared no expense in incorporating the most modern equipment' (*Motor Boat and Yachting*, November 25, 1938), which included a hydraulic steering system, a novelty in those days and new to Hillyard's, hot and cold running water, and a bath. There were 'quarters for a crew of two', making her something of a throwback to pre-Corinthian days.

Thus by 1939 Hillyard was well established as one of the premier yacht and boat builders in the United Kingdom, with his creations admired by many but looked down on by others as 'a bit common and cheap' and not really for gentlemen. It must be remembered that in those far off pre-war days, snobbery and tradition was very much to the fore in such activities as 'yachting'. It was not all that long before then that those in 'trade', such as Sir Thomas Lipton, were refused admission to the top yacht clubs and the soubriquet 'proper' for yacht builders and designers was limited to the likes of a select few such as William Fife, Camper & Nicholson, A.H.Moody, G.L.Watson and Alfred Mylne. Even Jack Laurent Giles and Fred Parker were considered interlopers and, for most people, owning a Hillyard was really 'beyond the pale'. As a result of the upheaval about to fall on the country in September of that year, all this would change by the time boatbuilding began again.

Chapter 9

AT WAR AGAIN

Initially Word War II had little impact on Littlehampton. The early days were known as the 'phoney war' which lasted from September 1939 to May 1940. The summer of 1939 was hot and long and the presence of groups of evacuee children from London made it seem, as one contemporary put it, 'little more than an over-large and long-staying Sunday School treat, sharing our beach with the children.' In contrast, that winter was one of the coldest on record for years. For a short period, the River Arun froze right over.

However, the horrors of war came home to Littlehampton in a very direct way at the end of May 1940 when, for nine days, an operation took place which ranks among the most significant events in British history (known as Operation Dynamo). A whole army was lifted off the beaches of Dunkirk by an armada of little ships most of which had been designed and built with nothing more than pleasure in mind. Around our coasts, over seven hundred craft, many from Littlehampton, were rounded up by the Royal Navy and, sometimes crewed by their owners, rescued 385,000 troops from under the German guns and bombers[*]. Almost a hundred of these little ships were lost, but many survived and are still afloat today, assiduously restored and maintained under the ever-watchful eyes of the Association of Dunkirk Little Ships[†].

Just before the event, Royal Navy officers came to Hillyard's looking for suitable boats. These they commandeered, along with supplies of blankets and stores taken from various yachts moored there. During all this, the people of Littlehampton could hear the gunfire from the other side of the English Channel, a sobering reminder of just how near the enemy was. David Hillyard and his men helped to

---

[*]   Brann, Christian: *The Little Ships of Dunkirk*, Collectors Books 1989.

[†]   See adls.org.uk

organise the requisitioned craft, although not many which the yard had built were involved. This is because those most needed were shallow-draught motor cruisers which could get right into the beaches and which were able to make their own way out and back. They took a couple of non-Hillyards which were stored or moored there (*Inspiration* and *Seagull*). But we know of at least five Hillyards which were involved in the action.

The only pure Hillyard motor cruiser which was involved was the 40ft *Iorana*. Her usual summer cruising ground was the West Country, but she was at Littlehampton when the call came. Having served and survived at Dunkirk, she was acquired by the Royal Navy in 1942. After the war she was eventually found and extensively refitted by Donald Berry, who cruised the Solent and south coast of England with her till the early 1960s, when she became a houseboat on the Thames. Today she is still alive and well and active once again in the Association of Dunkirk Little Ships.

The 42ft *Cygnet*, described in the previous chapter, was the 'fifty-fifty' built in 1930 for Mr A. A. Rowse of Morris Motors. She was a beautiful looking little ship but as she drew 6ft, her usefulness at Dunkirk must have been limited. However, she was manned by a Royal Navy crew who brought her back safely. Her later history is much sadder. After some years based in Devon, during which time her rig was altered to make her easier to handle, she was acquired by a John Hurrell who planned to sail her to South Africa for a family wedding. She was in poor condition by then and against contrary advice, Hurrell and his crew of three set out in October 1984. The ship was lost whilst crossing the Bay of Biscay, and neither ship nor crew were ever found.

Windsong, a 35ft auxiliary ketch, was one of the few sailing boats to be used in Operation Dynamo. In spite of the optimism of her owner, Mr G. L. Dalton, who reported that he was 'ready for sea and able to take thirty passengers' (which, as Christian Brann in his book* wrote: 'said more for his valour and patriotism than for the capacity of his vessel'), she had to be towed across the Channel by a trawler, the winds being so light. After a hairy first trip, others took her over for

---

*   Ibid.

a second visit to the beaches, where they distinguished themselves by recovering a group of soldiers. After several post-war owners, she still lends grace to the reunions of the Dunkirk Little Ships.

Two other Hillyards appear in the list of craft at Dunkirk, one being *Wings of the Morning*, a 12-tonner, built in 1933 for the then Lord Dunboyne and written up in *The Motor Boat* magazine at the time. She was a standard production ketch costing £750, but with some very interesting features, being adapted for all-year-round single-handed cruising. For this she originally had two sail plans, one for winter with a 406-square-foot Bermudan main and mizzen and one for summer of 576 square feet. Along with *Windsong*, she also happened to be at Littlehampton and both were sailed down to Dover by local men, where they were handed over to the Royal Navy.

Although we know that *Wings of the Morning* survived Dunkirk, it is not known if she and the other craft involved, *Lady Rita*, a 14-tonner built in 1938, are still afloat.

It has been suggested that the venerable 1925 7-tonner *Whaup*, mentioned earlier, also did duty at Dunkirk. The records show a vessel simply listed as *Fortuna* (one of *Whaup's* many aliases), without any detail, as having been involved in Operation Dynamo. A later owner, Group Captain P. A. Lombard, CBE, DFC, reported an interesting fact which came to light when the same boat had to have some planks replaced after being blown on to rocks at the entrance to Padstow Harbour in the 1960s. The damaged planks, which were of Oregon pine, were pitted with what he reckoned were .303 bullets, which led him to believe that she may have collected them off the beaches of Dunkirk.

After Dunkirk, the town of Littlehampton found itself in the front line. The nearby long, shelving beaches were ideal for use by landing craft, a fact not lost on the Germans. It was later learnt that Littlehampton would have been the centre of the planned landing-zone of the German ninth-army had Operation Sea Lion, the German invasion of Great Britain, gone ahead. Whilst the invasion never happened, Littlehampton's West Beach was used later in the war for a dress-rehearsal for the Allied D-Day landings. In anticipation of an invasion, scaffold poles and barbed wire defences were hastily thrown up on the beaches, which were then heavily mined. Pillboxes, roadblocks and batteries sprouted everywhere. Trade came to a halt in the harbour, which became a restricted area and was 'disguised' by the demolition of the light tower on the end of the east jetty. The distinctive wooden 'pepper-pot' lighthouse at the landward end was removed too. Both jetties were broken by the removal of the middle planks and were wired for demolition. In the event of an invasion, a barge, which was permanently moored to one of the jetties, was to be swung across the fairway effectively blocking the entrance.

The harbour became a base for light patrol craft and air-sea rescue launches. These were based on the Hillyard moorings and maintained by the shipyard engineers. The air-sea rescue launches had to be able to leave and enter the harbour day and night in rescuing downed airman, and in an effort to keep the entrance navigable at all states of the tide the harbour dredger, *Leconfield*, spent most of the war fighting a losing battle with the bar.

The harbour itself got off lightly. Although several residents were killed in bombing raids, the bombs which were dropped nearest to the Hillyard yard were in fields and the golf course nearby. No damage was suffered by the yard or by Butlin's Amusement Park just across the river. The nearest any of the Hillyard men got to a real live German was when an enemy plane crash landed on the riverbank nearby and the wounded pilot was carried in triumph along the road outside.

The yard men did, however, have fire-watching duties added to their daily work. They gathered each night in the office waiting for the air-raid warning siren. Some became members of the Home Guard, patrolling the town at night, often after a hard day's work. Some pre-war motor-boats were converted into fire floats and fitted with powerful pumps. In the event of an air attack, saving the yards along the riverbanks had priority over nearby dwelling houses. The yard had its own siren situated next to the slipway and its own fire-pump capable of delivering water anywhere within it.

Joe Robinson and his brother Alec were in command of one of the fire floats, a converted ship's life-boat. This came into its own one August afternoon in 1940, when the nearby RAF aerodrome at Ford was attacked by German aircraft and virtually destroyed*. As the main

---

*   This incident was witnessed by a young Antony Rushworth-Lund, then undergoing flying training, who later became the owner of Ransome's old Hillyard, *Lottie Blossom*.

water pipe had been fractured all the floats were sent upriver to pump water across the fields to extinguish the raging fires. The Robinsons recorded how they had a hard time holding the float in position against a strong tide and they returned exhausted.

With the commencement of the war, all private yacht building ceased but this in no way decreased Hillyard's workload which merely switched to work for the Royal Navy. Like many other boatbuilders, Hillyard found himself once again working for the Admiralty. As demand increased so he had to take on more men, and at the height of the yard's wartime operations his workforce expanded from forty to one hundred and forty[*]. One might think this would necessitate an increase in managerial overheads but that was not so, not being the way Hillyard handled these things. The office staff remained at virtually the same pre-war level, due in the main to the efficiency of an able local boy, Hector Billings. At first employed part-time, Hector went full-time when the war got underway and, with his wife working part-time but no other help, he somehow held the office together during those frantic war years.

Naturally, what was built at the yard underwent a considerable change and numbers increased dramatically. Small clinker-built motor launches with little single-cylinder Stuart Turner petrol engines were produced in their dozens, all under the motherly care of Hillyard's 'dinghy man', Bert Ponting. 60ft hard-chine rescue launches with double diagonal planking were built tucked into several semi-covered spaces. Spare corners were filled with partially built 45ft round-bilged diagonally-planked liberty boats. A visitor toward the end of the war would also have found them working on 25ft motor cutters, 16ft motor dinghies for survey work, 26ft motor whalers and several passenger launches sheathed in copper, designed for somewhere in the tropics. These boats were all built to Admiralty designs but no doubt with a large input from David Hillyard himself.

Harry Hicks had charge of building the largest craft to be built at the yard. These were Harbour Defence Motor Launches (HDMLs) to a design produced by J. W. 'Bill' Holt for the Admiralty in 1939,

---

[*]   Sharp, Nigel. *Troubled Waters: Leisure Boating and the Second World War*, Amberly Publishing 2015, p155

in response to the need for small warships to defend harbours and estuaries against infiltration by enemy submarines or small surface raiders. They were of round bilge design, 72ft overall (small enough to be carried as deck cargo on larger ships) with a beam of 15ft 10 in, a draught of 4ft 7in and a displacement of 54 tons. They incorporated eight watertight compartments, twin propellers and two underslung rudders, giving them great maneuverability. The earlier ones built at Hillyard's were driven by twin Thorneycroft diesels; the later ones by twin Gardner 8L3 diesels, the most powerful marine diesels built at that time. With a fuel capacity of 1,500 gallons, they had a range of 1,000 miles at 12 knots, or 2,000 miles at 10 knots. They also carried a ten-foot sailing dinghy in chocks on deck, something which would have delighted David Hillyard's heart. Designed to carry a complement of twelve officers and men they gained the reputation of being extremely sea-kindly boats, admirably adapted for their role of patrol work in estuary and coastal waters and beyond. They carried a variety of armaments, including guns, machine guns and eight depth charges which, together with 'asdic', made them effective submarine hunters. They were employed throughout the war all around the world in a variety of uses.

Unlike the better known 'Fairmile' Naval patrol boats which were built in large numbers but which came to the boatbuilder in pre-fabricated kit form, the HDMLs were built from scratch and were therefore only ordered from the better equipped and well regarded yards round the country. Hillyard's produced sixteen of these HDMLs out of a total of over four hundred built during the war years [*]. Their double-diagonal mahogany construction gave them strong and resilient hulls, but the construction demanded new skills and techniques from the shipwrights. Despite their size and complexity, the yard completed four in each of the years 1941-43, three in 1944, and one in 1945. After the war, a good number of the HDMLs were sold off by the Admiralty, both in Britain and wherever they happened to end their years of service; many were in the Mediterranean. These HDMLs were good looking vessels with long low graceful hulls and many were convert-

---

[*]   Nos.1005-6, 1056-59, 1235-6, 1269-72, 1401-2, 1458-9. No. 1460 was ordered but cancelled when the war ended.

ed into fine motor yachts or commercial work boats. These included some of the Hillyard HDMLs: No. 1236 became a workboat owned by a Qatar oil company for use in the Persian Gulf, renamed *Neba* and later converted into a motor yacht; No. 1271 became a Mediterranean based motor yacht renamed *Madonna Ta Pompeii*; and No. 1401 was also converted into a motor yacht, renamed *Keredon*. A good number of these craft ended their days gracing our estuaries and backwaters as houseboats. In quieter times, Hillyard's would later convert another ex-Admiralty craft into a 20-ton yacht re-named *Bristol Fashion* but it is not known who originally built the hull.

The other main wartime Naval activity in the yard was the building of landing craft. These Landing Craft Assault vessels (LCAs) littered the smaller sheds. In all, more than 2,000 were constructed by different boatbuilders around the country between 1940 and 1944 and over one hundred were built at Hillyard's. These were wooden, flat bottomed craft, 41ft 6in long with a 10ft beam and a displacement, fully laden, of 11 tons. They were powered by twin 65bhp Ford V8 petrol engines, driving two shafts, giving them a maximum speed of 11.5 knots. Their 64 to 68 gallon fuel tanks meant that they had a range of only between 50 to 80 miles. They were intended to be hoisted aboard a mother ship and slung out on arrival at their destination. They were the workhorses of the various sea-borne invasions which took place during the war, including of course D-Day in June 1944. Designed with a draught of only one foot at the bow they could deliver two tons of troops with their equipment over a dropped ramp right onto the beaches. They carried sufficient built-in buoyancy to allow them to float even when swamped, with self-sealing fuel tanks, should they be shot at and holed.

Tom Jeffers, who looked after this assembly line, called them 'oblong wooden boxes.' They required new techniques to construct. The wooden hulls had ¾in armour plate along the sides, ¼in over the engine-room, with bullet proof side decks, as well as steel bulkheads fore and aft. There was a supposedly bullet-proof shelter for the Coxswain, which was situated at the aft end in the earlier models, but was later moved forward to the bow on the starboard side, the space to port being fitted with a machine gun. The plating required riveting, a new departure for Hillyard's. The red-hot rivets were used direct from portable furnaces, and the loud, metallic clamour from the riveters was something which had never been heard in the yard before.

Some of the workers involved had never been seen in the yard before either! In spite of heavy boots and dungarees, there was no disguising their feminine forms; for the first-time women were employed in the yard. David Hillyard had always been very reluctant to take them on, believing that boatbuilding was not woman's work. However, now, with an increasing workload and a shortage of manpower, he gave in to the inevitable. He hired about a dozen girls to work on the LCAs, and by all accounts they were just as ready as the men to put in a long, hard day's work. Mrs May Goodhew, whose husband also worked there during the war, remembered cycling over the bridge from the town to the yard to start work sometimes as early as 7.00 a.m. and frequently working late into the evenings. She confessed it was tough work holding a dolly on the heads of the copper nails under the craft, while her companion clenched them above. However, like the others, she did it willingly because she wanted to contribute towards the war effort. She also met her husband there, a man more used to making furniture. Some of the women continued at Hillyard's for several years after the war, until they gradually fell away, many to get married.

Engineering and electrical work increased dramatically at this time, with the latter being contracted out to specialist firms. The problem of housing these extra workers' equipment was solved by clearing out the customers' personal stores, which became ideal repositories for wires, electrical instruments and the somewhat secretive electricians, who were always viewed with unwarranted suspicion by the others.

In 1941, Hillyard's nephew, Dennis Cullingford, joined the yard for a year, before he went off to do his military service. He remembers his uncle kitting him out on the first day of his apprenticeship. He was presented with all his tools enclosed in a strong, impractical leather bag and with the wry comment, 'I don't suppose you will have time to wear any of them out.' He had memories of the narrow, low ceilinged old Air Raid Shelter being turned into a veritable Dante's *Inferno*. The volume of engine installation work led to an increase in the need for large diameter copper pipes that had to be persuaded to

1. The High Street, Rowhedge, c1900

2. The Ferry, Rowhedge

3. Rowhedge Regatta

4. Congregation of the Mariners Chapel, Rowhedge;
Hillyard was aged 18 at this time

5. Hillyard, aged 16,
sailing his home built 16ft sharpie on the river Colne

6. Forrestts' Shipyard, Wivenhoe c1902,
where Hillyard served his apprenticeship.

7. Littlehampton c1906, as Hillyard would have found it

8. The chain ferry crossing the river Arun at Littlehampton

9. The swing bridge, which replaced the chain ferry in 1908

10. Littlehampton lifeboat, *The Brothers Freeman*, being launched for a shout; she was withdrawn from service in 1922

11. The Shipyard c1960; the 19-tonner *My Lady Ailsa* in the foreground

12. Views of the Shipyard

13. Hillyard's stand at an early Earl's Court Boat Show;
the 6ft pram dinghy on sale for £27

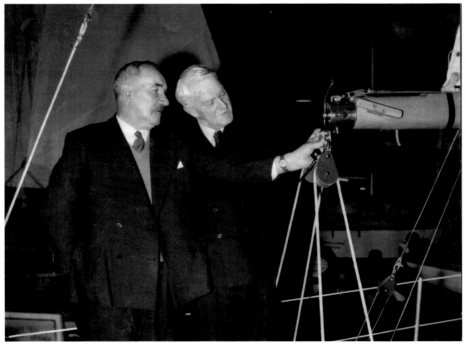

14. Hillyard with Reginald Moody at an Earl's Court Boat Show c1960

15. David Hillyard at the Shipyard

16. The Shipyard's wartime fire float – a converted ship's lifeboat

17. Women employed at the yard during World War II
to help build landing craft

18. The workforce expanded to some 140 during World War II

19. Harbour Defence Motor Launch (no. 1458),
one of many built at Hillyard's during World War II

20. Workers on their HDML

21. Probably the first yacht built by Hillyard
after his arrival in Littehampton in 1906

22. Hillyard motor cruiser the 40-ft *Iorana*, one of the many little ships
at Dunkirk in 1940 and still afloat today

turn acute bends. This was carried out in that building by the process of annealing the copper, then filling it with molten lead so that the pipe would not 'cripple' when bent. The heat for this process was obtained from roaring, red-hot monster Primus blow lamps.'The heat in that confined space was tropical', he used to say,'the sweat that poured forth was like the rolling of the Amazon… and the language…!!!'

David Hillyard's Admiralty contracts led to a strange spin-off. Being the man that he was, and unlike plenty of others, he felt it would have been morally wrong to profit from and make a fortune out of the conflict. He was therefore prepared to complete all war work at cost plus a minimal level of profit. Many boatbuilders in a similar position used the opportunity to profit greatly from the work, enabling them to update their plant and build shiny new sheds and slipways. Hillyard simply cut holes in his buildings to accommodate the larger craft. At one point the Admiralty sent representatives to his yard to find out why the bills they were receiving were so low. They discovered why and were so impressed by his honesty that the Admiralty never thereafter questioned his quotations or estimates. In fact, they often ended up asking him to quote for work which they knew he would never take on and then use his costings to browbeat other firms to match them. This appreciation was demonstrated by the Government awarding him an MBE at the end of the war, which he was proud to collect from King George VI at Buckingham Palace in 1946. This award no doubt left some hard feelings on the part of many other boatyard owners.

Admiralty work meant contact with Naval personnel and several officers who came to take over their vessels from the yard later became peacetime customers. Some learned about the ways of the River Arun the hard way, like one brand new young Midshipman who rushed into the yard with his small crew to take delivery of yet another new LCA. Facing a strong flood tide, with the threatening presence of the swing bridge just upstream, the Midshipman was advised by the yard staff, in the politest of language, to make sure he swung the bow of his vessel downstream before letting go. However, this young tyro in his shiny new uniform knew better. 'Let go for'd…let go aft…hard a'starboard,' and the LCA responded by drifting sideways up the river, props thrashing the water at full throttle! The bridge claimed yet another victim. As soon as the yard staff saw their newly built craft firmly wedged under the bridge on a still flooding spring tide, they sprang into action. Dennis Cullingford recalled 'a hundred pounding feet were heard racing around the in-tervening ground that lies between the yard and the bridge and once they arrived, everyone leaped into the cavernous hold of the LCA which, duly laden, sank down on her waterline. The Midshipman was brushed aside, suitable orders given and His Majesty's latest vessel was safely but unceremoniously steered back to the Hillyard moorings. Its first battle over, its impromptu crew discharged, the Midshipman reinstated, the vessel was finally seen heading down stream no longer needing a port navigation light, as the Midship-man's face could now fulfil that function!'

Recollections of Hillyard's at war are of early morning starts and work going on well into the night with bright electric lights illumi-nating the job in hand, safely screened behind blackout curtains and blinds, the efficiency of which were Hillyard's constant worry. Dennis also remembered the foggy day when he had the fright of his life when coming out of the Gents, he found himself almost eyeball to eyeball with an equally astonished pilot of a very low flying German Heinkel!

Although David Hillyard was prepared to do anything to help his country at this critical time, his nerve did fail him when the Admiralty suggested that he consider building the hulls of some midget subma-rines. Being the man he was, the idea initially appealed but when he was told that the work would be accompanied by the strictest security measures, he could not bring himself to do it. To him everyone and anyone was always welcome at his yard to see what was going on and he could not conceive having to hide some of his work away from prying eyes.

A sense of the coming return to normality was experienced when, immediately after D-Day, a letter was received from the man who was to become General 'Boy' Browning*. In June 1944 he had flown over the yard in a towed glider on his way to the landing grounds behind enemy lines in France. In this letter he confirmed his intention that

---

*   'Boy' Browning was married to the author Daphne du Maurier.

on his return from a somewhat 'pressing duty' he would come back and purchase the Hillyard yacht *Beaver*[*], then lying at the yard. He returned… and kept his word.

There was a huge pent-up demand for boats of all shapes and sizes as the war ended. But UK boatyards could not take advantage of this as the Admiralty retained control for some years and one had to apply for a licence to carry out any work over the value of £100 on any one vessel. Licenses were freely granted for work on fishing and commercial vessels but not for private yachts. There was also a woeful shortage of timber, supplies of which boatbuilders had to share with housebuilders and furniture makers. But somehow and slowly boatyards started working again, often returning to boats which had been started in 1939 and mothballed since.

Despite Vice-Admiral Sir Lancelot Bell Davies' experience, recited in the Prologue, costs were considerably higher in the immediate post war years than they had been in 1939. Whilst we do not have any comparable figures for Hillyard's, two almost identical 14-ton auxiliary sailing yachts built by the Berthon Boat Company in Lymington cost £1,500 in 1939 and £3,600 in 1948, their lead ballast keels increasing in cost by a staggering five hundred and forty one per cent from £78 to £500[†]. Bell Davies was a lucky man.

---

[*]   *Beaver* is the 28-ton Ketch referred to in the previous chapter, built for Major Younger.

[†]   Figures taken from Nigel Sharp's *Troubled Waters*.

Chapter 10

THE LINE GOES ON

At the end of the Second World War Hillyard was sixty-two. After the frenetic activity of the war years came the inevitable anti-climax. Admiralty orders dried up abruptly, naturally enough. They cancelled the order for the last HDML and orders for yachts could not immediately be fulfilled. Hillyard's did however still have several hulls in various stages of completion which had been stored in mud berths near to the yard at the beginning of the war.

In 1945 they completed a 5-tonner, which had been laid down in 1939, and recommenced work on a 10-tonner started in 1938 (it would be completed the following year), but apart from a 14-tonner there were no other new boats that year. 1946 was a thin year too, 1947 a little better, 1948 a struggle. It was not till 1949 that the order book began to fill up again, and then mostly with smaller craft. After the war, few people had much money and, as always, yacht ownership reflected the economic climate of the times. It was the 6-tonner together with the diminutive 2½-tonner of everlasting appeal which gave Hillyard's their bread and butter in the austerity of those post-war years.

The main problem facing all boatbuilders at that time was the shortage of decent timber and other materials. So much was being diverted into house repairs and rebuilding that rationing had been imposed. Unless they had stocks to draw upon, it was extremely difficult to find what was required, although Hillyard maintained that good timber could always be found if you looked hard enough. One timber which became available post-war was iroko, which began to be used for keels, stems, sternposts and deadwoods and, later, planking. Although described as 'the poor man's teak', iroko is by no means a bad timber. It is stable and reasonably resistant to fresh water, which mahogany is not. At this stage boats were usually planked in mahogany (pitch pine being no longer available) and were offered in iroko as an extra. With the post-war introduction of good waterproof glues, timbers and frames became laminated rather than grown or sawn. Decks and cabin tops were made using waterproof marine ply, a wonderful wartime bonus for sailing people, originally sheathed in canvas but later in glass fibre and polyester resin and nowadays in epoxy. Later still sails became Terylene, stoves used bottled gas, windows were Perspex and boats were regularly wired for electricity. But much of that was in the future. The period immediately after the war was a time of shortage and innovation.

Another real problem was sourcing lead which was in great demand, commanding sky-high prices. In order to meet the need, Hillyard looked around for any large yachts which had survived the war, bought them up and proceeded to remove their lead keels. These included *Palatina*, a large ketch built in 1891 and one of Charles Nicholson's early designs, whose remains still lie in the mud down river from where the yard used to be; *Aglaia*, a 70ft ketch built by Sibbick's of Cowes in 1902; and *Isoletta*, previously owned by the test pilot Neville Duke. Interestingly, the 60ft ketch *Isoletta* had been built in 1909 by Forrestts in Wivenhoe, the very yard where David Hillyard had served his apprenticeship. With those hulls which were not too damaged Hillyard ballasted them internally, modified the rig and sold them on. Some of the lead could also be sold on, which helped to balance the yard's books.

The first post-war standard hull came to be known as the 6-tonner, and a large number were built. It began life as a 5½-tonner and was then lengthened. According to the yard's brochures and Lloyd's Register of Yachts, the lengths varied between 27ft and 27ft 6in, with a beam of 7ft 6in, and a draught of 4ft 3in. In his advertising, Hillyard used the same photographs and internal layout plans for all these boats. They accommodated four people, two in each cabin, and there was a separate heads forward. The after cabin was shown with a wardrobe and dressing table with a galley in the main cabin. There was no chart table. The usual cockpit arrangement incorporated the petrol tank under the port seat adjacent to the wheel, which was mounted on the forward bulkhead, and the water tank on the starboard side. Originally sloop rigged with a three-quarter jib, they were later changed to a masthead rig. A few of the earlier boats suffered from excessive weather helm and this was corrected by an alteration to the rudder configuration. One 6-tonner was rigged as a ketch and several later owners have attempted to improve the boat's overall performance by adding a bowsprit and changing from sloop to cutter rig.

The 6-tonner has proved to be a rugged sea kindly boat with high freeboard, canoe stern and an inherently safe, deep centre cockpit. This was small by later standards and, at the request of some customers, Hillyard's built three with aft cockpits. Like most Hillyards, the 6-tonner was designed for comfort, not for speed, with a steady rather than a sparkling performance. Armed with a decent size auxiliary engine, this boat perfectly fitted many novice sailors' requirements and they sold in volume.

It is at this stage of the yard's history that Dennis Cullingford, David Hillyard's eldest nephew, comes into the picture. As mentioned earlier, he and his younger brother had grown up with their uncle's boats and business. When they were still in short trousers, they were often chased off the boats lying at Hillyard's moorings and were always ready with the irrefutable rejoinder: 'Don't you know who we are? We are the boss's nephews?' As we have seen, the young Dennis entered employment with the yard when he was sixteen, before he went off to war. After the War, as soon as he was de-mobbed in 1946, he began working alongside his uncle again. He already knew the trade well and by the end of the 1950s had taken over the designing side, with his uncle looking over his shoulder. He was responsible for some highly effective designs, still essentially Hillyards but incorporating his own ideas.

At the bottom end of the range he added what a Boat Show brochure at the time described as 'a 20-foot Sailing Yacht with a 6-foot beam and a draught of 3 feet 3 inches'. She was exhibited at the 1956 Boat Show for £495, with an auxiliary engine as an extra. Dennis remembered the event well. She was planked in soft wood and displayed in the hall in way of a strong drying draught; he arrived at the stand prior to opening day to find every seam had opened wide! Panic reigned for several hours as he worked flat out to make her presentable before the public started arriving. 'At least one could not fall between the planks when the show opened,' he recalled.

Dennis also introduced a new 5-tonner to the Hillyard range. The concept was a combination of good sailing performance with more commodious accommodation than to be found in the South Coast One Design, which was beginning to become popular and to which his 5-tonner was compared. She was a handsome, transom-sterned craft with a raised foredeck and low cabin top, 24ft 7in long, with a 7ft 6in beam and a draught of 4ft 6in. She could sleep three in comfort plus a fourth in a quarter berth and she even had a chart table, a rarity for a Hillyard. One couple who had previously owned four Hillyards (2½-, 5-, 8- and 9-tonners), believed that this 5-tonner had by far the best sailing performance of them all, an opinion endorsed by others. However, only five were built.

In 1954, the new 9-tonner was introduced, which has been de-scribed as the most successful Hillyard of all. Once again, the lines had a family likeness to the already popular 6-tonner and were drawn up by Dennis Cullingford. This model, together with the later 12-tonners, are the Hillyards you are most likely to meet around our coasts as more than eighty were built following the end of the war. The 9-tonners were selling in large numbers right through into the 1970s. At least one owner had three in a row! Three were built with an aft cockpit, two of them on the same keel! The was because the first was burnt out and only the keel salvaged. However, the stand-ard design was the familiar double-ended centre cockpit sloop. They had five fixed berths with a pipe cot in the forecabin and some were fitted with two heads. The galley was somewhat small and there was no chart table, an omission which several owners remedied in various ingenious ways.

Those who sail them speak highly of the amount of room available on board. That includes standing headroom in the main saloon and aft cabin, with sitting headroom in the forepeak; better than average for a boat of her size. The centre cockpit is a safe refuge for the family and lends itself well to a fixed open-backed wheel shelter which many had fitted later and which provides yet more space when cruising. Some 9-tonners have been used by liveaboards, making passages as far afield as Australia and Vancouver (see Chapter 13).

The 9-tonners were sturdily built. The owner of one, *Moomba*, comments, 'Having rebuilt her, I could see how well she was con-

structed.' Some have inevitably suffered from the long-term legacy
of degradation of the galvanized nails used for fastening the deck (a
problem to be found in other Hillyards as well). Her weight and long
keel mean that, while she carries her way well, she is not ideal for close
handling in the likes of canals or modern crowded marinas. Like most
heavy long keel yachts, going astern is always a bit of a lottery with no
certainty as to which way she will turn.

Many have expressed surprise at the 9-tonner's stability. It has
proved to be comfortable at sea and dry in rough weather. 'With eight
rolls in the main and no genoa she handled perfectly in a gale' or 'an
incredibly dry, high-sided boat—never wore oilskins any time I had
her' or 'amazing performer in heavy following sea' are the sort of comments frequently heard about its seaworthiness. At the other end of
the Beaufort scale, like most Hillyards, it needs a breeze to get it going, although the owner of *Golden Corn*, who sailed his 9-tonner regularly back and forth across the Irish Sea, says that he does not feel
that 'for her type and size passage making is in any way slower than
one would hope.' These Hillyards have been sailed widely, including
many Atlantic crossings.

A past owner of the 9-tonner *Trimley Maid*, the late Michael
Walden of whom more is written in Chapter 16 wrote; 'The Hillyard
9-tonner is the result of applying a true cruising concept with inbuilt
strength and fitness for function in every aspect of her design. The
hull shape, displacement, relative waterline length, plus 50% ballast
ratio, ensure stiffness in a seaway and seakindliness. High freeboard,
small centre cockpit and large decked area keep the on-watch crew
safe and dry, and subject to minimum pitching moment in a following
sea, a result of the canoe stern offering minimum resistance.' Although
some would have liked more beam and more roominess, for him, the
narrow beam below offers safe grab-rails and 'wedging places' for the
crew in a seaway.

One owner said: 'In 1985, returning from the Outer Hebrides to
Poole, I was caught in a full gale in the Portland Race—and I am here
to tell the tale!' Get the right balance and a 9-tonner will sail on her
own quite easily. The long keel allows the helm to be left long enough
to make a cup of coffee, go to the heads, or do some chartwork. To
reduce weather helm, and in the hope of increasing speed, several

owners have clapped on more sail by adding a bowsprit and converting their sloops into cutters. *Nantua's* owner, believing his 9-tonner to be under-canvassed, not only added a bowsprit with a substantial masthead jib, but also stepped a mizzen aft of the stern cabin with a 4ft bumpkin. This cured a weather helm problem and improved her performance considerably. Another owner found that a feathering prop substantially increased his boat's speed. The very fact that the 9-tonner has satisfied so many owners over such a long period of time demonstrates that, whatever her vices, this post-war design was certainly a winner for Hillyard's. She was one of the best.

Next in popularity to the 9-tonner was a redesigned post-war 12-tonner, again designed by Dennis. Based on the original pre-war design, she was in his words a scaled up 9-tonner. He gave her a bigger sail area and longer overhangs. Her standard rig was still a sloop but she could be ordered as a ketch, and several owners have subsequently converted their sloops to ketches. They were originally powered by a BMC 2.2 Commander, which some felt left the boat under-powered. Most of these original engines have been replaced over the years, usually with something a bit larger.

Like the pre-war 9-tonners, the 12s have six berths distributed between three cabins, with good stowage and headroom. It is said that the aft cabin is comfortable even in a gale. The size of the galley left something to be desired for some owners and others disliked the deep, non-self-draining cockpit, which meant that any water shipped on board found its way into the bilges. However, very seldom does this occur, and the deep cockpit is valued by many family sailors for the sense of security it brings. The 12-tonners have proved to be ideal liveaboard boats and have many long and intrepid cruises to their credit.

They are described as 'a no-nonsense, strongly built boat sailed by people who want reliability and comfort', and those who do sail one find it has few vices. Although like most Hillyards they are safe and secure rather than fast, they have a high reputation for coping with gales and heavy weather.

Svano, launched in 1959, is an interesting example of a 'stretched' 12-tonner. She was originally built for Tom Southern (see Chapter 13) who won the prestigious Royal Cruising Club's Challenge Cup and Romola Cup for successive annual cruises between Littlehampton and the Baltic, and the Balearics and beyond. At nearly 40ft, she has a sleek hull form which, together with a larger than standard sail area, give her excellent sailing performance, particularly upwind. A later owner logged 8 knots on a beam reach in a Force 3 to 4.

In the early 1960s, Dennis Cullingford was to add an 8-tonner to the range. These turned out to be very popular. They were 30ft long with an 8ft 6in beam and a draught of 3ft 6in. They had a chine hull and bilge keels, an aft cockpit and a canoe stern. Hillyard had the idea of building one without an iron keel at all, but with all internal ballast like the 18-tonner. Following a near capsize of this one on a trial sail, an iron keel was fitted before delivery. By this time buyers were expecting more and more by way of home comfort in their boats and to keep up with the competition Hillyard's were forced to follow this trend. The specification for these 8-tonners included Dunlopillo mattresses, four electric cabin lights, a well fitted out galley, and Terylene sails. They had four berths (with limited headroom for the two berths in the forepeak) and a separate heads compartment. They were powered originally by BMC Navigator or Captain engines.

A large number were built up until the mid-1970s. Dennis remembers the 8-tonner as being a 'fill-in' boat, built by Bert Ponting, the dinghy man, when other work was slack. Due more to Bert's temperament than the wishes of future owners, no two boats were ever quite the same. Rigged as a Bermudan sloop, she is said to need a Force 4 to show her real potential, although those who have experienced both feel that these were a better light weather boat that the 9-tonners. Owners certainly speak highly of their sea-keeping qualities. They have chalked up some long and notable cruises.

In the mid to late 1960s and in the 1970s, before orders for new wooden boats dried up completely, and probably as a result of rising prosperity, the trend was for larger and larger boats to be in demand. Hillyard's reflected this trend by introducing their largest standard design yet. This was a 22-tonner which was an impressive voluminous yacht capable of sailing worldwide in safety and comfort.

As a direct development of the smaller hard chine 18-tonner, the new 22-tonners followed the same concept. They were 42ft long, with an 11ft 6in beam and drew 5ft 6in. They offered considerably more space and comfort than their smaller sisters and incorporated a large sunken deckhouse saloon. It did not take long for owners to have a solid open-backed wheel-shelter built over the forward end of the open cockpit. Their hard chine construction created lots of space below and allowed for standing headroom up to the full width of the boat, even in the forepeak which accommodated a single berth. A comfortable forecabin was fitted with two single but spacious bunks and a hanging wardrobe. Aft of this cabin was a spacious galley, opposite to which was a heads compartment. Steps led up to the deckhouse saloon in which a double bunk could be made up. The tanks for fuel and water were located under the saloon. More steps then took you either up to the centre cockpit or down through a passageway under the cockpit seat to the aft cabin where there were two more single berths, together with hanging wardrobes, a dressing table and a separate heads/shower compartment. In this arrangement Cullingford and Hillyard anticipated modern yacht design, where this layout is now commonplace. The engine was situated underneath the cockpit in its own separate engine room, access to which was either from the saloon or from the passageway leading to the aft cabin. Some of these 22-tonners, including *Wendy Woo*, built in 1965, were fitted with the first examples of a pressurized water system designed specifically for yachts. Ascot gas water heaters were provided in the galley and in the two heads compartments and each cabin had its own built in gas-heated radiator (the risk of a gas explosion was immense, especially as the gas cylinders were stored in the engine room!).

These large sophisticated yachts were rigged as Bermudan ketches and carried a spinnaker and a mizzen staysail. They had excellent sailing qualities and at least one of these (*Wendy Woo*, the author's previous boat) was fitted from new with taller spars to increase sail area. The author and other owners speak highly of their sea-keeping qualities, while their spaciousness can make them an extremely comfortable home. They can make long passages in almost any weather, as some of them have done, being extremely stable at sea. One owner arriving in Littlehampton from Greece proudly pointed to a bowl of fruit on the cabin table which had been there all through the voyage. They have been sailed, often with only a husband and wife on board, all over the world. The owner of *Tarion*, a standard model, worked hard at making what was a heavy displacement boat even simpler to handle with the addition of a bow thruster, powered reefing, in-boom reefing, a powerful engine and a powered windlass. *Tarion* was cruised extensively from the UK to the South Atlantic, where she was sadly lost some years ago, driven onto the rocks on the island of Tristan da Cunha.

When first built, the 22-tonners were equipped with powerful auxiliary engines. *Santa Lucia II* still has the original 65hp Ford, while *Wendy Woo* was originally equipped with a 63hp BMC Commodore diesel (replaced by the author with a 70hp Beta diesel). One past owner, Sir David Mansel Lewis, described her as a 40/60 motor-sailor and spoke highly of her handling even in high winds as 'a classic boat and a delight to sail and to live aboard'. As mentioned above the engines are situated under the cockpit floor in a separate engine room with good all-round access, and into which one can descend to check the oil, water or batteries. (Dennis Cullingford, incidentally, related how *Wendy Woo* once demonstrated to him the joys of being a boatbuilder. On a Sunday afternoon some years back, he was just relaxing after a good lunch when the phone rang, 'Hello, this is *Wendy Woo*. We are in the middle of the Channel and have a fire in the engine room. What do we do?' Dennis said 'I told them, they did it and all was well').

*   *   *

The London Boat Shows at Olympia and then Earl's Court increased in popularity during the post war period and became an important shop window for exhibiting Hillyard's boats. David Hillyard would sit in state on his box receiving an endless stream of visitors, owners, past owners, prospective owners and many others who would like to be owners if they could afford it. He affably welcomed them all like a patriarch. At the first Olympia Boat Show held in 1955, the Duke of Edinburgh made a personal request to see him and they chatted together about their mutual enthusiasm. The Duke was particularly interested in the Exhibition boat, *Mavrodaphne*, a new example of the 6-tonner, as the Duke knew that an identical one had just been delivered to General Sir Richard Gale, who at that time was Commander-in-Chief of the British Army on the Rhine. Of the boat, the

Duke said, 'It is very good value for money.' It is a wonder Hillyard didn't clinch another sale—a 'By Royal Appointment' sign would have looked good at the yard! General Gale later followed up his 6-tonner with a 13-tonner, *Firenze*.

In 1958, at the age of seventy-six, David was accorded the honour of opening the fifth Olympia Boat Show. In this he followed in the footsteps of a lifeboat coxswain, a lighthouse keeper, Lord Hailsham, then first Lord of the Admiralty, and lastly Viscount Montgomery of Alamein; the succession highlighting the increasing importance of the event. He was no doubt invited, not only because of his long association with the event, but also because by that time his yard had produced more small yachts than any other yard in the country[*].

Speaking to the exhibitors in his opening speech, he said, 'Don't despise the young people who keep coming to you with all their questions. They have a wonderful influence and more knowledge than we credit them with. I remember one young man who came to me with questions. What happened? Eventually I built him one, two, three, and finally, six boats.'

It is said that in his old age Hillyard became more conservative when it came to design and that he came to prefer modest sail-plans in the interests of safety. This may have been so, but it did not detract from the popularity of his yard's output. He maintained a lively interest in the latest trends and Maurice Griffiths, the Editor of *Yachting Monthly*, recalled how at one Boat Show in the early 1960s he turned up at the magazine's stand to discuss the then emerging new lightweight diesels for small craft. Griffiths said, 'he later jokingly declared that we had convinced him to install diesels in all his future boats, which I believe he did.'

Soon after that Hillyard's stopped exhibiting at the shows, at which there was a looming and ever-increasing presence of GRP boats. The sheer expense of getting the boats there, as well as the cost of renting a stand, all combined to make the exercise uneconomic. The next boat that the yard would exhibit would be the GRP 'Moonfleet', design many years later.

---

[*] Up until 1958, there were more Hillyards listed in Lloyd's Register of Yachts than any other builder. After that the number of GRP yachts built each year far surpassed anything one wooden boatbuilder could produce.

Hillyard by this time was an old man, and although he hung on manfully, he did not have long to go. Denny Desoutter, then editor of *Practical Boat Owner*, told of a visit to the yard just before the old man died. He asked how Hillyard fared. 'Pretty well, thank you,' David replied, 'though I do have a bit of a job getting my leg over my motor-bike to come into work in the morning.' Denny thought he was joking but he was not. Hillyard carried on riding his preferred form of transport until the end and well after he really should have done so.

Hillyard attended the yard daily right up to three months before he died, peacefully at his home in Littlehampton, in 1963 at the age of eighty. Perhaps he summed up the story of his life himself when he told a local reporter at the time of the 1958 Boat Show, 'I'll go on building boats. I love the sea. It's in my blood… I can't help it.' Those who attended his funeral service in his beloved Argyle Hall paid tribute to his Christian faith and integrity, and many more customers turned friends mourned his passing. A great character had gone from the world of yacht design and construction, but thankfully not the name which had come to represent good, honest craftsmanship and value for money.

There are only a very few boatbuilders anywhere in the world whose names have become synonymous with the boats they built. People say, 'there's a Fife' or 'that's a Hillyard'. But that's about it. One built yachts for the rich and famous which are today worth millions of pounds. The other built ordinary boats ordinary people could afford and can still afford today. That is David Hillyard's legacy.

*   *   *

It was natural enough for Hillyard, who had no children of his own, to the leave the business to his eldest nephew, Dennis Cullingford, just as it was natural enough for Dennis to carry on using the Hillyard name. Over the coming years, despite growing difficulties and competition from GRP craft, Dennis enhanced the yard's reputation even further. The hand-over from uncle to nephew led to no break in the Hillyard tradition. Boats built after David Hillyard's death would continue to be built to the same high standard as those produced during his lifetime.

This was demonstrated in the very first commission received by Dennis after he had taken over. He was approached by Tom Southern, a previous owner of the 'stretched' 12-tonner, *Svano*, to design him a new yacht of approximately 50ft overall to be capable of taking him anywhere in the world. Tom Southern was one of the yard's best promoters, having cruised widely between the Irish Sea and West Coast of Scotland, the Baltic, the Mediterranean and the Canary Isles in his previous boats. The new boat was to be easy to handle by a crew of two, comfortable in all weathers, and able to cruise anywhere the intrepid skipper wished. The result was *Aguila*, a 52ft ketch with a centre cockpit and accommodation for seven. As befitted the largest yacht to grace the Hillyard fleet, she continued the tradition of having a double ended hull with the usual Hillyard canoe stern. She fulfilled every requirement of her owner and throughout his long ownership he had not one word of complaint about the boat or her gear. He gratefully remembered having spent his best years in and around Hillyard's.

A request by an owner of a 9-tonner gave birth to another line of hard chine boats. This owner had been told by his anxious wife that discretion was the better part of valour and that the size of the boat they handled should be more in keeping with their advancing years. They asked Dennis for a bilge keel boat that they could sail themselves but with a powerful engine to be used when the foredeck was no place for the crew. Accommodation was only required for two. Dennis produced a stubby looking ketch, 32ft long, with a pleasant airy doghouse and sheltered cockpit. She broke with Hillyard tradition in having a square near vertical transom rather than the usual double ended hull. This feature gave the vessel a more modern look (and was easier to construct). Powered by a 35hp Mercedes-Benz diesel the boat was essentially a motor-sailer, setting only 300 square feet of sail. The couple were pleased with the result which was launched in 1967 and named *Maymaid*. They cruised in her successfully for their remaining sailing years, based in Falmouth.

This boat was admired by another aspiring Hillyard owner, but she was too small, sleeping only two people. He approached Dennis for something bigger to sleep four. The result was what was to become the popular 11-tonner. They too were hard chine, bilge keeled craft, ketch rigged with a transom stern and were 33ft long with a beam of 9ft 6in, a draught of 3ft 6in and a sail area of 350 square feet, all a little larger than the 9-tonner. The first of these, *Maid of Shannon*, was designed for space and easy handling, and was built to a high standard. She too had a Mercedes-Benz engine*. She was kept in immaculate order by Ken Pausey for many years and won many prizes at various classic boat rallies.

Ten others followed, built to the same design. They gained a reputation as good sea boats, despite being shallow with bilge keels. Owners claimed them to be comfortable at sea and with spacious accommodation for four people. Ken Pausey reported *Maid of Shannon* to be satisfactory off the wind although she was in his opinion really a motor-sailor (and none the worse for that). Others like *Pangchi* (ex-*Forest and Vale*) have been modified with the addition of a bowsprit and masthead genoa. This, together with a larger main and mizzen, improved performance substantially. Like other Hillyards, the 11-tonners have made many notable cruises and have proved to be excellent sea boats. One owner, having crossed the Channel single handed at the time of that notorious 'Fastnet Gale' in 1979, complained that 'he had nothing to do as the boat looked after herself.'

The family likeness was continued with two larger craft coming out of the yard. The bigger of the two, *Nourlangie*, was 40ft long and ketch rigged. She carried all her ballast outside in a lead keel and was powered by a 100hp Perkins diesel. As to be expected of craft sharing the Hillyard pedigree, she had excellent sea-keeping qualities, although these were not appreciated by one owner on his first Atlantic crossing. He wrote back to the yard full of criticism of her performance. However, on his return from the West Indies, he shipped 'a man of the sea', as he described him, who he appointed as sailing master. Another letter arrived, this time full of apologies, confessing that having been taught an extended lesson in boat handling he withdrew his complaints as unfounded. The defects were all to be found in his seamanship and when sailed properly the boat 'was a dream'.

---

* These engines became the diesel of choice for Hillyard's in the 1960s but were never particularly successful and many owners experienced problems with them. Mercedes stopped production of small diesel engines at around this time.

With the same workforce, Dennis continued to meet the demands of a full order book throughout the 1960s and into the early 1970s. One of the changes he did introduce, and for which he will be gratefully remembered, was the setting up of a pension scheme for the employees. His customers continued to receive the same service and knew they were dealing with a man of integrity, a committed Christian just like his uncle.

Another custom which Dennis began was to put on board each new boat a Bible with the yacht's name embossed on the cover. He used to say that as he had built the owner a good boat it was only right and proper that there should be the best of all books on board the vessel. These volumes have become sought-after collector's items and replacements were often requested by new owners on acquiring a second-hand craft without one.

Despite the prosperity of this period in the yard's history, it did not take much to see that labour-intensive wooden boatbuilding was beginning to face stiff competition from the revolution beginning to overwhelm yacht building. Boatyards went over to building in GRP and newcomers arrived on the scene. They were soon able to undercut the cost of wooden construction and promised a trouble-free hull. In those days, GRP was offered as being practically indestructible, requiring no or minimal maintenance. We now know that the picture is not quite as simple as this, but GRP boats swept the market. Wooden boats became the desired possessions of those who could afford them. As Roger Witt commented in an article in the magazine *Practical Boat Owner*[*], David Hillyard's 'boats for the people' had become 'boats for the few'.

Although the yard continued to undertake a good deal of maintenance and repair of wooden craft, it produced only one new boat each year from 1975 to 1977 and after that nothing until 1981-2 when it had a 24ft new build on the stocks. This was *Isis of Arun*, and her owner remembered completing the painting, varnishing and interior work at the yard before her launch in 1983. She was a pretty boat with an aft cockpit and a well raked transom hung rudder. The building of a small wooden yacht at that time was unusual enough to cause

---

[*]   Issue of March 1982

comment in the yachting press. There simply was no demand for new wooden boats.

Finally, in 1984 the last wooden boat to come out of the yard was completed. She was called *Hapara* and was designed by her owner, with much tweaking of the design by Dennis Cullingford. She had distinct Hillyard build details but she had a transom stern and was rigged as a gaff cutter. She was the most expensive boat Hillyard's had built and was, according to yacht Surveyor John Lilley, very well constructed with a considerable amount of care. He remembers seeing her being built as a young man at the time his father kept the family Hillyard at the yard over the winter. John Lilley also says that at around this time the yard fitted out to a high standard a concrete 'Endurance' hull.

*   *   *

There was, however, a continuing and growing interest in the boats that had already emerged from the yard. In 1977 Robert and Pamela Keen, then owners of the 1964 built 12-tonner *Kalena Kay*, founded the Hillyard Owners Association with the aim of providing and encouraging 'the exchange of ideas, details of boats and sailing experiences between owners, past, present and future and with the builders.' They began to publish a periodical newsletter, *The Hillyarder*, which became a platform for owners to express their views and share their experiences. They also began to arrange social gatherings and occasional meets at venues around the coast. When they had to give up running the Association, Michael Joyce, a serial Hillyard owner and enthusiast, took over as Commodore and promoted the Hillyard cause so enthusiastically that the HOA, as the Association was known, became one of the most active associations of boat owners. Over the years he amassed details and sometimes photographs of upwards of six hundred Hillyards built since 1920, collected sales brochures which go back to 1929 and other ephemera relating to the yard and its boats. He also assembled a small library of books written around or about Hillyards and their voyages. In all this Dennis Cullingford, and then his son Simon, were of great assistance, dredging their memories to fill out the picture.

Hillyard owners, like other owners of classic sailing craft, are often fanatical enthusiasts who understand that they hold their classic craft in trust for future generations. Ask them about their treasured possessions and you will be showered with details and photographs, regaled with experiences, invited aboard to look around, and generally evangelized into buying a Hillyard for yourself. Many of us would be deterred by the degree of commitment required to keep these elderly wooden boats in good and sound condition, able to put to sea, and to ensure they do not become mere museum pieces. Hillyard owners spend literally hundreds of hours scraping, burning off, restoring, caulking, painting, varnishing and all the other things which make owning a classic like these almost a full-time undertaking. Wooden boats are marvellous creations but, unless they are properly and continuously maintained, the law of entropy (what you put together falls apart) will take over rapidly. The owners of *Daisy* (ex-*Big Fizzer*), a 1925 4-tonner, admitted that although they had owned her for nearly 12 years, they had only ever sailed her twice as it had taken them that long to rebuild her. John Balchin, the author of the original version of this book, once asked the skipper of *Aeolus* (ex-*Eolis*), one of the 6-tonners, 'How long have you owned her?' 'Thirty-seven years,' came the reply, 'most of that time refitting in my garden.'

When Rodney Spring found *Dudley* (ex-*D'Sel*), the experimental diesel electric 12-tonner, sitting on a platform at Bridport Station (don't ask how she got there) she had no decks and all her beams were rotten. He was gratified to learn something of her history as mentioned previously. This enabled him to identify previously unsolved mysteries like traces of wiring and all sorts of fittings and holes for which he could not see any use. Despite her far-gone condition, he was bitten by the bug and he set to to rebuild her from the inside out. It would be difficult to estimate what percentage is now original, but his efforts have resulted in the preservation of a unique craft.

Owning a Hillyard can easily become an addiction, as many have come to find out. One owner told of the time when, just as her husband had given in to her wishes to buy 'a sparkling white Tupperware boat', she was persuaded by her local yacht broker to look over a Hillyard 6-tonner. 'I stepped on board—and fell in love,' she wrote. 'I raced back to the brokers and slapped some cash on his desk...too late! *Norvad* had just been sold.' But it did not stop there. 'I was now a woman with a mission—no tacky, plastic boats for me. I wanted a 6-ton Hillyard.' She scoured the country looking for one, without success until one day by chance she saw an advertisement in *Classic Boat* for *Miss Ruth*. This time she was in time, in more sense than one, to buy and rescue her. Her surveyor discovered that when the sea-cocks where fitted the holding bolts had never been properly fastened and the seacocks were held in only by some thick grease in the holes through the hull. After a mere three years' work, 'she looked glowing' and served the family well in the waters of the Solent for several years.

Not all Hillyard owners are purists, which is not surprising when you realise the number of modifications which are made to boats over the years. Adjustments to the rig, the abandonment of galvanised stanchions for stainless steel, the position and size of the steering wheel (you can find them on different bulkheads, fore or aft, port or starboard side in the centre cockpit) and ingenious ways of supplying the frequently missing chart table are the sort of improvements that owners will proudly show you. All in all, however, they need to be highly commended for their efforts in keep the name of Hillyard alive and the fleet together.

Chapter 11

THE END OF THE LINE

In the summer of 1979 Dennis was joined by his son Simon, who had up to then been working elsewhere for a company building aluminium boats. Unlike Dennis, Simon was used to dealing with materials other than wood and was aware that the future of boat building lay in a different direction. He was ambitious and wanted to move the Hillyard business on into the twentieth century, as he saw it. Whilst the yard continued to be busy in repairs and maintenance, Simon believed that there would be great demand for a 'new' Hillyard built in modern materials and he wanted to cash in on their history of producing high quality and good value boats. Unfortunately, he failed in this as what he came up with was, to most Hillyarders, wildly expensive.

Soon after he arrived at the yard, Simon approached the well-known firm of naval architects, Laurent Giles Ltd, the firm founded by Jack Laurent Giles back in the 1920s, which was still in business in Lymington. He initially sounded out the possibility of a design for a 35-footer using the advanced wood-building systems which were coming on stream in the early 1980s. However, when they produced a specification, it was obvious that the product would be just as expensive to build as a traditionally constructed craft. After seriously considering taking on the building of plywood boats constructed from kits supplied by the well established firm of Whisstocks of Woodbridge, Simon went back to Laurent Giles to explore the possibility of producing their original concept in GRP. They lengthened the hull to 36ft, and the 'Moonfleet' was conceived.

It was a case of 'if you can't beat them, join them.' Building in wood was no longer commercially viable and Simon wrote, not unkindly, in the Hillyard Owners newsletter, 'It must be remembered that we are a commercial concern and not a traditionalist's charity.' There were those traditionalists among Hillyard supporters who thought that the way ahead was to use one of the traditional boats as a plug to produce a GRP version of the craft they already knew and loved. However, a new material really did demand a new design. Although the hull would be plastic, the interior would be wooden throughout in the Hillyard tradition.

The prototype Moonfleet which first went on display at the Southampton Show of 1987 was 36ft long, with a beam of just over 12ft and a draught of 5ft 6in. She was rigged as a masthead sloop and weighed some eight and a quarter tons. She had a long fin keel with a rudder mounted on a substantial skeg, and had a full-bodied hull built to above Lloyd's specification. The deck was an end-grain balsa/GRP sandwich and the deck moulding at the outboard edge formed a low bulwark capped by a mahogany rail. The whole assembly was, as one reviewer put it, 'confidence inspiring'. She had an external cast iron keel which was bolted through a keel stub which doubled as a bilge sump.

The deck and hull plugs were constructed at the yard, but the actual glass fibre moulding was undertaken by a specialist firm, Armadillo, which at the time constructed the hulls of a GRP version of the famous Vertue class of yachts, also designed by Jack Laurent Giles. The Moonfleet hulls were to be transported by road to Littlehampton, launched upstream at the Littlehampton marina, and then floated down to the yard to be hauled out again for fitting out.

The Moonfleet was a thoroughly well thought out modern design, the whole thing in the modern idiom but with a solidity and built-in strength in accord with the Hillyard tradition. As was the centre cockpit and the three-cabin layout. Laurent Giles came up with a design of which David Hillyard would have approved.

The design, construction and cabin arrangements were aimed at the upper end of the cruising market with liveaboards in the Mediterranean very much in mind; perhaps a mistake for a Hillyard. Accommodation was provided for two couples, or a couple and two singles, in a forecabin and in the now universally accepted aft cabin (with its own opening hatch). Each had en-suite heads and a shower. A further couple could be accommodated in the central saloon by folding down the table. The galley ran the full length of the starboard side of the saloon, and was geared for easy and gracious living, with extensive worktop, plenty of locker space, and a refrigerator as standard. In addition, there was a large chart table, a draining oilskin locker and an easily accessible Perkins 50hp diesel. In spite of the fibreglass hull, the accommodation was a tribute to the yard's skill with wood, being fitted out in American oak, beech or mahogany.

On deck there was the same feeling of quality, from double bow rollers to the stainless hoop handrail in the centre cockpit and the large lazarette in the stern. A double-spreader Kemp spar with in-mast furling and a Furlex self-furling foresail with all lines running to the cockpit made the Moonfleet easy to handle. She sailed well, as may be expected from her design stable, and was the kind of boat which appealed widely at the time. Sensible, conservative with the traditional Hillyard strength and quality, she was to use modern par-lance 'the real deal' but circumstances worked against the yard. One reason why she remained a dream for most was, of course, that this all came at a price. By 1990 the price to buy a Moonfleet was £94,300; even then with rampant inflation this was far in excess of what the average Hillyard owner was used to paying.

With such a promising product, it is sad to see that, with hind-sight, the Moonfleet was a miscalculation for three reasons. First, it would have been quite possible, and substantially cheaper, to adopt one of the yard's existing designs for construction in GRP (which is pretty well what Peter Nicholson, then Camper and Nicholson's chief designer, did with their Nicholson 36 and what Laurent Giles did with the GRP Vertue). Adherents of the 'Hillyard' brand, are gen-erally traditional people, tending not to be wealthy and not neces-sarily interested in all the expensive luxuries with which Simon kit-ted out the Moonfleets. Many people would have bought a 'proper' GRP Hillyard but in the event few went for the Moonfleet. Had they done this it would not have stretched the yard's finances the way the Moonfleet did. Second, it was always going to be a challenge, and a big ask for Hillyard's, to move up-market and try to compete against the well-respected (and financially strong) boatbuilders such as Camper & Nicholson, Moody and various newcomers who were beginning to produce GRP boats at that time. There was nothing unique or special about the Moonfleet to distinguish it from the well-financed, well-marketed competition. Third, Simon, as well as everyone else in the business, was about to enter another of the regular economic

recessions which littered the post-war years in the UK. These were
the times when luxury items such as yachts were the first things to
be axed from shopping lists. Well-funded and profitable businesses
would see themselves through the coming recession but Hillyard's,
now having to rely on maintenance and repair work and the up-front
costs of developing the Moonfleet project, was simply not in that
position. To put it crudely, they were rather caught with their pants
down, as we shall see.

Few actual orders came out of the 1987 Southampton Boat Show
or during the rest of that year. However, things appeared to be looking
up the next year when Simon wrote in the 1988 Winter issue of the
HOA newsletter*: 'by the time you read this article I hope that our
Moonfleet 36 build programme will be in full swing as we have just
won a large contract from a charter company which has been a great
boost for the boat.'

It was during that year that the owner of a 'proper' Hillyard got in
touch with the yard with what seemed to be a very attractive propo-
sition. He had plans, he said, to establish a charter fleet in the Mediterranean and the Moonfleet was the ideal boat. What was more, he
would be bringing his own yacht back to Littlehampton for a major
refit. A contract was signed although it is not now known how many
Moonfleets were to be built. The contract was a Godsend but it was
to be two years before the buyer turned up at the yard with his so-
called Hillyard and worse was to follow. No work ever started on the
Moonfleet charter fleet.

In 1990 Dennis retired and handed the yard over to Simon, who
incorporated a new company, David Hillyard Yachts Limited, to run
the business. It is not entirely clear what actually happened here and
whether ownership of the business passed to Simon's new company,
or whether this was retained by Dennis, with the new company simply
operating the business. This is most likely what happened. In the mean-
time, after a thirty-year absence, Hillyard's, now in the form of the new
limited company, returned to the London Boat Show, with the Moonfleet being exhibited in a prime site alongside the centre pool, where she
attracted a good deal of praise. Simon Cullingford wrote in the Spring

---

*   *The Hillyarder* Issue No.19 Winter 1988.

1990 *Hillyarder*[*] 'the result [of the Boat Show] has been a very healthy order book and we are in the process of increasing production capacity to meet demand'. However, this is not what came to pass.

There was a recession looming in the United Kingdom which led to civil unrest in 1991, the availability of credit was tightening and the time was not right to commit a large amount of scarce funds to developing a whole new area of business. Simon did however manage to sell five Moonfleets and in the Winter 1990 *Hillyarder* he wrote 'Moonfleets continue to proceed well with one in Chichester, another in Portsmouth, a third in Poole and a fourth shortly to go to Torquay, so there is a much better chance of seeing one!'[†] In all, Hillyard's only sold five Moonfleets, needing to have sold seven to break even on the project.

Thereafter it was downhill all the way for the yard, with Simon writing in the Winter 1991 *Hillyarder*: 'The past year has not been easy for anyone in our industry and wood boats have been no exception. The economy has slashed through anything described as a luxury and new boat construction, both sail and power, has been hit particularly hard... all aspects of boating have been depressed.'[‡]

Like some Greek tragedy, a series of events now followed which led to disaster for the business and precipitated it into insolvency.

First, the moulding company, Armadillo Plastics Ltd, which supplied Hillyard's with the hulls found itself, like so many firms at that time, in financial difficulties and threatened insolvency. To protect themselves, Hillyard's recovered the Moonfleet moulds. Although these were the yard's property, they could have become stuck in legal argument with any liquidator or receiver of Armadillo had they been left where they were. Wisely, Simon arranged for them to be collected and transported back to Littlehampton. There being no space in the yard, they were placed in the open in a nearby car park.

At around the same time the supposed 'saviour' of the Moonfleet project turned up at the yard with his yacht, which turned out not to be a Hillyard at all, but a large motor yacht which Hillyard's were asked to refurbish. All this was good business, and the men got to work with

---

*   *The Hillyarder* Issue No. 22 Spring 1990.

†   *The Hillyarder* Issue No. 23 Winter 1990.

‡   *The Hillyarder* Issue No. 25 Winter 1991.

a will. One day, however, a contingent of the men working on the boat presented themselves in the office 'looking like undertakers' holding out a package they had found on board, amongst other similar packages. As was suspected, they turned out to contain a serious quantity of hard drugs. The Local Customs and Excise were informed, the owner of the yacht was arrested and his vessel was seized by the Authorities. Eventually the owner was found guilty of drug smuggling and was imprisoned for a considerable time. No work had started on the Moonfleets for the proposed charter fleet and the contract for these boats was terminated. With no other potential orders in sight, this effectively ended the Moonfleet project. Even worse followed.

Mysteriously, one night the Moonfleet moulds were destroyed by fire. No one ever found out the cause, although many rumours abounded, some no doubt malicious. Whatever happened it was the end of the Moonfleet project and the end of Simon's dream. It also left the Hillyard business with a large debt with no longer even the slim prospect of financing it.

In September the same year, with the Moonfleet project and the finance of the business in tatters, Simon was forced to make many of the employees redundant and they were served notice. Then on 4 November 1992 Simon's company, David Hillyard Yachts Limited, which had been promoting the Moonfleet project, was put into voluntary liquidation. The company was insolvent and none of its employees received any redundancy money. Inevitably this generated huge bitterness among the workforce, many of whom had spent all their lives working at the yard. To be summarily dismissed after giving years of loyal service, without payment of a penny, was a sad and unhappy end and something which David Hillyard, had he still been around, would never have contemplated.

It has been very hard, after all this time, to establish what then happened, but it is clear that many debts went unpaid, boats and assets were seized by creditors, and the redundant workforce had to rely on emergency Government assistance. It really was an object lesson in how not to go about trying to transform a business from a specialist craft-based operation into a modern outsourced business without having sufficient financial muscle behind you. Surprisingly, despite the Cullingfords being in continuous contact with the HOA and many Hillyard owners, and Simon writing regular columns in the HOA newsletters which heavily promoted the Moonfleets, nothing at all was said in *The Hillyarder* about the demise of David Hillyard Yachts Limited, or of the failure of the Moonfleet project; the impression was given that all was well and that it was business as usual.

Business did continue at the yard as if nothing had happened, albeit with a reduced workforce. It may have been that Dennis had, wisely, retained ownership of the yard itself, with its plant and machinery, so that its business could carry on despite the insolvency of Simon's company.

Thereafter the yard built no further boats but did not go short of work, undertaking maintenance and repair work, mainly of Hillyards but of other vessels as well, renting out moorings for boats within the harbour, and storing boats both afloat and ashore. This continued throughout the rest of the 1990s. Simon had stopped writing his regular column in *The Hillyarder* and news of what was happening in the yard was scarce unless one kept one's boat there.

It later transpired, unbeknownst to most Hillyard owners, that big changes were afoot. In the late 1990s Aruncraft Limited, a yacht repair and engineering business based in the Littlehampton Marina, had to relocate as its lease had come to an end. A proposal was made to Simon that he and Aruncraft, together with one of its customers, should purchase the Hillyard business from Dennis, who by now was well and truly retired, and form a new combined business on the Hillyard site. Agreement was reached and a new company, David Hillyard Limited, was formed with three shareholders, Simon having the majority holding. For various reasons, and largely as a result of Dennis's caution at agreeing to such a major change to the business he had inherited, it took a long time to cement the deal, and it was not until December 2002 that it was completed. Simon announced it to Hillyard owners by writing in the Spring 2003 issue of *The Hillyarder*:

New Company formed at Hillyard Shipyard

In the middle of last December, the ownership of David Hillyard changed for only the third time in its 100 year history, when my father decided it was time to officially retire from the

business. My father started appearing in the boatyard as a child
in the 1930s and then as a trainee during the early war years.
The 1950s saw him becoming a manager and then in 1964 he
became proprietor following the death of my great uncle, David
Hillyard.

The last thirty years have seen changes in the marine industry and the boatyard's present existence is testimony to perseverance in the face of many uphill challenges faced by my father
during these last decades.

This situation presents many opportunities and to realise
them we have formed a new company called David Hillyard
Ltd., which has purchased the boatyard and all its goodwill and
assets from my father... The new company intends to continue
and enhance the tradition that is David Hillyard.

Alas, that is not what happened. There were now only ten employees,
perhaps a fifth of the yard's peak peacetime workforce, and the big
plans for expansion never came to pass. In 2005 Simon stated that
they planned to expand and create new Hillyard boats, quoting a huge
86ft 'Sahara' cruiser prototype designed by Laurent Giles. Nothing
came of this.

In 2008 the company announced that it had taken on the building of five part-completed boats, Sadler 290s and Sadler 340s,
bought out of the wreckage of Rampart Yachts, which had gone
into liquidation early that year. Simon also announced that the yard
had taken on the production, sales and marketing of the Broadblue
range of catamarans and were 'set to build the highly regarded
Broadblue 415 Catamaran*. Whilst one can hardly imagine anything further removed from the traditional slow heavy Hillyard
than a large hulking modern light-weight GRP catamaran, Simon
said at the time:

We are delighted to have secured both these deals. We have
acquired two brands which both lead their respective sectors

---

*   These activities were carried on via a separate subsidiary company set up by
        Simon called Hillyard Marine Services Ltd.

and both—in their own way—possess many of the attributes synonymous with Hillyard's—proven design; excellent sailing abilities; spacious well planned interiors and reputations for having loyal customer followings.

Even grander plans were then put forward by Simon. All boat production was to move to Portsmouth, they had orders for a projected ten boats secured for 2009 and would begin to actively market the new range to fill their planned 2010 schedule. The traditional work of repair, refit and renovation was to continue out of three strategic locations—Gosport, Chichester and Littlehampton with a projected base in Portland. Simon concluded his statement with these words:

> Now we can take both these names—Broadblue and Sadler—
> and develop high quality tailored boats which can 'go anywhere'
> and have the build attributes of a 'boat for life'. This is some-
> thing we have more than 100 years' experience of doing.[*]

Sadly, within a few months it was all over. Despite the grand announcements, the reality was quite different and these ventures failed due to a lack of working capital, not helped by a recession which hit the country hard that year and led to demand falling away. In January 2009, the business became insolvent and had to cease trading. The remaining nine employees were made redundant and steps were taken to sell the premises, where Hillyard's had been for over one hundred years, to pay off bank debts.

The final nail in the coffin was driven home on 22 February 2009 when yet another fire destroyed much of the little that was left. When Hillyard's finally ceased trading they had four part-finished Sadler 290 hulls in the yard, two of which were destroyed in the fire, the others being badly damaged. The workshop where they were was also extensively damaged. Thirty firefighters tackled the flames and several homes in the area were evacuated as it was feared there were gas cylinders in the buildings.

---

[*]   All this was reported in *Practical Boat Owner* on 30 October 2008 in an article
      headed: 'South Coast yard expands its range.'

For seven weeks before the business ceased to trade, Simon Cull-ingford had apparently been absent from the yard and the workforce were unpaid during this time.

Subsequently the Official Receiver wound the business up and the companies were struck off the Register, over one hundred and fifteen years after David Hillyard had first come to Littlehampton.

One of the former Hillyard directors, John Lambson, was able to recover some of the assets of the original Hillyard business and now trades under the name Aruncraft from premises beside the original Hillyard yard. Hillyards and other modern and traditional vessels are to be seen there to this day being worked on with the same skills and care as were exhibited by David Hillyard and Dennis Cullingford for all those years. Another former director recovered the company names by registering new companies with the names David Hilly-ard Yachts Ltd. and David Hillyard Ltd. in order to stop these well-known names falling into hands who might abuse them. These com-panies remain dormant to this day.

Simon Cullingford had no further connection with the business; he still lives locally and the author has tried unsuccessfully to contact him to discuss these events.

Finally, in the April 2009 issue of *The Hillyarder* there was a small footnote at the bottom of one page headed 'Tragic News from Little-hampton' which read:

> Sadly, we understand that Hillyard's (David Hillyard Ltd) have ceased trading. Our sympathy must lie with the Cullingford family and the employees of the Company. All members and owners of Hillyard yachts will feel the tragedy of this event most keenly and we can only hope that some continuity of ma-rine activity at this famous yard will prevail.'

Aruncraft still lives next door to the old Hillyard yard, trading as the Littlehampton Boatyard, but from much reduced premises. Interest-ingly they still retain within their modern-day telephone number the original Hillyard three number code '327' first used in 1923.

Today, the old Hillyard buildings stand empty and rapidly deterio-rating, seemingly used for little more than storage, with many shipping containers and caravans lying about where there used to be yachts. Most of the original buildings survive as does the original builder's plaque in one end wall stating '1837 SDO'. When I last visited Littlehampton in the summer of 2020 it was a sad forlorn place, unused and unloved with an air of dereliction and abandonment about it, full of ghosts and memories. Just another example of the industrial decay that can be found in all parts of the country where old craft-based industries have had to give way to our modern ways of doing things. The next-door yard, William Osbornes, who for many years, built highly regarded wooden lifeboats and smart high-powered motor yachts, has also closed. It looks likely that this whole area of Littlehampton's riverside will shortly fall into the hands of the residential property developers who for many years have been trying to get their hands on it. The local authority has up to now adamantly refused to consider such proposals but one day the developers will get their wish and move in, something which might have solved all Simon Cullingford's problems had it happened in 2008.

Part III

HILLYARD VOYAGES AND VOYAGERS

Chapter 12

THE EARLY YEARS

People who did not know about these things must have wondered why, if Hillyards were such wonderful sea boats, so few long voyages, if any, were undertaken by them in the years before the Second World War. People who do know about these things know that hardly any long voyages at all were undertaken in small yachts of whatever pedigree in those far off days. Corinthian yachting out of British harbours was predominantly a local thing with infrequent dashes to other British harbours combined occasionally with longer passages across the English Channel, the North or Irish seas. That was about it.

Of course, there were ocean voyages undertaken but these were carried out in large vessels with professional crews. The big boats, mentioned in earlier chapters, sailed the Atlantic to challenge for the America's Cup (in fact it was a rule under the original deed of gift of the Cup, that challengers had to cross the Atlantic on their own bottoms from their home port; no such adverse requirement was laid at the door of the defenders!). Ocean going yachts in those days were generally large beasts. Lord and Lady Brassey's yacht *Sunbeam* in which they circumnavigated the world in 1877 was 159ft long. The first 'yacht' ever to sail south of Cape Horn was a 133ft schooner, the *Coronet* (in 1885). There were of course exceptions. Joshua Slocum sailed around the world single handed in his 35ft long *Spray* between 1895 and 1898 and in the interwar years of the 1920s and 1930s there were very few who ventured offshore to cross an ocean or even to sail round the world. One of the most notable was the voyage of Irish patriot Conor O'Brien who circumnavigated in his 42ft long ketch *Saoirse*, arriving home in Ireland in 1925[*].

---

[*]   See the author's *Astronauts of Cape Horn*, The Conrad Press 2018.

Humphrey Barton, the well-known author, yachtsman and yacht surveyor, stated in his authoritative book *Atlantic Adventurers*[*] that up until 1939 whilst twenty-three small boats had sailed the Atlantic from west to east (considered the easier downhill way) only four small yachts had sailed from Europe to the USA via the Northern Atlantic route[†]. Amongst the four was the English, or rather Welsh, built boat which could easily have come from the Hillyard yard. She was the 30ft gaff cutter *Emanuel*, which her owner Commander Graham sailed singlehanded to Newfoundland in 1934[‡]. The vessel came from a yard with qualities like that of Hillyard's. It was owned and run by a Mr Anderson from ramshackle premises on the shore at Penarth in Cardiff Bay, South Wales, where he built a number of small yachts to his own designs which in looks, design and construction could have been Hillyards. Mr Anderson garnered the same loyalty in his customers as did Hillyard and Commander Graham went back to Anderson for his next yacht, the *Caplin*, which he sailed to New Zealand with his daughter as crew in 1939.

Another pre-war yacht mentioned by Humphrey Barton is *Driac II*, a simple gaff cutter equal to anything coming out of Hillyard's at that time. She was built for A. G. H. Macpherson, who sailed her on a long ocean voyage ending up in South Africa via the Mediterranean and as far east as Bali and the Spice Islands[§]. These voyages were the exception.

Nearer home some of the first Hillyard voyages before the Second World War for which detailed records exist were those undertaken by Dr L. B. Winter in two Hillyards, first *Magpie* and then his newly built *Brynhildr*. In fact, as we shall see, *Brynhildr* did cross oceans to reach Australia (where she is still well and sailing) but not on her own bottom but as deck cargo.

Dr Winter started sailing whilst a medical student in London in the 1920s. In the summer of 1932 he chartered the 29ft cutter

---

[*]   Barton, Humphrey. *Atlantic Adventurers—Voyages in Small Craft*, Adlard Coles 1953.

[†]   These were the *City of Ragusa*, a converted ships lifeboat, the *Little Western*, all of 16ft, the *Vraad*, an experimental 18ft steel lifeboat and *Emmanuel*.

[‡]   Graham, R.D. *Rough Passage*, Wm Blackwood 1936, various reprints.

[§]   Scott Hughes, John. *Macpherson's Voyages*, Methuen 1944.

Magpie which had been built by Hillyard's the previous year[*]. With four other medical students he joined the ship at Fambridge. Winter described her as: 'an attractive little vessel; painted black with a gold line, she had a transom stern, a fairly large open cockpit and the usual high coach-roof demanded by people who place a high premium on headroom'. They had an enjoyable cruise along the east coast as far north as Grimsby, and spent some time exploring the Wash. Winter wrote later in his book[†]: 'so impressed was I by the general excellence of *Magpie's* construction that I resolved to go to Mr David Hillyard if I decided to have my own vessel built'.

During the winter of 1932, Winter started a search for a yacht of his own but could not find what he was looking for—a gaff rigged cutter with a pole mast, about 30ft in length, with a good beam, a flush deck, stoutly constructed, of medium draught and with a reliable auxiliary. Early the next year Winter went to Littlehampton and laid out his problem to David Hillyard. After an hour's discussion Hillyard made a note of what Winter wanted and put forward a tentative figure for the cost, which Winter accepted. The boat was to be laid down in March and ready to sail at the beginning of July 1933. She was to be 30ft long and 10ft wide. The accommodation was to be similar to that in *Magpie*, worked out by Winter on the floor of his room in Manchester which happened to be 30ft by 10ft. Visitors no doubt speculated on the various chalk marks to be seen on his floor! The bunks and settees were to be at least six and a half feet long, as Winter was himself over six feet tall. The boat, to be called *Brynhildr*, was to be tiller steered with a transom stern and a large open cockpit (Dr Winter, a man of strong views, felt the risk of getting pooped and flooded was very much less than that of being washed overboard when half in and half out of a small self-draining well). She had a flush deck, apart from a skylight. Winter did not feel the need to have standing room when below and Hillyard, whilst expressing surprise that there was not to be the usual coachroof, agreed that a flush deck, well supported and planked with timber of unusual thickness, would

---

[*]   *Magpie* was one of the job lot of yachts bought for charter by Mr W.J.L.Watts in 1931, referred to in Chapter 5

[†]   Winter, L.B. *We Who Adventure—Cruises in British Waters*, Oxford University Press 1956.

ensure a dry boat below. In the forepeak were to be spacious sail lockers and a special locker where the oil navigation lights could be kept upright, filled and always ready for use. Winter decided not to fit a marine W.C. but to rely on a bucket with a detachable seat; space saving and hygienic. There was to be no electric lighting on the ship but gimballed paraffin lamps for cabin lighting. Winter decided against fitting stanchions and a life rail, believing them to give much less security than generally supposed. All in all, *Brynhildr*, was an exceptionally well thought out little ship, typical of what was then thought to be the ideal small cruiser, and typical of Hillyard's work at the time.

Winter resolved that *Brynhildr* should make her maiden voyage to Scotland and lay up there for the winter. With the same crew as on *Magpie*, they set off on 12 July running straight into the teeth of a north-easterly gale in the Thames estuary. The ship never faltered and the only fault was with the mast cheeks which allowed the shrouds to loosen. In Southwold, they had some new oak pads made up.

They made fast passage up the east coast and were soon in Scottish waters. They called in at Berwick and Fraserburgh. There, the local fishermen tried to persuade Winter and his crew to savour the joys of the Caledonian Canal rather than endure the perils of the Pentland Firth where they were bound. But no. Winter and his crew were determined. They put into Wick on 2 August and set off the next morning to find out what awaited them. Soon the tide took over and a northwest breeze began to increase. This is what Winter wrote about it:

There was scarcely any warning: off the Men of Mey rocks we saw the race just ahead and almost instantly we were in it. The ship became unmanageable, sinking suddenly into what appeared to be a deep hole in the water and then just as suddenly being projected on high; at the same time her bows were swung from west to north and then to south and east. Enormous pyramids of water appeared and disappeared all round us and all the while there was a deep roaring sound due to the stream surging over the uneven, rocky bottom.

They made it safely and put into the small harbour of Scrabster. From there it was plain sailing round Cape Wrath and down the west coast to end their voyage at Tarbert in Loch Fyne, where they left *Brynhildr* for the winter. They had covered 1,100 miles since leaving Littlehampton.

The next year they sailed *Brynhildr* to Orkney and Shetland. She remained in Scotland for more than twenty years and, except during the war, became a much-loved family holiday home.

So loved, in fact, that when, after the war, the Winters emigrated to Australia, Dr Winter put *Brynhildr* on the market with the greatest reluctance. He was secretly relieved when no one came up with a reasonable offer. However, Sydney Harbour is a long way from Mallaig, where she was finally laid up, and missing deeply the vessel in which he had invested so much time and care, Winter worked his passage home to England as a ship's doctor and arranged for *Brynhildr* to be shipped out as deck cargo to a new home in Australia, where she is still afloat and sailing today. She was transported on the Shaw Savill Line ship S. S. *Runic*, which left King George V Dock in Glasgow on 7 August 1957.

She has been kept in good trim and refitted as the years have gone by. Once, when renewing the cockpit coamings, a new owner found a pencil-written message from the past: 'Littlehampton, D. Hillyard, 12th June, 1933' and then two signatures, one illegible, the other 'D. Wilkin'. However, perhaps the best memorial these two shipwrights could have is that this small vessel, which is now over eighty seven-years old, was shown in 1983 at an exhibition in Sydney of 'thirty historic and unique vessels'. As we shall see in the next chapter *Brynhildr* was the first, but by no means the last, Hillyard to find its way to Australia one way or another.

During the pre-war period, many other voyages were undertaken by Hillyard's around the coasts of Great Britain, Ireland and the neighbouring continent, several of which are mentioned in Part III of this book (Hillyard People) but those undertaken by *Brynhildr* are the most memorable and were well written about by the owner*. They demonstrate the qualities inherent in David Hillyard's boats, which so many people found appealing and for which he rightly acquired his reputation.

---

*   Winter, L.B. *We Who Adventure*, Oxford University Press 1956 and Winter, L.B. *Nor They Understand*, Jacaranda Press Pty Ltd. Brisbane 1966.

Chapter 13

OCEAN WANDERINGS

It was only in the late 1940s and the 1950s that small boat voyaging across oceans really took off, as exemplified by those immortals such as the Hiscocks, the Pyes, the Smeetons, Edward Allcard, Peter Tangvald, Humphrey Barton and the others who inaugurated those Golden Years of small boat voyaging. Very soon Hillyards were to be found joining in the fun and this is where our account of Hillyard ocean wanderings begins.

Victor Clark and *Solace* (1953-1959)

During 1952, the same year in which Eric and Susan Hiscock set off in their newly built Laurent Giles designed *Wanderer III* on their first circumnavigation, a forty-four year old Royal Navy Commander's spirit revolted at what he described as the futility of 'their Lordships ordaining in their wisdom that the last few years of my twenty-seven year service in the Royal Navy should be spent at a desk'. The man was Commander Victor Clark and his was a distinguished career including service in European and Far-Eastern theatres of war, award of the Distinguished Service Cross, and three and a half years as a prisoner of the Japanese. After the war, Clark spent five years as Chief Training Officer to the Sea Cadets, during which time, tied to a desk, he managed to keep sane by planning a circumnavigation.

Faced with retirement the following summer and feeling like a caged bird yearning for fresh air and freedom, one day at the end of that year he casually dropped into a yacht broker's in West London saying 'I want to buy a yacht to sail round the world in.' He was shown various boats and the broker pointed one out in particular. 'That's what you want, sir—take you anywhere.' The man thought she was a little beauty but was far too much money for him. So, he started a search and after looking at over one hundred boats he chose the first one he had seen in that broker's office six months before.

*Solace** was not a typical Hillyard. She was built in 1929 for a Mr A.R.White who wanted her built to a design by an American, John Allen—believed a mis-spelling of John Alden, whose style the boat resembles, with its 'almost a schooner' rig. Surprisingly Hillyard agreed, against one of his major principles; maybe because at that time, with the Wall Street crash, and a depression looming, he needed the work. But Hillyard, probably unbeknownst to the owner, altered the underwater shape of the hull around the garboards and keel so as to avoid any possible claim for infringement of Alden's copyright (though this would be unnecessary with a properly licensed design). Hillyard felt he could, and in fact did, claim the design as his own. *Solace* was an attractive looking 34ft gaff ketch with a broad well-raked transom stern, a long low coachroof, and aft cockpit which was, unusually for a small yacht, surrounded by a high and ornamental timber taffrail. This gave her a distinctive appearance and certainly she did not look like a normal Hillyard. She turned out to be an excellent sea boat, able to sail herself perfectly on the wind with no attention to the helm. With her (most likely) double Alden-Hillyard pedigree she would hardly be anything but a proper ocean-going yacht.

Clark bought *Solace* in June 1953, proposing to be away on his circumnavigation that September. He had Humphrey Barton survey her, who pronounced her in sound condition and 'just the job' for Clark's purpose. After some modifications and with Royal Navy efficiency, Clark sailed away on Friday 4 September 1953 on what proved to be a five-and-a-half-year circumnavigation, west-about through the Panama Canal and across the Pacific. His voyage is well described in his book *On the Wind of a Dream*†.

Crewed at first by an experienced yachtsman, 'Chich' Thornton, *Solace* sailed south to Madeira, the Canary and Cape Verde Islands and thence to Barbados and Trinidad, where Chich departed. Clark

---

*   Victor Clark bought Solace from Lord Stanley of Alderley, a well-known yachtsman whose book, *Sea Peace*, describes the various yachts he owned which included the Laurent Giles designed double-ender *Argo* referred to in Chapter 6, which the author owned during the 1960s. Lord Stanley was also a friend of Arthur Ransome and they were fellow members of the Royal Cruising Club—see Chapter 15.

†   Clark, Victor. *On the Wind of a Dream*, Hutchinson 1960.

sailed on to St Lucia, where he was joined by a young West Indian teenager, Stanley, who stayed with him for the remainder of the voyage. Clark taught the boy navigation and seamanship and Stanley subsequently became the first qualified West Indian merchant skipper. Clark and his crew soon found out about *Solace's* capability for looking after them in bad weather, and her ability to self-steer unaided, even under full sail with the wind on the beam.

They had a few idyllic months exploring the Caribbean islands, then a difficult passage to Panama and on into the Pacific. They visited the Galapagos Islands, the Marquesas, the Tuamotu Archipelago, Tahiti and Rarotonga. Then by rights the voyage should have come to an end.

Their next port of call was the isolated coral atoll of Palmerston Island, 260 miles north-west of Rarotonga. Whilst anchored in the atoll the night before their planned departure, a sudden increase in the wind, plus a shift from east-south-east to between west and north, put them on a lee shore and in an extremely dangerous position. They were less than one hundred yards from large seas breaking onto the coral reef with a rapidly rising wind and sea. It was pitch dark and raining with the anchor chain foul of a rock and liable to part at any moment. The engine was useless. They tried to sail out but the cable parted and *Solace* was driven onto the reef. It was the top of the tide and *Solace* was lifted by the seas over the edge of the reef and flung on to the coral where she came to rest.

Clark wrote the following in his book about what he found when daylight came:

> There were a lot of long faces but little was said... The ship was obviously holed but did not look a wreck! But what a position to be in! On a tiny coral atoll with only seventy inhabitants, hundreds of miles from anywhere, thousands of miles from 'civilization' and not due to be visited by a ship for another nine months! I think I'm a born optimist, but my heart has never been nearer my boots than it was at that moment.

In normal circumstances *Solace* would have been declared a total loss, but the Palmerston islanders proved to be far from normal. All of them were descendants of a William Masters, who had taken over ownership of the island in settlement of a debt and who then colonised the atoll with his three Polynesian wives back in the mid-nineteenth century. Masters' descendants, starting with seventeen children and fifty-four grand-children, are now in their sixth generation and number over a thousand people scattered throughout the Cook Islands and New Zealand.

Those remaining on Palmerston Island were, as Victor Clark was about to find out, an extremely skilled and self-sufficient community, who still speak English as their first language. Against all the odds, the whole population turned out to drag *Solace* back over the reef, float her on oil drums across the lagoon, and haul her out for repairs. It took twenty-three days of sweated labour.

After all this, the prognosis was not good. She had a hole nineteen feet long in her starboard side, the planking ripped to pieces, the frames smashed, and the deck buckled. But the islanders were capable shipwrights. They felled some of their precious mahogany trees for new frames, protected the savaged hull from the sun with a palm-leaf shelter, and set about rebuilding her. Although she had to be re-planked later in New Zealand, this was not because of the islander's workmanship. It was a result of the poor quality of the timber used, which was all that was available to them.

The job took about eighteen months, taxing the ingenuity of the islanders. Their atoll is remote from any source of supplies and trading schooners call infrequently. An attempted air-drop of some much needed supplies was somewhat unsuccessful, in that a parachute failed to open and the bags burst on impact, leaving them with a jumbled mixture of glue, cement, copper nails, twine, bent cooking utensils, letters and papers. Clark became the subject of some lurid 'marooned sailor' articles around the world. Actually, he appears to have thoroughly enjoyed his stay with those delightful people and he repaid their efforts by conducting navigation classes, teaching the children Bible stories and how to read, and preparing over sixty sermons for their chapel services!

Once *Solace* was seaworthy again, Clark undertook a shakedown cruise to Rarotonga taking some islanders with him. He then ferried some of them to New Zealand where *Solace* was hauled out and the planking which had been fitted on the island was removed. As for the frames which had been fitted there Clark was told 'Don't you touch them. You won't get as good a job as that done anywhere in New Zealand!' The side was planked with new timber and the deck canvas was renewed. Then a new engine was installed, the rigging refitted, the vessel finally spruced up and declared fit for a return to England.

They left after nine months in Auckland to return to... Palmerston Island, which, Clark wrote, had 'an almost irresistible pull on the heart strings which will continue to my dying day'. The hurricane season was approaching but Clark had time to sail back to Palmerston before returning to New Zealand in December to wait out the season.

In April *Solace* returned to Palmerston once again and eventually left for home at the beginning of June. The whole island turned out on the beach to bid them farewell, singing a Maori hymn in harmony, saying prayers for a safe journey. Clark and his crew, Stanley, had to kiss nearly eighty people all in tears as they embarked.

From Palmerston, *Solace* visited Tonga, Samoa, Fiji, and the New Hebrides before leaving the Pacific. Then through the Torres Strait, the Timor Sea and into the Indian Ocean. On to Cape Town via the Cocos-Keeling Islands and Mauritius. From South Africa they headed not for Europe but for the Caribbean and St Lucia, so Stanley, his loyal and by now very accomplished crew, could see his family. Then they sailed home to England via Bermuda.

What a voyage it was and all done in an exemplary way by a talented and accomplished skipper and crew. *Solace* had proved to be the near perfect ship for such a voyage and arrived back in Plymouth in 1959, six years (less one week) and 48,000 miles after departure.

In 1962 Victor Clark took command of the schooner *Prince Louis* for the Outward Bound School, later replaced by the *Captain Scott* and only came ashore permanently in 1975 when he married. He taught for a while at the Emsworth Sailing School (what a marvelous instructor he must have been) and in 1994 at the age of eighty-six he completed his autobiography *Triumph and Disaster*. Clark died on 14 December 2005, aged ninety-seven. He was survived by his wife and their two daughters.

Keith Robinson and *Leiona* (1960)

In 1960, a year after *Solace* was in St Lucia on her way home, another Englishman was returning home slowly to England after his retirement, pondering the idea of a life wandering the world under sail. This time it was a retired Colonel, who like Victor Clark had a distinguished war record and had spent time in the far East. Circumstances found him spending November and December of 1960 having a look round the West Indies. Before he had left Malaya to return home, his General had given him an introduction to a friend in the West Indies, living in St Lucia. This invitation brought the Colonel to the island at just the same time as an Alan Keith arrived by air from England to get his boat ready for the Caribbean season of winter sailing. The soldier was Keith Robinson and Alan Keith's yacht was the Hillyard *Leiona*.

Robinson, whilst looking at the boats anchored in the harbour, was invited on board *Leiona* and he liked her from the start. He wrote: 'She was strong and good-looking, well-kept and gave a feeling of confidence and ability.'[*] She was an 18-ton cutter, 42ft long with a centre cockpit, and had been built by Hillyard's just two years before, in 1958. She had been sailed out to the Caribbean by the owner, Alan Keith. She was a big boat for her size, comfortable below, and Robinson thought she would suit him ideally.

Just as he was heading ashore Robinson remarked that he envied Keith, saying he had a fine boat. Keith's reply was a surprise in which he said that, with a growing family, he had actually ordered a bigger boat from Hilllyard and would have to sell *Leiona*. He went on to say that he was going to ship her home to England in the spring on a steamer, as she would be easy to sell there. The next morning, a deal was done and Robinson agreed to buy her for £1,500 less than Keith's asking price of £5,000 as Keith would avoid the shipping cost and insurance. Keith would hand her over in March the next year, 1961.

Robinson duly took over the boat intending to sail her across the Atlantic to the Mediterranean, which was to be his base. First though, he made a single-handed shakedown cruise through the islands south of St Lucia. He visited St. Vincent, the Grenadines (Bequia, Mus-

---

[*] Robinson, Keith. *Islands of Blue Water*, Adlard Coles 1968.

tique, etc.), Carriacou and Grenada. Keith Robinson found *Leiona* easy to sail single-handed and found she would steer herself on almost all points of sailing.

He then headed north for Antigua where he was stopping for a month to prepare for his transatlantic trip. On the way there he experienced the only 'fright' of his cruise. In the open sea north of Dominica, in a rising wind and with a large sea rolling in, his steering quadrant broke and the boat lay beam on rolling ferociously. He had a struggle to repair it and re-clamp it to the rudder stock. Eventually, with a slipping rudder, he made it, in the pitch dark, into a narrow twisting entrance to an anchorage in The Saints.

Nelson's Dockyard in Antigua's English Harbour, where Robinson went next, was a good place to prepare for his voyage. When *Leiona* arrived, Keith Robinson had no crew lined up, except for a vague promise from a French couple he had met the year before. He wanted to sail with four on board and soon he was inundated with offers; eventually leaving with a total complement of five. They left on 3 May 1961, a happy bunch looking forward to a month of sailing. This all came to a quick end that evening when the fitting for the backstay at the top of the mast broke. With the boat having no running backstays they were in danger of losing their mast. They rigged up a jury system of temporary stays from the upper crosstrees and decided to divert to Bermuda, seven hundred miles away but not far off their planned route. They stopped in Bermuda just long enough to have a new masthead cap made up and they also fitted two running backstays as a backstop.

It took them five days sailing to the north-east in light winds to reach the westerlies which were blowing hard. They soon ran into a typical North Atlantic gale. This scared the somewhat inexperienced crew but *Leiona* shrugged it off and the rest of the passage to the Azores was uneventful. They nearly decided to give the Azores a miss as the weather was good and the winds favourable, but the skipper wisely decided to put in to fill the water tanks and get some fresh food. They arrived at Ponta Delgada in early June to be told that they were the first yacht to arrive for two years. How things have changed!*

---

*   Ponta Delgada now has a thriving yacht marina, hosts the end of the AZAB

From Ponta Delgada their destination was Cape St Vincent, eight hundred miles away, which they first saw on 18 June 1961, five miles off to the north east—a perfect landfall. After an uncomfortable night and heavy short seas which bought *Leiona* to a halt, they made it into Gibraltar late the next day. There his crew left him and Robinson was once again alone on his boat, happy and satisfied with his achievement.

Now began the next phase of Colonel Robinson's life afloat on *Leiona*; wandering in the Mediterranean for several years, wintering one year in Mallorca, another in Volos in Greece. Robinson ended his book with these words:

> My few years of sailing and living in Leiona have made me sure that this is the kind of life I want. I would not now like to change it for any other. The past years have been good. Now I am thinking of the years to come. Rhodes and Istanbul and the Dodecanese would be good targets for next summer. And then perhaps Venice and Dalmatia after that, and back to Spain for the winter. Or a visit to the Caribbean. Or a summer in the French canals. Or the Balearics again. The scope is so wide that it is hard to choose. Maybe I will choose them all. My new life has had a good beginning.[*]

W. E. Rankin and *Penella* (1958)

Whilst Victor Clark and *Solace* were nearing home and just before *Leiona* was setting off on her new adventures, another Hillyard was setting out to sail for Australia. This time in the hands of a retired Royal Air Force Group Captain. We now have a sailor, soldier and an airman all sailing their Hillyards across the oceans at roughly the same time. In 1958, Group Captain W. E. Rankin and his wife set off from England to sail to Australia. Their vessel was the 17-ton staysail schooner *Penella*, built by Hillyard's in 1935.

In the early stages of their voyage the Rankins nearly lost her. The passage to Casablanca was undertaken late in the year and they ran

---

and other yacht races and is always full. When the author was last there, some years ago now, there must have been over one hundred yachts moored in the harbour.

[*]   Robinson, Keith. *Islands of Blue Water*, Adlard Coles 1968, pp 243-44.

into hurricane force winds*. The boat held up well, but they lost their steering and were nearly sunk by a well-meaning but incompetent ex-Liberty Ship intent on taking them off, when all they needed was a tow into port. Thankfully the ship went away, they got a tow from another vessel and made it to port.

Few details of their voyage survive but it is understood that after Casablanca they crossed the Atlantic to the Caribbean, thence to the Panama Canal after which they visited the Marquesas and Fiji ending up in Sydney in 1962, where *Penella* remained.

In 1971 Rankin sold *Penella* to another airman, Air Commodore Gordon Steege of the Royal Australian Air Force, who kept her for many years. In 1981 Steege wrote in *The Hillyarder*† that he had re-moved the old engine from *Penella*, which was the original one, then nearly fifty years old, fitted when the boat was built in 1935, They don't last that long these days! Interestingly the engine was an 18hp Thornycroft Model RJ2, slow revving, hand start and with a huge fly-wheel. This was the same type fitted into the lifeboats of the original *Queen Mary* Cunard liner. Steege replaced it with a shiny new 3-cylinder 34hp Lister.

It is not known whether *Penella* is still afloat and in commission as all contact was lost some years ago.

Tom Southern, *Svano* and *Aguila* (1959-1966)

Whilst all this was going on in the late 1950s and early 1960s another yachtsman became captivated with Hillyards and became yet another 'serial' owner. He went on to have one of the largest Hillyards built specially for him.

D. F. 'Tom' Southern bought his first Hillyard when visiting one of the combined Motor/Boat Shows looking to buy a motor car. Tired of the noise and bustle, he retreated into the calmer area of the Boat section and came across David Hillyard's stand. Having recently lost his wife, it struck him that cruising under sail would be an excellent way to keep his young family together. He ordered a 9-tonner and on delivery, taking Ben, one of Hillyard's staff as skipper, he set out

---

*   This passage is written up in the April 1959 issue of *Yachting Monthly*.

†   No. 8 Summer 1983.

for North Wales having never sailed before. By the time they reached Penzance Southern reckoned that he had got the hang of things and sent Ben home. Sure enough, he got the boat safely to Anglesey and later cruised in her as far as the Baltic.

In 1958 he was back at Littlehampton, to order a new bigger boat, more experienced and now enamored with yacht cruising. He described this new boat as follows in the 1959 log of his first venture in the new vessel[*]:

> *Svano* is a new boat this year of 13 tons TM. in which Mr Hillyard has combined the comfort of his standard yachts with a finer hull and increased sail area. The name, Norwegian for a swan, reminds us of a very beautiful anchorage on the west coast of Norway. Her dimensions are 40 feet O.A., 32 feet W.L., 5 feet 3 inches draught and 9 feet 9 inches beam with ballast divided between an iron keel and inside lead. As a masthead sloop the sail area can be varied from a working area of 620 square feet to over 900 square feet when using the large reaching sail of 520 square feet. This latter was a great asset and boomed out took the place of a spinnaker.

After a single day's sailing trials, Tom Southern set straight off with a crew of three to sail to the Gulf of Finland, most of the time beating into strong Force 7 winds. He reported that the boat never faltered in her stride and was exceptionally dry. After nearly nine days at sea, all into the teeth of a strong north-easterly, they made their first landfall at Brunsbuttel, the entrance to the Keil canal to take them through to the Baltic. They then cruised, stopping often, through the Danish islands and then along the south coasts of Norway and Sweden until they reached Helsinki, where they stopped and, as Southern put it in his log, 'I now had to return to England to find whether I still had a business left and then to return with my family...' On his return they went on to Kotka which was the end of their outward cruise. They returned around the top of Jutland and arrived back in Littlehamp-

* Acknowledgments and thanks to the Royal Cruising Club who retain copies of the logs of all of Mr Southern's cruises in *Svano* and in his later Hillyard *Aguila*.

ton on 1 September 1959 after a total of thirty-seven days at sea and some 3,300 miles made good, though they had sailed nearer 4,000 miles through the water. It was an impressive first cruise in a new and untried boat and a real tribute to the quality of the boats' designer, builder and, of course, skipper.

Over the next three years Southern made three more exceptional summer cruises. In 1960, he sailed to Spain, Portugal and Morocco, in 1961 to the Balearic Islands and in 1962 to Madeira and the Azores, with a short excursion into the Mediterranean on the way. On this last trip, they left Littlehampton on 25 May 1962 with four people on board, arriving in Gibraltar on 14 June, having stopped at Portimao and Cadiz. Following a quick trip to Ibiza they left for Madeira on 14 July reaching Ponta Delgada in the Azores on 28 July. Soon after leaving the Azores for Spain they nearly lost a man overboard. After the staysail halyard parted, they hoisted a crew member to reeve a new one. Unfortunately, when he was being lowered, his bosun's chair became tangled in the rigging and on freeing himself the crew member fell into the sea from quite a height. With a big sea running it was difficult to keep him in sight and to retrieve him, which they eventually managed to do. It was a fright for all of them. They made it to Corunna on 17 August 1962 and were back in Cowes on 8 September. Another fine cruise nearly marred by a tragedy. Southern commented in his log that he would always in future use a downhaul on a bosun's chair and he also said, 'a lifejacket would seem desirable too!' (These were little used in those days.)

In 1964 Southern was back at Hillyard's discussing with a young Dennis Cullingford the design for a 'go anywhere' yacht. The result was the largest, and probably the most expensive, yacht to have been built at the yard, which was named *Aguila* and launched in 1965. Southern set out his requirements for the ship to have the luxury of space below, a large unobstructed cockpit and a motion that would enable life at sea to be a pleasure rather than an endurance test. She was very much a development of all that had gone before in that she was double-ended, long keeled and rigged as a ketch with a well sheltered centre cockpit. She was 51ft long had a 12ft beam and a draught of 6ft 6in. She displaced 19 tons and had a working sail area of 920 square feet; planking was 1 and $^5/_{16}$in mahogany on grown oak frames with a backbone, stem

and sternpost of iroko. Her deck was of ⅝in ply with a ½in teak deck
laid on top. There was a separate and sound-proofed engine-room
where one could work in comfort and space. This contained a 62hp
Thorneycroft diesel and an air cooled Yanmar generator. Below decks
the accommodation was spacious, incorporating a forepeak to house
sails, spare ropes, warps, etc. , a two berth stateroom was located next
followed by a separate toilet compartment containing a basin, shower,
dressing table and linen cupboard. This lay forward of the saloon at
the aft end of which was a commodious galley and a navigator's desk,
with all necessary instrumentation, a Sailor radio, Heron D/F, echo
sounder and chronometer. Access to the aft stateroom was through
a passage running past the engine. This alleyway had along its length
lockers for oilskins, tools, bosun's stores, bonded stores and paints for
a whole year. The aft stateroom had its own toilet compartment. All in
all, she was the ultimate cruising yacht that could be built at that time.
Southern wrote of her: 'On a trial trip to Vigo, *Aguila* beat out of the
Channel in winds of up to Force 7 and then across the Bay in comfort
at 150 miles per day. She is beautifully balanced on all points of sailing
and needs little helm. Waves seem to be much smaller now.'

The next year Southern took *Aguila* on what he described as 'a
cruise to the West Indies'. With a complement of four (two of whom
proved to be 'an unfortunate choice') they left Littlehampton on the
afternoon of 30 September 1966. A week before they reached Madeira they ran into a ferocious gale which *Aguila* handled perfectly;
the only damage being the skipper's false teeth which he bit in two
when shouting too loudly at two novice crew who were not enjoying
the proceedings at all. They then had light winds on the short trip to
Las Palmas, the most westerly of the Canary Islands. On 17 November, after a fast Atlantic trade-wind crossing, they sighted the loom
of the lights of Barbados. Having landed the two novices, *Aguila*
began a leisurely cruise the length of the Caribbean islands starting
in the south at Grenada and visiting, amongst others, St Lucia, Martinique, The Saintes, Antigua, St. Kitts, Anguila, The Virgin Islands,
then on to the Bahamas and Bermuda and then home via the Azores
and Spain. They found strong following winds in the North Atlantic
but *Aguila* handled the seas well and they arrived in Horta on Fayal
in the Azores at the end of a gale on 27 May. They moved on to

Ponta Delgada on San Miguel a few days later. They left on 6 June on their last passage to England where they arrived back at Littlehampton on 5 July after a voyage of 11,500 miles. Aguila looked in better condition than when she left and suffered only minor electrical and mechanical trouble during the entire trip. A tribute to her builders, skipper and crew.

Records are scarce as to Tom Southern's wanderings after this epic voyage and by 1975 *Aguila* was, according to Lloyd's Register of Yachts, no longer owned by him but by a John Roberts. The author understands *Aguila* is still sailing today.

Frank Mulville and *Iskra* (1970-1993)

The next ocean voyage undertaken by a Hillyard was in a quite different type of boat and with a quite different type of skipper.

The skipper was named Frank Nugent Blood Mulville, who died in November 1997. He is remembered as one of Britain's finest sea writers. He wrote nine books, all accounts of his own life and sea travels. As the *Independent* newspaper said about these in their obituary of Mulville: 'His observations and fearless self-analysis raise them to the level of literature'. He was the youngest of seven children, whose parents had met in Argentina. His father was an Irish/Australian engineer. Frank was born in Dinard in France. Holidays were spent in Brightlingsea on the east coast, where he was introduced to the smacks and Thames barges that worked and traded in the Blackwater and the Colne, on the banks of which David Hillyard was born. He developed his understanding of how boats sailed with models on the round Pond in Kensington Gardens, near where he was brought up. He maintained a respect for traditional rigs and hull forms for the rest of his life.

During the depression of the 1930s his father took him back to Argentina and his book *North Star to Southern Cross*, written in 1993, poignantly described his travails and traumas as a foreign youth in a Spanish-speaking boarding school, as well as how he discovered the freedom of the Pampas and the colourful romance of Gaucho life. The book won the 'Best Book of the Sea' award that year.

By the time World War II was declared Mulville was a pupil at St. Paul's School. He promptly left and apprenticed himself to the Merchant Navy Blue Star Line, trading between Britain and Argentina.

In 1943 his ship, the *Celtic Star*, was torpedoed and the forty-five sur-
vivors spent four days in a lifeboat. Frank stepped the mast, hoisted
the sails, discovered the joys of ocean sailing and resolved to have his
own boat. Their rescuers landed Frank in Sierra Lone where he joined
the Royal Navy Volunteer Reserve and rose to the rank of Lieutenant.
Working on Naval tugs he was part of the Salerno and Anzio landings
when he acquired his first boat, a sailing dinghy called *Ratty* in Soren-
to. He carried her aboard the tug and sailed her in the harbours they
visited throughout the Mediterranean. His ship was towing a floating
dock from Iceland to Australia when peace was declared. There he met
and married his first wife, Mary, who later joined him in England.

Jobs were scarce and life was hard for Mulville after the war and he
tried window cleaning, journalism and selling pressure cookers door-
to-door. He started Tape Typing, a secretarial and printing company
which was successful and remained in business for many years after
the war.

In 1950, now with his second wife Celia, he sailed his first proper
boat, an 18ft converted lifeboat named *Santa Lucia*, across the Bay
of Biscay to Spain. He next bought an Essex smack, *Transcur*, which
was the subject of his first book, *Terschelling Sands*, published in 1968.
Then came his third and largest yacht, *Girl Stella*. An old and somewhat dodgy 40ft gaff ketch, she had been built as a Looe lugger in
Porthleven in 1896 by unknown builders and converted into a yacht
in 1935.

Tired of working life he looked for something more fulfilling. Mulville, a lifelong socialist and a Labour Party member, became determined to discover the truth about post-revolutionary Cuba and wit-
ness the life of Cubans shortly after the Russian/USA missile crisis.
He set off across the Atlantic with Celia and their two sons and sailed
Girl Stella to Cuba. On their return trip they made a fateful decision
to stop on the island of Flores in the Azores. Trying to enter a small
harbour they hit a rock which opened up an old wound in the old
boat[*]. Later in another harbour further along the coast and open to
the east, they found themselves trapped with a strong onshore wind.

---

[*]   Mulville had discovered a corroded keel bolt and rot in the boat's keel whilst
        hauled out at St Lucia on their way to Cuba. He patched it up as best he could
        but secretly suspected a major problem.

With the boat leaking badly, they failed to extricate themselves and were driven onto rocks. *Girl Stella* broke up and sank.

Back in England, nursing his humiliation with the loss of his boat 'striking at the core of his ego', Mulville determined that he had to make the voyage to Cuba again in order, as he put it 'to purge myself of the stain which would otherwise colour the rest of my life'. Having received from his insurers only half what *Girl Stella* was worth, he set to to find another boat. He came across a 30ft gaff cutter lying hauled out in an east coast boatyard 'run down, unloved, dirty and hopeless' as he put it. She was then called *Calva* and had been built by David Hillyard in or around 1930 (in the days before the 1946 fire in the yard destroyed most written records). Mulville was not impressed and thought her most unsuitable for a singlehander. Mulville had decided to make the return voyage to Cuba alone. But he bought her, renamed her *Iskra* (a Slav word meaning a spark or a small flame) and set about adapting her for his needs.

At first, the only thing about *Calva* he liked was the chubby cheerful visage of a carved wooden dolphin fixed to the bow just below the bowsprit. Initially Mulville thought he would get rid of it but later came to treasure the animal. Later he wrote:

> I have always believed it is the quality of humour that carries Iskra through when times are rough. I can feel it in her. There is a suggestion of wisdom, too, in the dolphin's wide-set eyes, his broad forehead, even the zany grin carried the hint of a deeper concern for our safety. He is like a Buddha, genial and grave. All suggest the swift movement I have come to expect of Iskra—her ability to sail herself out of trouble, her instant response to a sudden demand and her dogged capacity to keep going, week on week, month on month. The dolphin imparts to the ship the intelligence which is the birthright, inherited from his kind.

Very soon, Mulville came to appreciate *Iskra's* qualities. He commented that Hillyard was new to designing yachts when he built *Iskra* in 1930; Hillyard had not yet broken with the tradition that demanded of a boat the ability to beat back to harbour in a storm without an engine. He thought that later Hillyards lost this characteristic as they became 'fat' to accommodate engines and smart living quarters. He wrote: 'After Iskra they became good, comfortable, solid, safe, slow and boring, as they remain to this day'.*

Mulville came to love his boat, though slowly at first. She was stiff, dry, safe and sailed fast. He fell too for the friendly comfort of her. He described her cabin as like the drawing room of a country cottage, with her oil lamps held in place by two more dolphins. She was snug when times were inclement outside as well as being an airy place, lit by portholes and a well-proportioned skylight.

In September 1970 Mulville, Iskra and the dolphin left St. Peter Port Marina on the isle of Guernsey on their solo voyage to Cuba. They put into Vigo, leaving there in early October bound for La Palma, the most westerly of the Canary Islands. On this passage Iskra made good time, averaging 130 miles per day. During this trip, Mulville woke suddenly one night to find the iron slab of a ship's side hurtling past just yards away. It was a near thing and Mulville was even more surprised to read the name of the ship as it passed—the Cavalheiro Arujo—Lisboa. It was the very same ship that had brought Mulville and his family home from Flores after the sinking of Girl Stella. To be nearly run down by a ship which had earlier rescued you was a strange coincidence which troubled Mulville greatly.

It took thirty days from La Palma to Antigua. After a break in English Harbour, Mulville sailed for Cuba arriving at Baracoa, lying at the eastern end of the island. He described his time in Cuba as strange; he was part prisoner, part celebrity and part tourist but always at the whim of someone else. At first his boat was impounded and two soldiers were put on board to guard him. Then he was flown to Havana where he met people from his previous visit. Then he was given permission to sail along the coast to Havana provided he put into specified ports and harbours to be presented to the locals as some kind of hero by a kind of guardian/warden who would drive

---

*   Not everyone will agree with this statement by Mulville but there is an element of truth in it. There is no doubt that the early boats like Iskra, Solace and Brynhildr were exceptionally seaworthy and did not have to rely on powerful auxiliary engines to get out of trouble, as is invariably the case today—we are all motor-sailors now!

along the coast following him in an old beaten up Cadillac. He was required to take a Cuban as crew, who soon fled after the first spell of bad weather. He was then on his own, in winter, sailing a coast with few navigation aids, having to enter and leave strange ports in accordance with a timetable dictated to him regardless of weather conditions. Mulville wrote it was the hardest thing he had ever done. *Iskra* behaved perfectly throughout and they left Havana homeward bound on 1 April 1971. It was a difficult trip with gale force winds at the start. He had no choice but to battle through it as he could not land in Florida and ships from Cuba were prohibited from visiting the Bahamas.

In 1974, after *Iskra* underwent a major refit, Mulville sailed her single-handed to the Bahamas to attend his grandaughter's first birthday, arriving back in Bradwell in Essex without a mark on her. Next he had the idea of filling *Iskra* with copies of his books and sailing them to America, there to sell them using *Iskra* as a sort of floating book shop. In 1980 he set off with 400 copies of each of two of his books, sailing via the Azores and then direct to Newport on Rhode Island. This time he started the voyage with his third wife, Wendy, aboard until they reached the Azores. He sailed a very overloaded *Iskra* 2,181 miles alone from Ponta Delgada to Newport in thirty-four days. After the voyage, in which he nearly lost his life whilst climbing the mast to retrieve a wanton halyard block in the midst of a full gale, falling out of his bosuns' chair, he left *Iskra* in Rhode Island whilst he returned to England to try to salve his business. The next year with Wendy aboard they gently cruised through Maine to Canada laying the boat up for the winter. The following spring Mulville sailed *Iskra* to Halifax in Nove Scotia and then, alone again, back to England arriving in Falmouth after a heavy weather passage. After that the couple sailed thousands of miles together around the Atlantic—south to Buenos Aires, to Brazil, the USA, Bermuda, the North Cape of Iceland, Scandinavia, Spain, the Canary Islands, the West Indies and Africa.

After all that, *Iskra* was laid up for a well-earned rest just off a grassy quay in Maldon in Essex, with Mulville musing 'soon we shall both want the Dolphin again for another venture, perhaps to Argentina to see my cousins.'

In 1992, with Wendy as crew, they sailed *Iskra* to Santander in Spain to visit the Altimira caves. On their return, after a horrendous crossing of Biscay in a north-westerly gale they stopped at Brest for the Classic Boat Festival being held there for the first time[*]. Tiring of the hustle and bustle of that amazing collection of yachts, barges, fishing smacks, square riggers and everything and everyone involved with classic boats (and it seems at times half the population of France) Mulville decided to divert on their way home to Ireland and the west coast of Scotland[†].

By Saturday 5 September they were sailing to the west of the Mull of Kintyre heading for the island of Gigha to stop for the night. They made it just as it was getting dark and picked up a mooring in Ardminish Bay next to a deserted trawler. It was blowing hard but they appeared comfortable. During the night the wind got up to a near gale from the south and the moorings became untenable. There was little they could do; it was too late. Their warps to the buoy broke and *Iskra* was driven first into the trawler suffering dreadful damage and then, breaking free from her, onto some rocks. Mulville tried to get an anchor down but it would not hold. It was all over. A helicopter arrived and plucked them to safety.

Over the next twelve months, they removed everything from the stranded vessel, dragged her over the rocks back into deep water where she barely floated with a number of bad leaks. *Iskra* was towed to Craobh Haven where she was hauled out and rebuilt.

The year after her stranding Mulville and Wendy sailed her round the north of Scotland back to her home mooring off Pewit Island in Bradwell Creek in Esssex. Mulville finished his book about this latest adventure of his with the words: 'As we rowed ashore, the dinghy heavy with our gear, we took a last look at *Iskra*, peacefully at rest for a spell. She looked much as she has always looked, bearing no scar, carrying no mark to tell of her adventures—perhaps a little smug having extracted from us everything she wanted'[†]

---

[*]   Where they met a number of other Hillyards who had sailed from England for the event.

[†]   The author attended that memorable event and it was everything that Mulville described in his book *Rescue and Recovery*.

[‡]   Mulville, Frank. *Rescue and Recovery*. Seafarer Books 1997.

One strange coincidence involving all the owners and Hillyards mentioned above is how the island of St Lucia, one of the smallest and least visited islands in the West Indies, played a part in their stories. Victor Clark found his ideal young West Indian crew, Stanley, living there on the island. Stanley accompanied Clark and *Solace* round the world. Keith Robinson found his Hillyard lying there on a mooring, Tom Southern took his *Aguila* there on his Caribbean cruise and it was there on the island that Frank Mulville discovered the wound in his boat *Girl Stella* which led to her loss.

Conrad Jelinek and *Carousa* (1974)

In June 1974, Conrad Jelinek, with his wife Wendy and their six-month-old daughter Nicola, set sail from Malta in their newly acquired 6-ton Hillyard, *Carousa*, which had been built in 1932. She was not dissimilar to *Iskra*, who had been built at much the same time and was much the same size. The main difference was that *Carousa* was not gaff rigged but was a Bermudan sloop.

Six years later and with 22,000 miles under her keel, they landed at Eden in New South Wales, Australia, having visited Greece, Gibraltar, the West Indies and the USA. After traversing the Panama Canal they went to the Galapagos Islands, the Tuamotu Islands (known as 'the dangerous archipelago'), the Cook Islands, Brisbane and finally Eden.

It was a remarkable voyage in a small boat with a small child. Little has been written about it but Conrad did write in a letter to *the Hill-yarder*[*]:

In Gibraltar I re-rigged her from sloop to cutter and for the Pacific a square sail and a raffee[†] pulled her steadily and easily before the trade winds. A highly modified Q.M.E. self-steering gear did virtually all the steering, the only foreigner being a wonderfully reliable MD2 Volvo.

Wherever we have been 'Carousa' is admired and coveted and with good reason, for she has carried us safely and com-

---

[*]   Issue No. 3 Autumn 1980.

[†]   A three-sided sail hoisted above a squaresail.

fortably through all weathers. It is with a feeling of inestimable satisfaction and pride we relax ashore admiring 'Carousa' at anchor, knowing she will carry us many miles more.

The Jelineks then settled in Eden, buying 12 acres of virgin bushland. Conrad worked skippering a trawler whilst in between times clearing their land. *Carousa* remained their prized possession for many years.

Of such stuff are true pioneers and Hillyard owners made!

Angela Langley and *Wumpus* (1978)

The 1970s was not a period when women sailors abounded and it was therefore a surprise to be told* that in 1978 two young women sailed alone to the West Indies—and in a Hillyard.

Angela Langley had been sailing for quite a while and had done all her RYA qualifications by the time she went looking for a boat in which to sail away in search of a new life—destination Australia. Her search had taken her a full year when she decided on the Hillyard *Wumpus*, a 9-tonner built in 1964. The vessel had been well loved and looked after by her one and only previous owner and was in very original condition. But much work was required to prepare her for extended passage-making. The original canvas decks were glassed over, the rigging was replaced with stainless steel, the mast was re-glued, jiffy reefing was added to the boom. The boat was stripped out inside and repainted, the seacocks checked, the keel sandblasted and all the keel bolts were renewed. This being 1978, there was no GPS, nor two-way radios, which then were expensive, heavy and power hungry. There was no solar anything. By today's standards, *Wumpus* was extremely basic inside and out. A Hydrovane wind-vane self-steering gear was added.

As for crew, Angela wanted to sail double-handed with a female crew, and after advertising for someone in *Yachting Monthly* she found Liz Hammick. Liz turned out to be the perfect crew; she had previously crewed on a voyage to New Zealand.

Wumpus looked the part when they departed with wooden ratlines up to the spreaders and the shrouds spouting much baggywrin-

---

*   The author was alerted to this voyage by Ann Hammick, doyen of the Ocean Cruising Club and Editor of its estimable journal, *Flying Fish*—one of the girls was her sister, Liz.

kle. They left Jersey in mid-September and were soon tested by a gale in the Bay of Biscay. They arrived in Bayonne battered but happy. The leg to Madeira was the girls' first passage using celestial navigation and they were satisfied to have Porto Santo and then Madeira come up right on target. After a week in Funchal, they left on 14 November and soon got into the rhythm of the long trade-wind passage to the Caribbean. They stood three-hour watches during the night but were more flexible during the day. Angela described how they spent most afternoons sitting on the floor of the centre cockpit, well sheltered, doing their tapestries and playing scrabble! They suffered the inevitable damage from involuntary gybes but managed to hold everything together. They ran the engine every few days to charge the batteries but electrical use was minimal. Their only problem was they got through numerous fan belts as the alternator was misaligned. They ended up using a supply of their nylon stockings plaited together.

Eventually Antigua came up over the horizon and the girls sailed into English Harbour on 11 December 1978 at the end of their twenty-seven-day transatlantic crossing.

Bill Finnis and *Didycoy* (1983)

Bill Finnis and his wife, after some extensive cruising between Holland and the Mediterranean in their 12-tonner *Didycoy*, took off in 1983 on a six-year circumnavigation. He eventually wrote up the lessons garnered from this 40,000-mile trip in a book[*].

Bill has some appreciative things to say about his boat, particularly in terms of her seaworthiness and solid construction. In all the miles they sailed and in all the various weather conditions they met, *Didycoy* seldom shipped green water on her foredeck. Her long keel made her well behaved in the heaviest weather and under normal conditions she would practically sail herself. Whatever may be said about double-enders not being pooped, their experience demonstrated that they can be, although this only happened twice during the whole voyage. Then they were saved from the full force of the breaking sea by the aft cabin and the deep centre cockpit. Finnis also tells of how the latter saved their lives during 'a close encounter' with a reef in the San Blas

---

[*]   Finnis, Bill. *The Passage Maker's Manual*, Waterline Books 1993.

islands. Despite being laid over horizontally and completely washed over by pounding surf, they were protected by the depth of the cockpit and the doghouse.

Bill Finnis had no problem with *Didycoy's* relatively slow speed. He points out that, even at the maximum hull speed of around 8 knots, the noise of the bow wave prevented anything like ordinary conversation, let alone sleep. He was quite happy to make 120 miles a day. His only regret was that, because of the amount of gear they had to take, the internal volume of the 12-tonner proved to be a little too small. His ideal would be a craft of the same proportions, but with a beam of around twelve feet.

The Finnis's sailed the conventional route west-about around the world, initially following 'Hum' Barton's oft quoted rule for getting from the United Kingdom to the Caribbean—'sail south until the butter melts, then turn right.' They took six years over their voyage, travelling via the Panama Canal and then across the Pacific to Australia and home via the Indian Ocean, the Suez Canal and the Mediterranean. It was an extremely competent and well exercised voyage about which there are few available details other than what can be gleaned from his book. Bill Finnis did write an account of his voyage in a book titled '*Didycoy—Six Years Around the World*' but this is now out of print and hard to find.

The Symes-Davidsons and *Tallulah May*

Inevitably with time passing and the Hillyard fleet getting older and, in many cases, frailer and with yachtsmen's ideas of what makes an ideal ocean cruiser changing (mainly the perceived need for installing all todays modern electronic gizmos), fewer and fewer long ocean voyages are being undertaken by Hillyards. There are however a number of people who are still attracted to the idea of taking an old simple wooden boat on such an adventure, unencumbered by much of today's 'must have' accoutrements which adorn the sterns, masts, stainless steel hoops, gantries and cabin tops of the so-called 'proper' ocean cruising yachts.

One such family who exemplify the Hillyard tradition are the Symes-Davidsons who at the time of writing were still on an ocean odyssey which started in 2011, when they purchased a run down

1969-built 13-tonner Hillyard called *Trifle*. She was a 'stretched' version of the well-received 11-tonner ketches: hard-chined hulls with transom sterns and bilge keels. She was roomy enough to accommodate the Symes-Davidsons and their four children, of whom two were under three at the time. She was in a poor state and was transported to their rented home in a very landlocked part of Somerset.

There they gave her a thorough refit. Chris Symes-Davidson wrote:

> We decided very early on to replace or repair everything that needed doing with the very best quality materials we could find. All through-hull fittings were replaced with bronze, wiring is all tinned copper. All plywood was Lloyd's registered; decks were epoxied using West system resins and woven roving. Iroko was used, bought as boards, cut and planed to size. French oak was used for frames and ribs, whose quality is more consistent than with English oak. Where planks were replaced we used copper boat nails, roved to fix them. The joints were treated with cuprinol, primed, caulked, primed, stopped with lead putty and primed. New side decks were laid, the engine was taken out, refurbished and replaced. New tanks were fitted, all plumbing and electrical wiring was renewed. At the end of it she was nearly a new boat and was given a new name—*Tallulah May*.

It was an object lesson on what to do with an old Hillyard to make her fit for some ocean-bashing.

By 2015 *Tallulah May* was back in the water and ready for the off. Five years ago Chris and Mandy with their two youngest daughters, set off on an extended live-aboard cruise. To date they have visited Northern Spain, Portugal, Morocco, various Atlantic islands, the Caribbean, North America and Canada. When they left they said they would return in five years time but in 2020 they were still in Canada, enjoying every day and having th time of their lives.

One hundred years after the first Hillyard was built the Symes-Davidsons and *Tallulah May* are still showing others how to do it.

Part IV

HILLYARD PEOPLE

INTRODUCTION

Generals, greengrocers, authors, admirals, fraudsters, vicars, airline pilots, doctors and academics, house builders, lords and knights of the realm, farmers, drug dealers, opticians, naval and military men and, last but not least, dreamers of the day. David Hillyard and his men will have seen all these and many more such folk coming through the gates into the yard, buying their boats or mooring them on the river, on the quays, or in the mud berths.

Sailing, the smell of the sea and the lure of open oceans is strong stuff and many cannot resist it, whether they can afford it or not. For these people, ownership of a small yacht becomes a necessity to be had at all costs. For the very rich, displaying their wealth via a smart mega-yacht is an essential part of the vision they try to present to the world. The very poor will scrabble around for every last penny to acquire a boat of their dreams, however unsuitable or unseaworthy. Many people, including no doubt many Hillyard owners, put reason to one side when faced with the nostalgic sights, smells and sounds of a traditional boatyard, where dreams can be given full rein and the vision of a new life brought to fulfilment. But boat ownership, as they soon discover, brings difficult decisions, discomfort, debt and often fear and fright at the sea's capriciousness. It is an oft repeated phrase, but no less true for that, that a yachtsman is genuinely happy only twice during the ownership of his dream—the day he buys her and the day he sells her.

It has always amazed the author (who is also a lawyer) how buyers of yachts too readily put reality behind them when they find the boat of their dreams. They will often agree to spend more for their boat than they paid for their houses but without any investigation into whether the seller actually owns the vessel he is offering, and often they will buy without a survey. Or they will rely on a survey the seller produces, purporting to have been carried out 'recently' by an unknown surveyor, probably with no qualification and offering no

23. 2½-tonner *Dawn II*

John Rossetti

24. 2½-tonner *Mynute*

25. 4-tonner *Twinkler* - the oldest known Hillyard, built 1922

26. 5-tonner
Fyne Spirit

27. 5-tonner
Wembury

28. 6-tonner *Mavrodaphne*

29. 6-tonner *Miss Ruth*

30. 9-tonner *Trimley Maid*

Douglas Coulson

31. 9-tonner *Hannah*

32. 11-tonner *Pangchi*

33. 12-tonner *Snoqualmie*

34. 13-tonner *Sanchia*

35. 13-tonner *Sequoiah*

36. 16-tonner *Misty Morn*

37. 18-tonner *Maffick*

38. 22-tonner *Wendy Woo,* once owned by the author

39. 28-tonner *Aquila*

*40. Ragged Robin III
ex-Lottie Blossom*

41. Nancy Blackett,
both boats owned by Arthur Ransome

42. Nevil Shute's *Runagate*

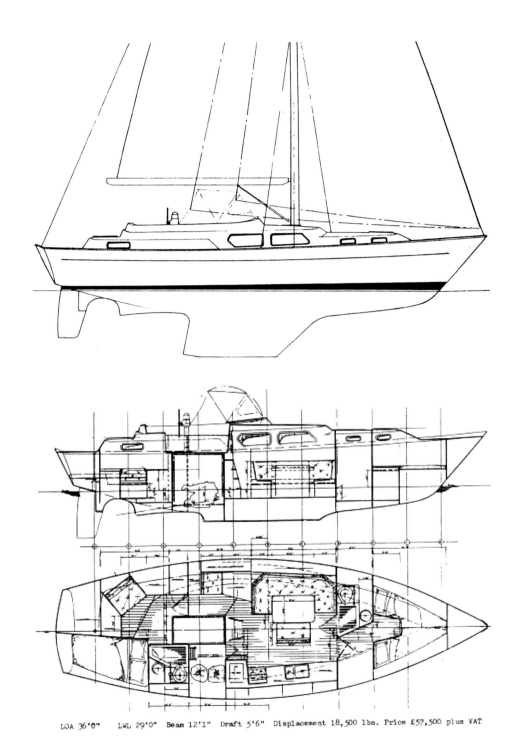

LOA 36'0"   LWL 29'0"   Beam 12'1"   Draft 5'6"   Displacement 18,500 lbs. Price £57,500 plus VAT

43. Moonfleet, designed by Laurent Giles and built in GRP

protection to the buyer.* Many yachts are not registered, others are on the so called 'Small Ships Register' which affords no protection at all†. Many people try to sell boats which they do not own. The secondhand boat market gives many opportunities and rich pickings for fraudsters and charlatans.

David Hillyard himself would have been aware of all this and he could only too easily have fueled the dreams and visions of deranged folk who, all too often, try to build or buy quite unsuitable boats with no money to pay for them and with no skill or experience to sail them. For this reason Hillyard, someone with his feet planted firmly on the ground and never given to flights of fancy, was often thought of as difficult, fussy and choosy in that he could, and did, refuse to build for people he did not think capable of handling his creations. Whilst he was a businessman through and through, he cared enough for his customers not to let 'the bottom line' influence him in deciding whether to take on a commission. Most small builders of wooden craft in the last century were perpetually short of money and many, sad to say, lacked Hillyard's ethics and took on any job that came their way and which produced a deposit enough to pay yet one more week's wages to the men. Companies folded, deposits were lost, crooked yacht brokers tried to sell the same boat to two buyers (this happened once to the author), customers were overcharged and cheated, many a horror, mistake, or deliberate cost cutting (or use of cheap unsuitable timber) was hidden by numerous coats of paint, or bilges were filled with concrete. But Hillyard sailed on regardless, punctilious to the last, with a dedicated and loyal band of followers and customers (and employees) all begging for more. Money was important to him and necessary, but only just the right amount to ensure that the yard did not fall into a

---

*   I came across one buyer who did just this when buying an old wooden boat. The copy survey the seller produced referred to the boat as having a GRP hull suffering badly from osmosis! 'Oh', the buyer said, 'I was told that was just a mistake'. In fact the boat suffered from broken frames and rotten garboards.

†   This was introduced by the UK Government so yachtsmen going abroad could produce a 'certificate' showing the 'registered owner'. It does no such thing. Anyone can register themselves as an 'owner' by making a simple declaration which is accepted without any investigation. It is no proof of ownership at all. A bit like a motor car's log book.

loss and so that customers felt they were getting a good deal. In this he succeeded magnificently for nearly a century.

In this section we look at a number of the people who over the years have owned Hillyards, sailed them, helped in their development, promoted the 'brand', written about them and restored and rebuilt them. They can genuinely be called 'Hillyard people'.

Chapter 14

THE EARLY YEARS

There were from the start famous names among the Hillyard customer lists. In the first few years after World War I buyers tended to be Generals, Admirals and other men with distinguished military careers, along with medical men, lawyers and other professionals, many of whom would keep coming back for more. As cruising in small boats became more popular, buyers came from all over and were of all types. We have mentioned many of these in earlier chapters of this book but there are others worthy of note and who by their writings, voyaging, or efforts to keeping the Hillyard fleet together, have made a contribution to the history and legacy of the Hillyard fleet, and Hillyarders past and present. Amongst these people from those far-off inter-war years, we describe two, namely:

Sir Bertram Clough Williams-Ellis

The diminutive 21ft centreboard cutter *Twinkler* built by David Hillyard in 1922 is considered to be the 'first' real Hillyard and is certainly the oldest surviving one. As we keep having to recognize, yard records from that time are non-existent but from a study of Lloyd's Register of Yachts and from records held by owners of this particular vessel it has been possible to re-create its history and ownership over the last one hundred years.

Twinkler was exhibited in 1922 at what was effectively the first London Boat Show (which was then called The Marine and Small Craft Exhibition and was held at the Royal Agricultural Hall in Islington), and was bought by Clough Williams-Ellis in 1927. He was then forty-four years old and he owned *Twinkler* until 1939. It was during this time that he completed the building of his famous Italianate village of Portmeirion in North Wales. *Twinker* went through a number of subsequent owners, who kept her going, and in 2010 was bought by Professor Ted Evans and his wife, Dr Diana, about whose life we write later in this section. They kept her for many years and are primarily responsible for this little ship being in such good condition today.

Clough Williams-Ellis was knighted in 1972 and he died in 1978. In accordance with his wishes he was cremated and his ashes went to make up a marine rocket which was fired into the sky as part of a New Year's Eve firework display over the estuary at Portmeirion, some twenty years after his death.

Sir Giles Rolls Loder, Bart.

Sir Giles was an English aristocrat of the old school. Born in 1914, he inherited land and money when he was only five and was educated at Eton and Trinity College, Cambridge. He and his family have been synonymous with West Sussex gardening and horticulture, owning over the years some magnificent gardens at Leonardslee near Horsham, High Beeches near Handcross, and Wakehurst near Haywards Heath. The names Loder and Leonardslee are familiar to gardeners all over the world, many of whom have never been near the garden to which Loder devoted much of his life. He had a lifelong fascination with machines and studied engineering at Cambridge, where he became interested in sailing and boat design. During World War II he worked at the Vosper Shipyards on technical and design aspects of new vessels for the Royal Navy.

Loder, as a very wealthy schoolboy, first encountered Hillyard at one of the early boat shows, and the pair started talking boats so long and earnestly into the night that they were actually locked into the Aggie, the exhibition hall where the show was being held. A result of this discussion was that in 1931 at the age of seventeen Loder became the proud owner of a mahogany lug-sail dinghy, with which he had great fun sailing in Poole harbour. In 1934 he felt it was time to graduate to a 2½-tonner, but his mother thought that was much too small. So he settled for a standard 9-tonner, *Laranda* which, despite a long bowsprit, was under-canvassed for her size. 'She was very sluggish in light airs and pulled and was hard-mouthed in strong ones', Sir Giles said. However, he discovered that her canoe stern made her a good sea boat.

In 1936 Sir Giles had Hillyard build him his first *Selig* (Giles backwards), which was a one-off design of distinctive Hillyard shape, 38ft

6in long, 10ft beam with a 6ft draught. Sir Giles incorporated a number of ideas derived from his earlier experiences, including a flush deck and a dog house. He also had a permanent backstay fitted, not much in evidence then when most boats were gaff rigged. 'It takes much of the worry of a tall Bermudan mast off one's mind' he said. Rigged as a cutter, she sailed well. Fitted with a teak laid deck and a Grey petrol engine, *Selig* cost something in the region of £1200, according to *Yachting Monthly*, which published the boat's lines in an issue of 1937 making the comment: '*Selig*'s lines are those of a handsome and nicely moulded cruiser hull with ample forefoot and balanced overhangs'.

Sir Giles found the aft cabin particularly useful for the extra guest or the paid hand. If the latter, 'he, his pipe and his snoring were well isolated from the owner's quarters!', Loder wrote. When he brought her back to Littlehampton, the yard workers went in terror of the paid hand who did everything ever so correctly—soft shoes on board and the rest—and insisted everyone else did too.

Loder sold *Selig* during the war and moved over to motor cruisers. Hillyard built him three. In 1947 he launched *Golden Oriole*, a 40ft, twin screw motor yacht (TSMY) based on the standard 18-tonner hull. This was followed by *Golden Seal* in 1950, basically an 18-tonner lengthened to 46ft and 24 tons, and finally in 1954, *Golden Beaver*, a motor-sailer of 50ft and 28 tons. Dennis Cullingford designed the hull of the latter, and Loder designed the upperworks.

Golden Beaver was a handsome looking yacht, warranting an article in the June 1945 issue of *Yachting Monthly*, which published her sail and cabin plans. She had an 11ft long deck saloon, half sunk to avoid windage, with large windows, and was generously fitted out. It was this feature which caused Humphrey Barton real misgivings when he was commissioned to bring *Golden Beaver* home after a long trip south. As this involved crossing the Bay of Biscay, Barton insisted that the windows should be boarded up, as he considered them to be a menace and completely unsafe in rough weather. However, after the crossing and once safely moored back in Littlehampton, 'Hum', as he was known, was man enough to apologise to Hillyard for his adverse comments. Hum admitted that, despite the rough weather experienced in the Bay, not one wave had in any way threatened the safety of those large saloon windows.

Golden Beaver had 'all mod. cons.' for her day, with a spacious galley, a bathroom with a sit-up bath, and a pressurized hot and cold
water system. She was powered by a 72hp Gardner diesel with a 33in
propeller, which gave her a cruising speed of 8 knots. Under sail, with
her ketch rig of some 600 square feet of sail, she could make 8.5
knots on a beam reach. On the aft deck she carried a Fairey Duckling
wooden dinghy nesting inside a West Wight scow, both launched by
the topping lift on the mizzen boom, so that guests could have some
small boat fun whenever they were in harbour.

Sir Giles commented that when it came to his non-standard boats,
Hillyard would never give him an exact quote, but with a twinkle of
his blue eyes, would say, 'You get what you pay for.' When the account
eventually came in, often long after the boat's completion, it was always very moderate. Loder commented 'his only overhead being his
motorcycle he rode to work on.'

Loder was a member of the Royal Yacht Squadron and was a regular at Cowes Week, often skippering *Kaylena*, a well-known 12 Metre
yacht. Family holidays with his wife and two sons were often taken
exploring the European inland waterways. At other times, away from
the sea, he and his wife went on ambitious journeys to the Amazon
or the Antarctic to look at the wildlife. Loder died in February 1999.

Chapter 15

AUTHORS AND STORYTELLERS

Two well-known authors and writers of fiction in the early to mid-twentieth century were Hillyard devotees, both of whom wove their yachts and sailing exploits into their books. These two are:

Nevil Shute Norway

Better known as Nevil Shute he was born in Ealing in 1899, although most people think of him as being from Australia, to where he emigrated in 1950. He trained as an aircraft engineer and started sailing by chance when he and a friend from his prep school days, Oliver Sturt, answered a notice in *The Times* personal column for two undergraduates to crew for an elderly Southampton solicitor, Mr Hepherd, in a yacht called *Aeolia*. She was an engineless, 1888-built, straight stemmed 28-ton gaff cutter with massively heavy gear. This cruise took them to the Scilly Islands, a cruise to which later featured in Shute's first published novel *Marazan*.

This voyage made a profound impression on Shute. He described the voyage in his autobiography *Slide Rule*[*], and it laid the foundation for a recreation that endured for the rest of his life. Voyaging under sail became a thread throughout his novels. In many of these sailing becomes a means of escape and a way of getting away from it all. In *Pilotage* (published posthumously) the protagonist escapes to sea from his failed marriage. David Anderson in *In the Wet* sails his boat to escape the pressures of flying in the Queen's Flight. The Corbett family try to escape from the horrors of wartime bombing by taking to their yacht on the Hamble River, even if it means cramped living on board with a baby and two small children. In *Trustee from the Toolroom*, Jack Donnely, the illiterate Oregon fisherman, escapes from sophisticated Hawaii to sail south to 'the islands' and this provides

---

[*]   Shute, Nevil. *Slide Rule*, William Heinemann 1954.

Keith Stewart with his only affordable chance of reaching Tahiti in the *Mary Belle*.

Shute began his engineering career with the de Havilland Aircraft company. In 1924 he moved to Vickers, where he was involved with the development of airships, working on the R100 project. All this work stopped when the counterpart R101 suffered a fatal crash in 1930. In his autobiography, Shute was very critical of the R101 design and management team. He teamed up with an aircraft designer and in 1931 they started Airspeed Ltd to build aircraft. They began in a former trolleybus garage in York and, after many initial setbacks, their Envoy aircraft was chosen for the King's Flight and a military version became the standard multi-engined trainer for the RAF. Shute developed a hydraulic retractable undercarriage, and for this and his work on the R100 he was made a fellow of the Royal Aeronautical Society.

In 1933 Shute moved Airspeed Ltd south to Portsmouth. This brought him back to the Solent and the Hamble River, enabling him to resume sailing. This was initially on a friend's 1908 Estonian-built 30ft sloop called *Skerdmore*. In 1938 he left Airspeed and had some success with his novels *Lonely Road* (1932) and *Ruined City* (1938), for both of which he had sold the film rights. He now had the funds to commission a new yacht. The same year he went to see David Hillyard in Littlehampton and the result was the building of an 18-tonner which he called *Runagate*. She was 40ft long, 11ft beam with a draught of 5ft. She was rigged as a schooner with a sail area of 640 square feet, and a Victor oil engine was installed.

Shute had used the name Runagate for a yacht in his then un-published book *Pilotage**, which he had written in 1929. In this book one of the main characters, Peter Dennison, had been helmsman on a yacht *Runagate*. A paragraph reads:

---

* Pilotage was published posthumously in 1961, along with a novel written in 1923, *Stephen Morris*, as a single book. An *Observer* review of the book said, 'An example of trim, professional storytelling with technical know-how (splendid accounts of flying, driving by night, and sailing) giving extra thrust to the narrative'.

'Here we are,' he said. 'I thought we should find it. *Runagate,* fifteen ton, helmsman P. Dennison.' He ran his eye rapidly down the letterpress. 'Here we are,' he said. '"Much interest will be centered on the *Runagate,* whose helmsman, P. Dennison, is only sixteen years of age."'

Shute had little time to sail *Runagate* before the outbreak of war, although legend has it that he was actually afloat sailing in the English Channel when war was declared on 3 September 1939. In 1940 he applied to the Royal Naval Volunteer Reserve in response to their call for 'elderly yachtsmen'. He hoped to be given command of some small naval vessel, perhaps a trawler or drifter, where he could go on writing. After only a few days at the RNVR training centre, HMS *King Alfred* in Hove, Shute was furious at being directed to a technical department rather than to go and fight. But he was a technically qualified engineer, had run his own aircraft construction business (Airspeed) and had most recently been involved with the development and testing of secret weapons. His skills and experience were soon noticed by the Admiralty. Shute was to spend the war years 1940-1944 working in an office in London as head of the engineering section of the Department of Miscellaneous Weapons Development, a branch of the Admiralty, colloquially known as 'Wheezers and Dodgers'. They were responsible for the development of various unconventional weapons with, as he put it, 'occasional trips to the sea to see my things go wrong'. He developed the Rocket Spear, an anti-submarine missile with a fluted cast iron head, and the 'Panjandrum', a weird and massive rocket-propelled explosive-laden two wheeled cart designed to be launched from a landing craft to breach concrete defences. (It was scrapped after a trial run went badly wrong, nearly killing the watching top brass from the Army and Navy!)

Shute's own sailing exploits and his war time experiences all provided background for his later novels. The central theme of *Most Secret* is the use of a French fishing boat for raids on Brittany ports. A Sunday afternoon trip by Bill Duncan and Janet Prentice from Beaulieu to Lymington featured in *Requiem for a Wren*, set in waters that Shute knew well but were transformed by the huge buildup of vessels in preparation for the D-day landings.

Shute's writings on sailing are, of course, based on how things were in his time. When as an undergraduate he embarked on that first cruise in the *Aeolia* in 1919, most craft either had no auxiliary engine or only a temperamental one, so that manoeuvring in confined waters required considerable skill. Sails, often of flax, were generally heavy and they and all attendant gear required considerable manhandling. Shute writes of the discomforts of being at sea, of cooking on Primus stoves, of trimming and filling oil lamps, and of fetching water in canvas bags from the shore for filling the ship's tanks. The details are all there in his novels, serving to inform the reader but never bore with too much detail. For the most part his characters have a sense of release in being at sea, where their worlds are shrunk to considerations of course, tide, and weather, and battling with an element that is generally benign. There are exceptions such as the wrecking of the *Sheerwater* in a hurricane and Donald Woolfe's terror during a storm as he sails across the Atlantic single-handed.

In 1945 Shute was in the Far East and on his return he picked up the threads of a civilian life by getting *Runagate* out of mothballs. He resumed sailing her from his house, Pond End, on Hayling Island. He had two daughters, who sailed in dinghies, and his many friends were invited to go sailing with him on *Runagate*, to whom he lent her on occasion.

In 1950 Shute emigrated to Australia and made his home in Langwarrin in Victoria. High taxation and what he felt to be the decadence of Britain, with the spirit of personal independence and freedom dying, led him to leave the 'Old Country'.

Runagate was sold before he left England. His house in Australia was close to Port Philip Bay where he continued to sail but he never again owned a boat like *Runagate*. Shute died in January 1960.

Runagate exists today and is currently still afloat but in poor condition in a marina in Newcastle-upon-Tyne. The Nevil Shute Norway Foundation, an organisation dedicated to the writing, wisdom and philosophy of Nevil Shute, has for some time tried to set up a trust to raise money to buy and restore *Runagate* and make her available for charter in much the same way as the *Nancy Blackett* Trust has done with Arthur Ransome's old yacht (see next section). Alas, no progress has been made and despite the current owner being determined that 'one day' he will complete her renovation, the signs are not good. She is still in her original state and exactly as she would have been during Shute's ownership, save for the addition of a wooden shelter over the fore part of the cockpit. The Nevil Shute Norway Foundation visited the boat some years ago and now have a comprehensive photographic record of the old boat and her condition.

Arthur Ransome

Of all English writers in the twentieth century, Ransome is the one most associated with the sea, sailing and 'messing about in small boats'. He was born in 1884, fifteen years before Nevil Shute, and died in 1967, seven years after him. They both started their sailing activities in the 1920s and both incorporated their sailing experiences in their fiction, but Ransome is of course the best known, mainly as a result of *Swallows and Amazons* and its sequels.

Ransome became one of the finest English writers of children's books and many a yachtsman or yachtswoman afloat today was brought up on a diet of his books. He initially used real topographical features transplanted to the fictional places he wrote about, but after he moved to East Anglia he started to use real landscape and geography in his books. Thus one can use the maps printed in his books as a guide to those real areas. His own interest in sailing, and his need to provide an accurate description, caused him to undertake a voyage across the North Sea to Flushing. His book *We Didn't Mean to Go to Sea* reflects that passage and he based his fictional yacht *Goblin* on his own boat *Nancy Blackett*, which in turn took its name from a character in one of the books in the series.

After a year at what is now the University of Leeds, Ransome went to London determined to become a writer. He married in 1909 and wrote two biographies, one of Edgar Allan Poe, and one of Oscar Wilde which embroiled him in a libel suit with Lord Alfred Douglas, Wilde's 'Bosie'. In 1913, suffering from ill-health and financial problems brought about by the bankruptcy of his publisher, Ransome left his first wife and travelled to Russia. At the start of the Great War he became a foreign correspondent and covered the Russian revolutions of 1917. He sympathized with the Bolsheviks, became close to their leaders and met Evgenia Shelepina, who was Trotsky's personal secretary. In 1919 he was forced to flee Russia and he and Evgenia made their way to Estonia, where they set up home together and Ransome started on his sailing exploits. In 1920 he acquired a 17ft dinghy called *Slug* which he sailed off Tallinn. The boat leaked like a sieve and it says much for Evgenia that, after their first eventful spills and sinkings, she was still enthusiastic. After that, in 1921 he acquired an even smaller and less seaworthy boat with a tiny cabin. She was called *Kittiwake*. The bunks were too narrow for either of them to sleep properly at night and the boat was extremely tender and prone to capsize. Ransome wrote: 'If I shifted my pipe from one side of my mouth to the other I never knew what might happen.'

Next, Ransome had Otto Eggars, a well-respected German naval architect, design him a boat. This was *Racundra*. She was a fine-looking vessel, a typically broad Scandinavian double-ender, 30ft long with a huge beam of over 11ft. She was ketch rigged, very strongly built, with a shallow draught and a lifting centreboard. The couple sailed her from Talinn around the north Baltic and these were probably their happiest cruising days. Ransome wrote to Evgenia, after a visit to the 1924 London Boat Show, 'we are jolly lucky to have got such a stout lump of a boat as *Racundra*'. The book Ransome wrote about their voyaging in her, '*Racundra's First Cruise*', was an immediate success.

In 1924 Ransome married Evgenia and, leaving *Racundra* in the Baltic, the couple returned to England, where they settled in the Lake District. He sold *Racundra* to the writer and sailor Adlard Coles, who sailed her back to England, now renamed *Annette* II. This was at Ransome's insistence as he did not want anyone else to use her original name. There he set to and wrote the book for which he became best known, *Swallows and Amazons*, the first of the series that made his reputation.

In 1935 the Ransomes decided to leave the Lake District and move to the east coast of England. They rented a property known as Broke Farm at Levington where Ransome had a view from his upstairs study of Levington Creek, Harwich Harbour and the open sea. It was now that Ransome became, as he has been described, 'not quite a sailor who wrote children's books in his spare time'. Looking for a boat for him to buy, a friend of Ransome's (the yacht designer William McC Meek[*]) found him a 7-ton cutter for sale in Poole. Ransome travelled to see her and bought her for £525 in September 1935.

The boat had been built by Hillyard's in 1931 for a retired solicitor, who named her *Spindrift*. He sold her on in 1933 to a young man who, using money inherited on his twenty first birthday, changed her name to *Electron*. Ransome disliked this name and changed it again, to *Nancy Blackett*. He found her an excellent sea boat but heavy to sail shorthanded and with poor accommodation, which his formidable wife Evgenia loathed. She took against *Nancy* from the start because of the basic simplicity of the little Taylor paraffin stove to starboard of the companion way and a little white earthenware housemaids bowl to port. She seems never to have made any overnight passages in her.

Despite buying her late in the season, Ransome decided to sail *Nancy Blackett* to her new home on the River Orwell in Suffolk and very nearly lost her on the way. He ran into a full gale after leaving Poole Harbour and, meeting the full force of the ebb tide running out of the Needles Channel, was almost swept on to the Shingles bank. Many readers will have been there and experienced the ferocious seas that can build up in that narrow passage with wind against tide. When they arrived at Yarmouth, they found the lifeboat crew, who had been alerted by the coastguard, all ready to go to their aid. The rest of the trip was not without incident but they made it. Ransome summed up the whole experience, 'It had been extremely uncomfortable but at least it had shown me that Meek had found me a wonderful little boat'.

It was not long before *Nancy* was immortalised in print. She was faithfully and accurately portrayed under the pseudonym *Goblin* in the next book he wrote, *We Didn't Mean to Go to Sea*, even to the extent of having *Goblin* fly Ransome's Royal Cruising Club burgee. He drew the line, however, at giving her the same Official Number as *Nancy*. In the book Goblin's number is 16856 as opposed to Nancy's 162814

[*]   McC Meek, a well known yacht designer of the time, was the man responsible for the interior design of the diesel-electric Hillyard, *D'Sel* referred to in Chapter 8 above.

(maybe there is some simple coded message in this!). The book has a simple plot: Whilst waiting for their father to return from overseas on leave, the 'Swallows' are allowed to sail aboard their father's yacht the *Goblin*, but with a young man as skipper and provided they don't go outside the harbour. They all promise not to. The wind drops, they anchor and the young skipper goes ashore for petrol, where he has an accident and does not return. The fog comes down, the tide floods, the anchor drags and *Goblin* drifts out to sea. The weather worsens, the wind gets up, a gale blows and the *Swallows* have no alternative but to sail on. They reach Holland, where their father makes a pierhead jump from his steamer to bring them safely home. *We Didn't Mean to* was published in November 1937 and was an immediate success. 'Perhaps the best of all...' rhapsodized *Punch*.

The book is probably the first introduction to cruising that many a youngster has had, with *Goblin*, the fictionalised *Nancy*, becoming their ideal boat. The cliff-hanging suspense in the tale about four youngsters in a gale in the North Sea is balanced by the more pastoral description of cruising the Walton backwaters in another of his books, *Secret Water*.

*   *   *

As a result of his wife's dislike of *Nancy*, Ransome went early in 1938 to see Harry King, the renowned boatbuilder at Pin Mill on the River Deben, about a new boat. This all despite his much-repeated axiom, 'fools build and wise men buy'[*]. It was agreed that Fred Shepherd, a well-known South Coast yacht designer, was to produce the design which King would then build. Shepherd drew a canoe sterned yacht 35ft long and 10ft wide. Rigged as a Bermudan cutter she had a 50ft mast of which Ransome was somewhat in awe. Her hull was not unlike what Hillyard was producing at the time, but had an aft cockpit and no stern cabin. Below, her accommodation comprised a large airy saloon with 6ft headroom and two long 6ft 6in settee berths, a splendid galley, a chart table and a coal stove. There was a single bunk in the forecabin with a toilet right forward. They wanted to call the boat *Molly*, but the name was already in

---

[*]   This statement appeared first in his book *Racundra's First Cruise*.

use. Evgenia's second choice was *Selina*. When Harry King said that he had an Aunt Selina, Ransome said, 'Then we shall call her *Selina King*'. She was launched on 28 September 1938, with a war in Europe looming.

Nancy Blackett was sold, much to Ransome's regret, but he was pleased at how well the buyer looked after her, his even renaming his home 'Blackett Cottage'.

Ransome spent a happy 1939 until the outbreak of war sailing his new vessel, which he declared was 'a grand ship'. Unlike Nevil Shute, Ransome took no part in the war, being fifty-five when it was declared. The Admiralty did not want him and he would have nothing to do with the Home Guard. They moved away from the east coast back to the Lake District, where they bought a house on the shore of Coniston Water. There Ransome wrote a book every year until the end of the war.

In July 1945 the Ransomes moved to London and settled in a flat in Weymouth Street. He was now sixty-one, his health was not good and his doctors forbade him from sailing *Selina King*. This led him to declare what he needed was a sort of 'ketch rigged marine bathchair'. For this, he went to see Jack Laurent Giles, one of Britain's leading yacht designers who was in practice in Lymington. Ransome was exact in his requirements—a craft needing the minimum of work to sail but providing the maximum comfort for two with shallow draught (to explore the creeks and harbours of the east coast) yet with standing headroom below, ample lockers and storage space, with a tall cupboard for oilskins beside the companion way. Giles took up this interesting challenge with gusto. What emerged was a 28ft 3in long Bermudan ketch, drawing 3ft 6in with a 9ft beam. The sail plan divided between two masts was arranged for ease of handling. The mizzen mast was at the front end of the cockpit, with a small 8hp Stuart Turner engine under a bridge deck.

But it all went wrong from the start. Ransome hated the name Giles had given the boat—*Peter Duck*, saying it should be plain 'P.D.' The boat was built by Kings in Pill Mill and launched in 1946. Ransome was angered that he hit his head on a low transverse beam, at the aft end of the bunk, which gave only 2ft 6in headroom instead of the three feet shown on the plan.

Evgenia hated the boat as well. She said that under sail 'she looked ridiculous and in rain she leaked everywhere'. As a result of all this, and Ransome's general unhappiness with the boat, he decided to finish with the sea and sold the boat to Giles and his partner, Humphrey Barton, for £1,200, barely covering his costs. A month later he changed his mind and bought her back (by which time Giles and Barton had gone ahead and named her *Peter Duck*) losing some £300 in the process. When at last Ransome took her out for a sail, the main boom was too long and did not clear the mizzen, the mainsail was too long in the foot, the anchor chain did not fit the winch, the engine would not turn the boat to port when in reverse, the deck leaked everywhere and Ransome fell out of his bunk in the middle of the night, declaring it to be too narrow.

Slowly things got sorted out and Ransome had some good times on *Peter Duck* in 1947. No sailing was shown in the log for 1948 and 1949, during which year all the lead ballast was stolen whilst the *Duck* was laid up in West Mersea! The Ransomes moved back to the Lake District in 1948 and stayed there until the autumn of 1950, by which time Ransome was sixty-seven. They moved to London and bought a flat in Hurlingham Court overlooking the Thames at Putney, by which time *Peter Duck* had been sold.

Throughout 1951 the Ransomes were stuck in a noisy London flat with no boat. In July of that year Ransome, having decided that despite his failing health he would still be able to handle a boat and desperate to get sailing again, visited David Hillyard in Littlehampton and his diary records: 'Saw and liked his 6-tonner. Sloop, central cockpit, wheel steering, 27-ft x 7-ft 5-ins x 4-ft 3-ins. Evgenia decided the Hillyard would do, though she would have preferred a 10-tonner. I (coward) think that a 10-tonner would be too much for me'. Evgenia had already chosen the name for her—*Lottie Blossom*. This name came from one of the Ransomes' favourite books, P. G. Wodehouse's *The Luck of the Bodkins*, in which there is an American film star with this name who kept an alligator in a wicker basket with which to deter customs men from uncovering her smuggling activities.

Whilst they were pondering whether to go ahead and order a similar boat, some well-meaning friends warned them off Hillyards because they said the yard had taken to building their boats without a beam shelf running around the inside of the hull just below the deck and fastened to the frames. Ransome tackled Hillyard and his foreman, Tom Jeffers, about this. They told him that they used a thicker top strake, being the topmost plank, and this was done for additional strength and not to save money.

Meanwhile, deciding what to do, the Ransomes chartered from George Jones (later to become a long-term owner of *Peter Duck*) his pre-war 5-ton Hillyard sloop called *Barnacle Goose*, in which they spent a happy few weeks in September ditch-crawling around the east coast rivers meeting old friends. On one occasion they got caught in thick fog off Harwich, sailing close to the Cork light-ship, just like the similar incident in *We Didn't Mean to Go to Sea*.

Ransome spoke to Hillyard at that winter's boat/motor show in Earl's Court, who said Ransome didn't have to decide for a month or two in case his rheumatism and other problems prevented him from sailing. 'Jolly decent of him', Ransome wrote. After a week, Ransome ordered the new boat and Evgenia was left in charge of the internal arrangements. The boat was to be ready by 1 April 1951. Ransome wrote in a letter, 'with incredible idiocy we have bought a new 6-tonner which is to be launched on 1st April…making bankruptcy loom before us.'

The boat was indeed ready by that date, causing Ransome to write, 'this is the first time I have ever known a boat-builder keeping, so to speak, an appointment.' After some bitterly cold weather, the Ransomes set off on 19 April for Chichester Harbour where they were to keep *Lottie Blossom*. The next day they took her upstream to Birdham Pool. Ransome wrote: 'Quite good. Sailed herself but, of course, does not point high. Comes about admirably. Heaves-to quite well'. Then Ransome's health problems erupted and he had to be rushed back to London where he had an operation on his prostate.

Recovering from this, the Ransomes spent the rest of the year exploring the waters of Chichester Harbour and the Solent but still he was not satisfied with his new boat. They found the centre cockpit too small for two large people. They could not get used to the wheel steering and Ransome believed she could never, with her centre cockpit, be a true single hander. So once again, after having sailed *Lottie* only elev-

en times and covered less than two-hundred miles, they were resolved
to find something better. Ransome wrote in his log on 8 September
1952, 'talking of *Lottie Minor* with identical hull but tiller steering and
a real single-hander which *Lottie* can never be.'

Back at the yard, Hillyard proposed a 6-ton aft cockpit sloop like
one he was building for a General Gale and anticipated no difficulty
in selling *Lottie*. Evgenia wanted the new boat ready by April and this
was agreed. She was given a free hand to get the accommodation she
wanted. Ransome wrote that the new boat would be something like
Goblin, probably meaning her real-life model, *Nancy Blackett*, a boat
Evgenia disdained to go on board. Hillyard's soon found a buyer for
Lottie Blossom. She was sold to Sir George Mallinson for £1,425* on
condition that he changed her name. She became *Ragged Robin III*, of
whom we shall hear a lot more later.

During the building of '*Lottie Minor*', the Ransomes spent much
time in the yard on board her near sister ship, *Bimbi*, being built
for General Gale, the construction of which was further advanced.
The main cabin of the new *Lottie* was to be ten feet long and as
luxurious as possible, with settee bunks each side and a further
bunk in the fo'c'sle, as well as a W.C. and a sail bin. There were
the inevitable arguments with Evgenia, with David Hillyard always
taking Tom Jeffers with him when facing up to her, being too scared
to do this alone!

The new boat was now duly registered with the same name as the
old one and she was ready for Evgenia's birthday on 11 April 1953.
There was no launching ceremony and there were problems with the
engine on a trial sail. After one false start, they left the yard for Chichester on 25 April. The new aft cockpit *Lottie*, although not a pretty
ship with a pronounced high coachroof, suited the Ransomes splen-
didly and they spent the summer wandering around the Solent, at last
in a vessel with which they were satisfied.

In June they took *Lottie* to Spithead to see the huge armada of
naval ships assembled for the Queen's Coronation Review. By the end
of June they felt happy enough with their boat to sail to Cherbourg.
On arrival they anchored in the Avant Port amongst a contingent of

---

*   She had cost Ransome £1,589.

British boats and next to *Destina*, a Harrison Butler-designed cutter, owned by fellow Royal Cruising Club member, Lord Stanley of Alderley, who had the previous year sold his boat *Solace*, another Hillyard, to Victor Clark in which he circumnavigated the globe as described earlier. The Ransomes had a pasting on their return about which Ransome wrote: 'Lottie proved herself a good little boat, though groaning and squeaking horribly during the worst of the battering. It sounded like wood working on wood and we think must have been mast strains transmitted through tabernacle and cabin trunk.'

They wintered the boat in Littlehampton and left for the 1954 season at the start of May. It was all to turn out most unsatisfactorily. *Lottie* was damaged when a larger yacht dragged into her in the Beaulieu River, they had a difficult passage both to and from Cherbourg, had continuing engine problems, and they both injured themselves when picking up a mooring after the engine had let them down once again. They then took *Lottie* to Littlehampton where they told Hillyard they were winding up. Ransome wrote: 'G (Evgenia) has been long decided that we to stop and I suppose we are a bit old... for *Lottie* easily the best sail of the year. So now I swallow the anchor with one gulp and henceforth think exclusively in terms of fishing.'

Little is known of the second *Lottie* after this, save that in 1990 Roger Wardale[*], who wrote a book about Ransome's yachts[†], found her in a Surrey garden where her then owner, Chris Barlow, was attempting to restore her. After that she disappeared without trace and was believed to have been destroyed. This was confirmed when my wife, Josephine, who many years ago used to work alongside Chris Barlow in a large pharmaceutical company in Guildford, managed to track him down. He confirmed to her that *Lottie* was indeed broken up at some time in the middle of the 1990s. What a sad end for the boat which Ransome and Evgenia considered to be their favourite boat.

What about Ransome's other boats? The first *Lottie* is still going strong as *Ragged Robin III* (see below). *Racundra* remained in

[*]   One of the founders of the Arthur Ransome Society.

[†]   Wardale, Roger. *Arhur Ransome under Sail*, Sigma Leisure 2010.

Britain for many years, part of the time in the hands of a member of parliament. She then passed into the hands of Rod Pickering who found her in a very poorly state in Tangiers. He restored her and planned to sail her home to Britain. In 1978 he set out calling at Madeira, the Canaries and the Cape Verde islands, thence to the Caribbean where he foundered on a reef near Caracas in Venezuela and the boat is no more.

Selina King survived the war and has had an adventurous life since Ransome sold her; one which would make the perfect subject for a book! Sold, re-sold, bought back by a previous owner and sold again all on the eastern coast of North America, used for charter combined with drug smuggling in the Caribbean, she was last heard of in Canada in the welcoming hands of a shipwright with great plans for her restoration.

Nancy Blackett is of course extremely safe and well looked after in the capable hands of the Nancy Blackett Trust* where her future seems assured.

Peter Duck, despite Ransome's criticisms and dislike, went on to inaugurate a class of boats sold under the same name. They were highly popular, although my experience of them mirrors Ransome's views. My father, then a retired Admiral, bought one in a fit of 'downsizing'. He could never get on with her and hated her. Despite Laurent Giles describing the class as a 50/50, my father called her a 0/0. One time when I was sailing in the Solent with my father on his Duck (which he re-named *Scaup Duck* , not being able to bear her original name of *Salutation*), with steep short standing seas running against a strong ebb tide, we seemed to sit in the same hole, under both sail and power, making no progress whatsoever. However, generations of the Jones family, who have owned *Peter Duck* since 1957, love and cherish their 'dear old Duck', which is a fitting postscript to what was a difficult period in Ransome's life.

The lively subsequent life of the first *Lottie*, now *Ragged Robin III*, is described below.

After the Ransomes swallowed the anchor in 1954, they rented a cottage in the Lake district every summer for several years, until they

---

*   See https://nancyblackett.org/

settled into their last home between Windermere and Coniston over-looking the secluded Rusland valley. Ransome was as much at home with simple farmers and country folk as he was with his fellow writers and smart cronies in the Garrick Club or the Royal Cruising Club in London. He died in 1967. Evgenia died in 1975.

Anthony Rushworth-Lund and *Ragged Robin III*

When Anthony Rushworth-Lund began to look for a seaworthy boat which would take him and his family through the French canals to the Mediterranean and back, he was told very dismissively by one 'large, breezy Solent agent', 'Well, I suppose you can always get a Hillyard. You know the boat I mean—five tons Thames. You see them all over the place.' But that, in fact, is just what he did. In his various writings Rushworth-Lund betrays no awareness of the earlier history of the boat he had bought. She was *Ragged Robin III* (ex-*Lottie Blossom*) and he was to detail her subsequent voyages in a book. She was, he admits, all that her agent told him, slow to windward but with won-derful accommodation for her size, soundly constructed and safe in really bad weather.

With typical British reserve, Rushworth-Lund neglects to men-tion in his writings his past life, which included a very distinguished career in the Fleet Air Arm. All we learn is that he was married to Ve-ronica and had two children, a son Crispin and a daughter Hermione. And having bought *Ragged Robin III* he overlooks her illustrious past owner and her previous name.

Rushworth-Lund took his new acquisition to 'David Hillyard's ex-cellent yard at Littlehampton' for a few modifications, including the provision of steel sheerlegs by which the mast could be lowered or raised for passage through the French canals (although he used pro-fessional yard help for the latter manouvre, on occasion he found it possible with just the help of one friend). Towing an 8ft sailing din-ghy, the family set off for France, the canals and five years cruising around the Mediterranean before returning by way of the Canal du Midi and the Bay of Biscay.

They joined the French inland waterways at Rouen, where with the help of some barge hands they used the sheerlegs to lower the boat's mast. Thereafter, until the Mediterranean, *Ragged Robin III* became 'a peculiar type of motor boat, with a keel that was far too deep and a large lump of timber lying along her deck from stem to stern'. They enjoyed Paris, the tranquility of the northern French canals and the quiet unfrequented River Saône. At Lyons it was all different. The Rhône was then completely untamed and a pilot was a necessity. It was in those days a vicious river, angry and turbulent, full of reefs and rapids and rocky islands. Rushworth-Lund describes this well and how, on stopping for the first night, whilst anchoring his vessel was carried backwards down the river at some three knots whilst steaming upstream at full throttle. Nowadays it is all different, the river has been canalized and one passes gently through some enormous locks, one over twenty-metres deep.

They had an ideal time in the Mediterranean, despite the odd *mistral* in the Golfe de Lyons and a storm on their way back from Corsica to Monte Carlo. From there they made their way home via Marseille, the Camargue, the Canal du Midi, the Bay of Biscay and then the Brittany canals to St Malo and home. The whole trip, undertaken by Rushworth-Lund, his wife Veronica and their two young children, Crispin and Hermione, is described delightfully in his book, *By Way of the Golden Isles*[*].

The vessel proved to be excellent for his purpose and he testified to her essential strength and sea-worthiness, particularly in coping with the savage power of the storm they encountered between Corsica and the French mainland.

Rushworth-Lund ends his book with the following words: 'I looked back at the brave little yacht lying snugly to her cable, not very clean, a little weather beaten. She had not been round the world, nor had she drifted with the trades over the South Seas. She had done nothing very spectacular but she was unique...'

Shortly after publication of his book in 1963, Rushworth-Lund sold *Ragged Robin III* and bought a 40ft Gauntlet, *Gay Gauntlet*, in which he undertook some long cruises, one to the Mediterranean and another to the Caribbean. Interestingly, the Gauntlets, a series of yachts built by the prestigious Berthon Boat Company in Lymington,

---

[*]   Rushworth-Lund, Anthony. *By Way of the Golden Isles*, Chapman & Hall 1963.

were all double-ended and their hulls bore a distinct likeness to much of Hillyard's work.

After this, Ransome's old boat went through a series of owners, some of whom were Ransome enthusiasts. Between September 1991 and July 1992, Peter St John Howe, whose love of sailing was inspired by Ransome, thoroughly destroyed Ransome's conclusion that the original *Lottie/Ragged Robin III* was not suitable for single handed sailing, by sailing over 1,000 miles in her on his own. In 2000 *Ragged Robin III* came into the distinguished hands of Hillyard (and Ransome) devotees Professor Ted Evans and his wife, Dr Diana, whose story follows.

Chapter 16

OWNERS AND ORGANISERS

The Hillyard fleet, originally some eight hundred strong and now amounting to some three hundred assorted vessels, would never have been maintained, renewed, re-built, improved, sailed, loved and cared for as well as it has been had it not been for a devoted band of owners and guardians, past and present, enthusiasts to whom we all owe a huge debt of gratitude. In this chapter we examine many of these people who, whilst they may not have crossed oceans or undertaken derring-do voyages, have year after year quietly maintained and sailed their boats and in many cases been responsible for getting owners together, assembling and recording the boats and their voyages, and establishing and running the Hillyard Owners Association. Here are some of them.

Ted and Diana Evans

Ted Evans is a most unusual and accomplished man and was a university professor (in Auditory Physiology), a member of many professional societies, international committees and editorial boards, recipient of many honours and awards, a specialist in communication and neuroscience, author of numerous publications on hearing, tinnitus and hearing loss from the points of view of physiology, psychophysics, cochlear implants and computational modelling. Oh, and as if that were not enough, he is an Arthur Ransome enthusiast and a well-known yachtsman to boot. To say he has had a full life is an understatement. His wife, Diana, is a General Practitioner, as is his daughter.

All went well with their annual sailing cruises until 1995 when Ted suffered a near-fatal heart attack whilst lifting an anchor off the island of Iona in the Western Isles of Scotland. Ted says he was only saved by the then novel treatment of the insertion of a couple of stents in his coronary arteries. Ted and Diana bought their first Hillyard in the same year. She was *Twinkler*, built to Hillyard's own design in 1922. She is

the oldest Hillyard remaining afloat today, still in commission, referred
to in Chapter 4. She was exhibited by Hillyard at the first Boat Show
he attended in 1922. Then she was offered for sale at a price of £150,
or £190 with a 3hp Stuart Turner engine fitted (£5 extra for a reverse
gear). She was a sweet looking boat and was shallow draught (3ft 6in)
with a centreboard—ideal for the east coast where Ted and Diana kept
her. They sailed *Twinkler* each summer roaming between Lowestoft in
the north and the Thames Estuary in the south in what was considered,
when she was built, to be a boat 'most suitable for Christchurch or Poole
Harbours or similar waters'*. Ted undertook a rolling programme of
modifications and repairs to the boat, including a replacement of the
engine and converting her to a cutter rig with a new bowsprit. She was
in excellent repair when she was sold in 2011.

However, whilst retaining *Twinkler*, Ted and Diana in 2001 bought
another larger Hillyard, also discussed earlier, namely the 9-tonner
Ragged Robin III, previously owned by Antony Rushworth-Lund,
and before him, as *Lottie Blossom*, Arthur Ransome. Ted also retired
in 2001 and he and Diana moved into a flat in Woodbridge in Suffolk,
overlooking the river Deben and the Tidemill marina.

From then until 2016 they undertook a relentless series of summer voyages in *Ragged Robin III*, visiting France and the South Coast
of England in 2003, the Netherlands in 2004 and Germany, Denmark and Sweden in 2005. The next year saw them back in the same
waters. In 2008 they were in France and Brittany. 2009 and 2013 saw
them re-visiting Holland and, finally, in 2016, this time without a
mast, they investigated the otherwise inaccessible inland waters of the
Netherlands.

These voyages are meticulously described on Ted's web site†, along
with lots of other fascinating information, deliberations and information about *Ragged Robin III*'s first owner, Arthur Ransome, and Ted's
personal philosophy, his life and his yachting experiences generally.

For their 2008 cruise, Ted called his log 'By Way of the Golden
Isles', a reference to Rushworth-Lund's Mediterranean trip in the
1950s in *Ragged Robin III*, described in Lund's book with the same

---

*   *Yachting Monthly*, Dec. 1922

†   tedevans.net

title. That year Ted and Diana and their crew sailed over 1,500 miles from the east coast to the Southern Brittany and Normandy coasts. One motivation for their cruise was to attend an international meeting of the Arthur Ransome Society in Falmouth that May. The whole cruise was carried out in text-book fashion and they met many other Hillyards on their way. On their return via Normandy they called in to the ancient harbour of Honfleur. Whilst waiting to go into the old harbour, entered by a lock, they were accosted by an impressive looking individual with: 'You, very pretty boat. We give you free mooring in the *Vieux Bassin* for as long as you like.' They were shown to a perfect berth, for them and for the profusion of artists who line the quayside, outside the medieval 'Lieutenance' building, a much-reproduced monument. Ted remarked in his account: 'there are some advantages in having a funny-looking old boat!'

For 2009 they visited Holland again about which Ted said, '*Ragged Robin's* cruise of July 2009 mainly consisted of fleeing from bad weather'. He titled his account 'Sailing with a Rear-View Mirror' on account of the fact that much time was spent, whilst avoiding bad weather at sea, traversing canals where a good look out is required behind one to spy barges and large cargo ships coming up fast. When they returned across the North Sea and brought up in the Walton Backwaters after a six-hundred and sixty-mile cruise, anchored surrounded by beauty and calling curlews they asked themselves: 'why do we ever go away?'

2010 found them in Belgium 'in search of Flemish Art and Architecture'. Bad weather delayed their departure but eventually they had an ideal crossing of the North Sea to Zeebrugge from where it is possible to travel 'mast up' along a short canal to Bruges. After visiting the historic centre and enduring a huge pop concert that night, they headed up another canal to Ghent, where they were faced with Ghent's annual pop festival! They moved on to Antwerp, again via a 'mast up' canal. Arriving back in England via the inshore channels along the Kent coast, finally ghosting into Harty Ferry and the East Swale for a magical evening as night fell, they again said: 'why do we go away?'

Their final cruise in *Ragged Robin* was a 'mast out' cruise through the inland canals, rivers and seas of the Netherlands in 2016. As always, the cruise was carried out with precision and care and they visited those places Hillyards normally cannot reach. By now the Evans's were in their eighties and this cruise was their swansong in *Ragged Robin*, after which they decided it was time to make a change of direction. They put their much-loved vessel, which they had continually improved and kept in immaculate condition, on the market and finally parted with her in 2018. They found someone who loved the boat as much as they did and the buyer, Mark Dyson, now looks after Arthur Ransome's old boat as well as the Evans ever had.

Not wanting to give up the sea completely, Ted and Diana bought a 25ft Broads motor cruiser called *Unicorn*. In her they have continued to cruise, first throughout the Norfolk Broads then, based at Ely in the shadow of the cathedral, exploring the Great and Little Ouse, the rivers Nene and the Cam and sections of the Grand Union Canal. Long may they be able to continue to do so.

Whilst Ted and Diana sailed no oceans, nor battled hurricanes in the Atlantic nor experienced the joys of sailing into palm fringed Pacific atolls, they demonstrated what could be achieved whilst pursuing extremely successful professional careers, with cruising limited to a few weeks' holiday each year. They also found in retirement the time and money to undertake the endless maintenance, improvement and repair work involved in keeping an old wooden boat together over seventeen years. They are an exemplar to all of us of what we owners (or guardians) of our old boats should aim for.

We also owe them a great deal, for without their perseverance Ransome's boat might no longer be with us and the original *Lottie Blossom* might have suffered the same fate as her younger sister, the second *Lottie*, which as we have seen was sadly allowed to become a wreck and then destroyed in a suburban garden in the middle of England some fifteen years ago.

In addition to everything else, Ted Evans has been heavily involved in the Arthur Ransome Trust for many years, first as its Treasurer and now as Vice President.

Ray Whitaker

In the late 1950s Ray Whitaker, like most people at that time, had virtually no money but, along with his wife Sue, had a burning desire to buy a boat. After an unstructured search amongst the myriad of small boatyards which litter the harbours, creeks and backwaters of the east coast rivers, they eventually found a yard in Maldon on the River Blackwater, where the proprietor deigned to speak to them, even when they told him they only had two hundred pounds to spend. After hankering for a Blackwater sloop (three hundred and twenty five pounds), a Dauntless (four hundred and fifty pounds) and a West Country-built cutter without an engine (three fifty) the couple were pointed in the direction of 'a little Hillyard'. She was propped up ashore in the yard under a green cover.

'*Puffin*, she's called', they were told, 'she's oldish—built in 1936— but she's in good condition… You can't get that sort of work nowadays, except for fancy prices.' 'How much?' Ray asked. 'Three fifty—like the other one but you get a few extras thrown in. There's a new dinghy and this cover that's on her now. You can say the boat herself is well under three hundred and she's a bargain.' 'I'll send you a cheque' Ray said.

That is how they came to own *Puffin* and that and the subsequent exploits of these two innocents afloat are all cleverly described in Ray's book *Two and a Half Ton Dream** in which he wrote humorously of their first season afloat in their dream-ship. They went no further than Pin Mill on the River Deben but Ray Whitaker invokes evocatively the pleasures of east coast pottering in a boat perfectly suited for the job and which they came to love. This is what he wrote of their first week-end trips from Maldon:

> We pottered. There is no other word for it. We did nothing remotely ambitious. We never went further than West Mersea. We investigated every creek that branched off the main river— Maylandsea, Goldhanger, Tollesbury. We would row ashore in the dinghy and find a patch of fleshy, cushiony vegetation on the lonely creek bank and lie there in the sun, with bees buzzing over the fragrant, salt-washed grasses around us. Occasionally a sail passed us, or a boat's engine throbbed for a while, but most of the time we were lapped in absolute peace, absolutely alone. We might have been a thousand miles from the everyday

---

*   *Two and a Half Ton Dream*, Ray Whitaker. Herbert Jenkins 1959.

haunts of men. Over the weeks we got to love our small boat more than ever, and to know and love too our lonely, beautiful Essex river in all its moods, from glassy calm to semi-gale—or our version of a semi-gale.

Puffin must have been one of the very early 2½-tonners, a gaff rigged sloop with a single-cylinder 4hp Stuart Turner engine, and the Whitakers' exploits demonstrated just what perfect little boats they were, which introduced so many people to the joys of simply messing about in boats.

Ray's book is out of print but second-hand copies are available and I would highly recommend it. If any book recreates what it was like to cruise small boats in the late 1950s it is this one.

Robert Keen

It was Robert Keen along with his wife Pamela who first had the idea of forming an Association for owners of Hillyards and others interested in the breed.

He was born in 1934 in Gravesend in Kent and spent his childhood there and in Swansea. He started life studying to be a Franciscan priest but after two years decided the monastic life was not for him. In 1964 he entered the business world and by 1968 had become managing director of a European public relations network. In 1975 he joined the Xerox corporation as Director of international external affairs. During this time, he and his family moved to his wife's hometown of Lymington, with Robert commuting to London. Getting tired of this, he decided to work and live in the New Forest. He bought some land in Lymington and started a soft fruit farm, where he successfully put his business talents to full use.

Throughout his life, Robert was a deeply spiritual man and developed an interest in the ethics and morality of big business. He began to teach corporate governance and business ethics at Bournemouth University and in 1998 achieved an M.A. in theology from Southampton University. Later he became a senior research associate at St Edmund's College, Cambridge.

He and his family had been sailing for many years when in 1973 he bought a Hillyard, the 9-tonner *Toccatina*. She had been built in

1962 named *Pacanda*, later changed to *Alcestis* and then to *Toccatina*. We shall hear more about her later. In 1977, with a growing family leading to them needing more space, they sold *Toccatina*. They bought a larger 12-tonner, *Kalena Kay*, built in 1964.

It was during their ownership of *Kalena Kay* that the Keens founded the Hillyard Owners Association. A meet of Hillyard boats was held in Lymington in September 1977. Some eighty owners and guests attended a meal held at the Lymington Yacht Club. The Association became popular amongst the boats' owners, the number of boat meets and get-togethers increased, the Association introduced a newsletter, and this became a great medium for members to exchange ideas and report on voyages.

But the fruit farm was too time consuming for the Keens to properly look after the Association and at the 1977 meet they handed it over to Michael Joyce who formalised the Association with a committee and it went from strength to strength.

In 1985 *Kalena Kay* had to be sold for a tractor*. Her place in the family was taken by a Hillyard 4-tonner called *Zeegul*. They changed her name to *Buff* (Robert Keen had served in the Buffs during his National Service) and Pamela Keen admitted that she thought the 4-tonner sailed better than ether of her larger sisters and more like a big dinghy. They kept her, pottering around in the Solent, until 1993. Robert Keen died in 2011.

Robert Keen's hero was St Thomas More and he often used to quote these words of St Thomas: 'You must not abandon the ship in a storm just because you cannot control the winds.'

Michael Joyce

Michael and Nicky Joyce were both born in 1922. Michael started life as an engineer and served with distinction with the Royal Engineers during World War II. He spent time in India and Burma, ending the war as a Major. He married Nicky in 1944 and they lived and worked

---

*   Not the first yachtsman who had to do this. The famous Argentinian yachtsman Vito Dumas had to sell his beloved *Lehg II* to buy a tractor for his ranch. Later he bought her back and sailed her around the world alone through the roaring forties in the middle of World War II (see Dumas, Vito. *Alone Through the Roaring Forties*. 1960 Adlard Coles Ltd.)

together for the next sixty-seven years. After the war, and a period as a singing duo, calling themselves 'Their Masters Voice' miming to gramophone records, Michael became one of the pioneers of the then emerging public relations industry and Nicky set up a translation business. They were both very successful. They lived in Chislehurst in Kent and then moved to a house on the bank of the Thames at Gravesend. Michael took up sailing in the early 1970s by buying a GRP Hurley 30, on which I crewed frequently. He was also a qualified pilot, often flying his own aeroplane to his holiday home in France.

In 1977 Michael and Nicky bought their first Hillyard from Robert and Pamela Keen. She was the 1962-built 9-tonner *Toccatina*. In early August of that year Michael planned to take *Toccatina* to the West Country. He told me he that he did not have a log to measure distance. I had recently acquired a boat which came with a beautiful unused original all-bronze Walker trailing log and I offered to lend this to him for his trip. I was much alarmed when Michael telephoned me a few days later, on 12 August, to tell me that *Toccatina* had caught fire and sunk in the Solent the day before. The first thing I said, before even asking whether he and Nicky were alright, was 'where's my log?' To this day I feel ashamed of myself.

This is what happened that day. Having left Lymington with a friend, Brian Hart, they had caught the tide and were heading out past Keyhaven on their way to Poole. 'Strong smell of petrol down here', called Nicky from below and when Brian lifted the engine hatch to turn off the supply, there was a blinding explosion and the bilges were in flames from stem to stern. The fire extinguisher made no impression and smoke thwarted their attempts to get at the radio. Michael and Brian leapt for the foredeck, Nicky exiting through the forehatch. After what seemed to be an age, they got the liferaft over the side, 'fearing' in Michael's words 'that any moment the flames would ignite the petrol tank, filled to the brim at Lymington, scattering boat and passengers across the Solent.'

Brian was now in some pain having, it was later discovered, dislocated his shoulder in the explosion but as befitted an ex-Para, remained calm and in control. With some difficulty they all took to the liferaft and cut free, watching *Toccatina*, her sails now well alight, making her way towards Keyhaven. Eventually they were picked up by a passing fishing boat. No sooner had they made themselves comfortable when a Coastguard helicopter appeared and plucked Brian away to the Royal Navy Hospital at Haslar in Gosport. The Joyces were landed at Lymington with only a deflated liferaft to their name. 'It was a very odd feeling,' said Michael, 'to step ashore in one's own country without being able to establish one's identity; no passport, cheque book, credit cards, car or house keys—nothing but your word! And as for *Toccatina* she was picked up by a fisherman in his role as an Auxiliary Coastguard, and what was left of the hull, burnt to the waterline, was towed into the Keyhaven shallows, where her charred remains rest to this day.

Not put off at all by this, the following month Michael and Nicky attended the meeting of the Hillyard Owners Association arranged by Robert Keen at the Royal Lymington Yacht Club. Here Michael was appointed Commodore. For the next twenty-one years Michael served in this role, producing newsletters, enrolling Hillyarders and charming everyone with his humour and infectious enthusiasm. During these twenty-one years, he published an annual Members' Handbook, kept the Association's accounts, and organized dinners and rallies in London, Cowes and elsewhere. The dinners were memorable affairs in somewhat grand venues, all polished brass and silver Race Trophies, including the Royal London Yacht Club on the Esplanade in Cowes and the Naval Club in Mayfair during Boat Show time in January; dress being blazers and club ties for the men and 'as fashion and good taste dictate' for the ladies. Michael assembled for the Association a mass of information, photos and books regarding the boats, their owners and voyages, and the history of the yard.

After the demise of *Toccatina*, the Joyces bought what was probably their favourite and certainly most successful Hillyard, the 12-tonner *Millstream* built in 1962. They sailed her every year around the south coast on both sides of the Channel, attending various rallies of Hillyards and Hillyarders. By 1988, Michael, who was then sixty-six, was finding *Millstream* too big and they decided to 'down-size'. They sold her and in June of that year bought *Lina Arni* , one of the Cullingfords' 'new' 11-tonners, which had been built in 1972 with the name 'Chicago'. These were comfortable motor-sailers, hard chine hulls and with a transom stern, rigged as ketches.

In 1992 they attended the first Brest Classic Ship Festival, a huge very French affair attended by thousands of ships, yachts, boats and dinghies and what seemed like millions of people. Also a good contingent of Hillyards. The author also attended and met Michael and Nicky there. Frank Mulville attended with *Iskra*. Michael had difficulties in the trip out to Brest, experiencing problems with *Lena Arni*'s Mercedes engine and he had a hard and difficult return passage, meeting much heavy weather. Michael, who was beginning to show the first symptoms of Parkinson's disease, which was to plague him in later years, decided it was time to quit cruising. He sold *Lena Arni* the next year. It was 1993 and he and Nicky were both sixty-nine years old.

However, nothing was going to stop Michael and it was really all my fault that he bought his next Hillyard. At that time I had a boatyard on the Milford Haven waterway in West Wales, which specialised in the restoration of classic wooden boats, and we had in the yard a small 2½-tonner called *Koala* which had been built in 1936. Michael and Nicky were staying with us in our house nearby and Michael saw the little boat and thought she would be ideal for him to keep on the River Medway for a bit of gentle pottering to keep his hand in. I am not sure if Nicky approved. We did some work on the boat, not a lot was required—a testament to Hillyard's construction, the boat being over fifty years old—and a friend of Michael's who had a large 4 x 4 vehicle towed *Koala* back to Kent and the Medway.

At that time Michael and I actually bought another Hillyard together! She was very much a long-term project. *Mignonne* was stored in the middle of a very muddy and isolated Welsh farmyard half-way up a barren, windswept hillside in the Presseli Mountains. I had been told some time before of the existence of a decaying Hillyard up in the hills and that the farmer was about to cut her up for firewood. I had no idea how she got there. She had nothing with her but a mast and boom and some rusty pigs of iron ballast lying alongside in a thicket of weeds. You could see daylight through her planking and her deck was shot. No rigging, engine or any gear. She was a standard looking 5-tonner and had been built I think in 1950. Anyway, we offered a minimal price and moving her to Pembroke Dock cost more than that! I then got cold feet about the whole project, paid Michael back his half share, and passed her on at cost. She ended up with a young man with a dream. I learnt recently that *Mignonne* is alive and well kept on the Milford Haven waterway and now fitted with an un-stayed mast and a junk sail. I am pleased that Michael and I managed to save her from the Welsh farmer's chainsaw.

Michael continued to look after the Owners Association until 1998 when he handed over to Michael Walden (see below). Nicky died on 14 June 2011 and Michael died seventeen days later on 2 July. They were both eighty-eight and had been together for sixty-seven years.

Michael Joyce did almost more than anyone to get and keep to-gether the community of Hillyard owners and to promote public rec-ognition of this fleet of classic boats. Until Parkinson's disease got the better of him he was always brimming with ideas as to how to assist others and keep the fleet together.

One plan he had, which he discussed with me at length, was to try to gain communal ownership of the Hillyard shipyard in Little-hampton and the surrounding area to preserve it for the future and for it to become a centre for wooden boats, boatbuilding and repair. Not only for Hillyards but for all wooden boats generally, making the Ropewalk area of the town into a sort of mini 'Mystic Seaport', the large wooden boat centre in Connecticut in the USA, where a maritime museum is the centre of a large harbour where classic and heritage vessels moor, where there are facilities for their repair and upkeep along with training facilities for wooden shipwrights. Michael discussed this proposal with the local council and with the National Maritime Museum at Greenwich, where he was a volunteer helper and guide, and had much support from both organisations. Unfortu-nately, mainly due to Michael's worsening heath, this came to nothing but would it not have been wonderful?

Michael Walden

Michael Walden was born in February 1933 in Trowbridge, Wilt-shire. He joined the Merchant Navy at sixteen and then joined the family bakery, chicken processing and egg packing business. Michael was a keen sportsman and took up competitive canoeing. Later he be-came involved with the campaign to restore the Kennet & Avon canal.

At the age of thirty-five, when back problems led to his having to give up competitive canoeing, Michael took to sailing. His first yacht, in 1968, was a small Caprice called *Aquarelle*. He then had a Lysander, *Caerulea*, followed by an Invicta, *Mary Blake*. In 1983 he bought a Hillyard, the 9-tonner *Trimley Maid* built in 1971. Michael described her as his magic carpet on which he could fulfill his dreams. Based at first in Milford Haven, later moving to Poole, Michael cruised in *Trimley Maid* to South West Ireland, La Rochelle, and the North Brittany coast. In 1985 he sailed to Barra in the Hebrides to celebrate the seventy-fifth anniversary of the Clyde Cruising Club.

During 1988 and 1989 he undertook an Atlantic circle sailing *Trimley Maid* to the Caribbean and back to England, sailing over 10,000 miles in ten months. Michael wrote: 'it will come as no surprise to [Hillyard] owners that she proved near ideal for a blue water cruise; handling 50 knot winds and 40 foot seas like the true thoroughbred she undoubtedly is.'

Ports of call on the way out were La Corrunna, Oporto, Cascais and the islands Porto Santo, Madeira, Salvagem, Gran Canaria, Tenerife and Grenada. The last 3,000 mile leg took thirty-four days. In the West Indies they visited The Grenadines, St. Vincent, St Lucia, Martinique, Dominica, Guadeloupe, Antigua, Nevis, St Kitts, Saba, St Maarten and Anguilla. From there they headed for Bermuda thence to Faial in the Azores and home to Poole. They had difficulties on the way, of course, and Michael said it was a constant major challenge to keep everything repaired and running. They encountered six gales which 'got our adrenalin going' but really were no problem as they reefed down in good time.

In 1993 he sailed to the Azores, the next year taking part in the Bristol Festival and cruising to North Wales. In 1997 he sailed to West Ireland visiting Cork and Kerry. Michael continued making annual cruises until 2014, by which time he was eighty, when he sold *Trimley Maid*. Michael joined the Hillyard Owners Association in 1983, becoming Commodore in 1998, when Michael Joyce retired.

From then on until his own retirement in 2010 Michael was an indefatigable Commodore, ensuring that membership thrived, leaving the Association in robust health. Michael died in 2014, aged 81.

As a postscript to this tale, *Trimley Maid* was sold to Grant Jamie-son-Hesk, who having completed the Atlantic Rally for Cruisers in a friend's yacht, decided to undertake the same transatlantic trip in his new boat in 2017. Thus, in November 2017 *Trimley Maid* set off on her second Atlantic crossing. In the rally, Grant and his crew, Gabriel, were the last to leave Las Palmas on Gran Canaria, after a mishap with the rigging, and were the last to arrive in St. Lucia. However, as a fitting consolation prize, she was voted Most Beautiful Yacht in the ARC. Grant and *Trimley Maid* returned to England in 2019 via the Azores.

Hugh Thomas

Hugh Thomas was typical of many a serial Hillyard owner who, although never undertaking any long or arduous voyages, stayed loyal to the brand and bought larger and larger boats as the years went by and the family grew older, more successful and more prosperous. For this he and his family deserve a mention, quite apart from the fact that he built the 22-tonner *Wendy Woo*, which I owned for several years, and he would have gone on to do great things on a retirement voyage had not illness cut short his life.

Thomas owned and ran a successful building company, living and working in Falmouth, Cornwall. They had two children, Nicholas and Wendy, from whom I obtained much information about their boats. Wendy is now in her early seventies and married to an American. They divide their time between San Diego in California and a cottage on the Helford River, where she sails a Cornish Crabber. Nicholas is in his sixties and is a merchant navy skipper who drives tugs and oil support vessels in the Arabian Gulf.

The Thomas' first Hillyard was, as it was for so many, a 2½-tonner which I am told was built for them in the mid-1950s with the name *Bambino*, but I can find no record of a Hillyard with that name. Then in 1958 came a 9-tonner, perhaps Hillyard's most popular model. She was called *Spinaway*. Nicholas was just three at the time of her launch. Three years later, in 1961, they ordered a 12-tonner which they called *Doojie*, this name being the family's nick-name for Nicholas.

After another three years, Hugh Thomas ordered one of Hillyard's new 22-ton hard chine ketches, wanting a larger ship for longer voyages. She was to be called *Wendy Woo*, which was Wendy's grand-mothers pet name for her granddaughter. *Wendy Woo* was launched in 1965 and was one of only three of these large Hillyard's built. The others were *Tarion*, later lost when she went ashore on rocks off the island of Tristan da Cunha on a world voyage, and *Santa Lucia II* which is still sailing today. *Wendy Woo* was built to a higher than normal specification, with teak upperworks instead of the usual ma-hogany and with taller masts than those originally specified. Inside, she had superior joinery, two toilet compartments, one with a shower, pressurized hot and cold water, a refrigerator and a separate engine compartment and large fuel and water tanks. She was well planned and fitted out for long voyages, which Hugh Thomas planned to un-dertake on his retirement.

From 1965 to 1973 the family cruised extensively in *Wendy Woo*, taking part each year in the Royal Cornwall Yacht Club's annual race to L'Aber Wrac'h in Brittany. *Wendy Woo* invariably came in last but always gave a good party on arrival. They also visited harbours in Normandy and Hugh became a member of the Deauville Yacht Club.

Sadly, Mr Thomas died suddenly of a heart attack whilst fitting out *Wendy Woo* for the 1973 season. He was only fifty-two. *Wendy Woo* was sailed back to Littlehampton to be sold strictly on the basis that the new owner undertook not to take her back to Falmouth.

Sir David Mansell Lewis

Another loyal Hillyard owner was the squire of Stradey Castle on the outskirts of Llanelli in Carmarthenshire, West Wales, Sir David Mansell Lewis. In his time the castle was virtually unchanged since it was built in 1850, a rambling rather grand Victorian pile surrounded by an 1,800 acre estate. Then slightly faded, it has now been resur-rected by his descendants into a smart venue for weddings and other functions. Sir David was, in his time, Lord Lieutenant of Dyfed and his wife must have had the longest maiden name of anyone who had ever part-owned a Hillyard, Lady Rosemary Marie-Gabrielle Mon-tagu-Stuart-Wortley-Mackenzie.

Sir David had been sailing and cruising all his life and first owned a Harrison Butler Z Class four-tonner (not dissimilar from and only slightly larger than the ubiquitous Hillyard 2½-tonners) and then a

29ft Norman Dallimore design. It was in 1971 that Mansell Lewis bought the Hillyard 12-tonner *Nandhi*, which had been built in 1965. He kept her, as he did with all his boats, in Burry Port, a small and somewhat malodorous drying harbour in the Loughor Estuary, access to which was, and is, extremely hazardous over drying and continually shifting sands. The estuary is adjacent to the Gower peninsula, near Stradey Castle and is rarely visited by yachts, although there is today a small marina in which boats are kept afloat behind a tidal barrage. During World War II the estuary was used for testing shells and other munitions and for years afterwards the Navy regularly swept the area for unexploded armaments. There were for many years persistent rumours that anthrax biological warfare shells had been tested against sheep in the estuary during the war.

Sir David was an active, adventurous and fearless sailor taking family and parties of friends every summer to Brittany, Northern France, Ireland, the Isle of Man and Scotland where they became well known to residents and visitors alike. Sir David was extremely hospitable and as his son, Patrick said to me, 'he was one of those people who simply liked the human race and everyone he met'.

In 1991 he deserted *Nandhi* and acquired the 22-tonner *Wendy Woo*, described above. He was now a member of the prestigious Royal Yacht Squadron, which entitles its members to fly the white ensign, otherwise reserved exclusively for fighting ships of the Royal Navy. Proudly flying this, *Wendy Woo* took up residence on a drying mooring in Burry Port, alongside a motley collection of decaying Welsh fishing boats, supported and kept upright at low tide by two massive wooden 'legs' which took at least two people to lift into place. With a long keel and a draught of nearly six feet, she cannot have been an easy boat to handle in the small confines of the harbour or to navigate over the drying and unmarked approaches to it.

Sir David continued with his summer travels and happy partying, equipping *Wendy Woo* with one and a half berths in the forepeak so she could sleep seven and a half people. His son Patrick complained that he always had to sleep in the saloon sharing a double berth which was created by dropping the saloon table. However, the voyaging continued with, it must be said, the boat getting dirtier and dirtier as the years passed and as Sir David's health deteriorated. Steve Tiffin, now

Commodore of the Hillyard Owners Association remembers going on board *Wendy Woo* and being offered a cup of coffee in a disgustingly dirty mug.

In the late 1980s, Sir David became involved with the Sail Training Association and was the principal organizer of the 1991 Tall Ships' Race which that year was to start from Milford Haven. He planned to enter *Wendy Woo* in the race but illness prevented it. When I bought the boat some years later she still sported the sail number 'T S 14'—probably the only Hillyard able to claim to have been a Tall Ship!

Over the following years, Sir David's health declined and from 2006 until his death in 2009 he was hardly able to use *Wendy* Woo, although he continued to visit her at Neyland Marina in Milford Haven where she was berthed. I bought *Wendy Woo* from Sir David's executors in 2011 when she was in a dreadful state.

Dennis and Doug Coulson

The Coulson's are another family where two generations became inextricably linked with a series of Hillyards and who, whilst not necessarily sailing great distances or venturing into unfamiliar waters, yet again demonstrate how Hillyards can come to dominate people's lives. This is what Doug Coulson wrote about the boats he and his father had owned:

> A growing family soon found my Father picking up a copy of Bristows Book Of Yachts, to see what would be suitable as a replacement for Carella, the 25ft strip-planked David Cheverton Caravelle sloop that my parents had owned from new, which had served the family for three seasons.
>
> A visit to the ramshackle Hillyard sheds in Ropewalk, Littlehampton in 1967 was followed by a trial sail in a Hillyard 9-tonner. The perfect type of boat for the young family had been found, and an order for a new one to be built quickly followed. The princely sum of £4,411 10s was paid, and the new Hillyard was ready for launching in the Spring of 1968. The boat needed a name. My father, Dennis, being a retired Royal Marine, thought the name 'Hannah' would be suitable. She was named after the famous Hannah Snell, a young

woman who served many years disguised as a Marine. Being a palindrome, the 'double ended' name further suited the hull shape. *Hannah* was delivered to Portsmouth by Ben, a Hillyard's employee.

And thus the Coulson family adventures with *Hannah* and their many years of Hillyard ownership had begun. The moorings officer at Portchester Sailing Club, knowing the expanding young family would have to transport themselves in relays out to the boat, allocated a handy swinging mooring just adjacent to club's slipway. This was to be her mooring for the ten happy years in my parents' ownership.

Hannah was one of three Hillyards at the club. The 9-tonner *Columbine*, belonging to the Commodore of the Club, lay farther upstream and downstream lay the former Dunkirk Little Ship, the 12-tonner *Windsong*, owned by Peter Whitfield. Just downstream and around the corner in Fareham Creek lay the 22-tonner *Wendy Woo*. Sailing was confined to South Coast waters whilst the family gained confidence. Being Solent based though, there was no shortage of destinations to choose from.

From an early age I became a bit of a Hillyard 'enthusiast'. Yarmouth on the Isle of Wight was a popular destination, and it would never disappoint for some Hillyard spotting. Before even entering the harbour I would be looking for wooden masts visible over the breakwater and picking out the Hillyard ones. Being allocated a berth alongside another Hillyard was especially exciting! Three Hillyards were regular sights there: *Trooper II* (12 tons), *Gander of Headley* (9 tons) and *Maid of Shannon* (11 tons). It was many years later that I got to know and became good friends with *Maid of Shannon*'s owners of long standing, Ken and Margaret Pausey.

The Coulson family became more adventurous and *Hannah* was sailed across the Channel. The drying fishing port of Barfleur in Normandy became a firm favourite for summer holidays. Upon entering Barfleur for the first time, the sight of another 9-tonner greeted us, lying alongside the quay wall. She was *Outcast*, owned by John Junor, then Editor of the *Sunday*

Express. He introduced himself, and he became good friends with my parents. Junor also owned a house there and for many years *Outcast* was a permanent fixture during the Summer months. It was no surprise to see her featured on post cards on sale in the local shops!

As the family grew older, my parents felt that we had outgrown *Hannah*, and maybe a bigger boat should be considered. Two larger Hillyards were viewed in 1977. The first, *Misty Morn*, was a lovely 16-tonner belonging to Major Webb, and berthed on the River Hamble. The second was the distinctive navy blue hulled 14-tonner *Romper*. We had known and admired her for a long time. Both Hillyards were lovely but thoughts turned to maybe having another Hillyard built for us. A trip was made to the yard and Dennis Cullingford's office. As it happened, the keel, stem and sternpost of a cancelled order of a 16- tonner lay in the yard ready for use. A quote to complete the build was prepared and sent to my Father.

Plans changed and the thought of a 'plastic fantastic' and something a little faster eventually saw *Hannah* delivered to Littlehampton in 1978 to be sold. There was not a dry eye amongst us when we parted with our *Hannah*, but there was the excitement at the idea of a brand-new fiberglass yacht, which was being fitted out for us. *Marquesa* was a Laurent Giles Bowman 40 (not to be confused with the later Chuck Paine designed Rival Bowman 40). She was lovely, but it wasn't the same. She wasn't a Hillyard. We had six happy seasons with *Marquesa*, cruising across the Channel and to the West Country but by early 1985 my parents grew restless and she was sold.

Towards the end of that year, during a browse in my local newsagent, I spotted details of a 16-tonner for sale under Hillyard's listings in *Yachting Monthly*. I bought the copy and took it home. Despite a few less than favourable comments about the amount of maintenance another wooden boat would require, we fondly remembered *Misty Morn* and my father conceded there was nothing to lose by taking a trip to Littlehampton. As we walked into the yard unannounced, Dennis Cullingford was just stepping out of his office. 'Ahh Mr *Hannah* isn't it? Can we build you another yacht?'

So we viewed *Moonflower*, built in 1972, *Misty Morn*'s identical sister. It was love at first sight. There was something about the 16-tonners and by early 1986 she was ours. She was very original and 'as built', having had little use in her time; the perfect boat for the family, now bringing along partners and friends. Over the eight years my parents owned her, family cruises were enjoyed in the West Country, the Channel Islands, France and down to Spain.

We attended the festival of Dournanez in 1988, fondly remembered as a great event. We encountered Michael Walden in his 9-tonner *Trimley Maid* for the first time. His infectious enthusiasm for all things Hillyard was evident from the moment his dinghy bumped alongside in the harbour.

Moonflower was usually wintered at Hillyard's. The Winter of 1987/88 was chosen for a refit, which necessitated her being brought into the main shed next to the slipway, indeed she was hauled out the day before the 'Great Storm' of October 1987. The refit saw a new engine fitted, a rewire of the boat, tanks overhauled, plus removal of all old paint and brightwork. During the refit rot was found in her forefoot, which necessitated renewal of that whole section. As luck would have it, the sections of the cancelled order of the 16-tonner a decade earlier were still lying in the yard, and its forefoot section was grafted into Moonflower! We shared the shed that winter not only with an old friend from Portchester, *Columbine*, but also a recent purchase by my brother, a Colin Archer built in Norway in the early 1960s, which had lain in a shed in Devon, unfinished and never launched, which he had transported to Hillyard's for fitting out.

If there could ever be a downside of wintering at Hillyard's, it was occasionally the lack of progress with the jobs list, due to distractions! Admiring someone else's boat would invariably lead to an invite aboard for a quick look, which in turn led to the stove being lit for a cuppa... or the drinks locker being opened!

Amongst some of the friendships established with other owners was Mike Radford on his 20 tonner *Santa Lucia II*[*] and Jan Plomp on his 18-tonner *Leiona*, a much travelled Hillyard[†], which was being lovingly restored by him. Ted Hargreaves on his 13-tonner *Dorenda Ellen* had not long returned from a Transatlantic with his young daughter Niki, and they were a familiar sight around the yard whilst their boat underwent a refit.

1992 saw me becoming employed at Island Harbour Marina on the Isle of Wight. Accommodation was required, and *Moonflower* fulfilled the role perfectly for the first few months, but understandably my parents wanted to be able to go sailing, so the acquisition of a small Hillyard seemed a perfect solution to the problem. Two 6-tonners were viewed, *Bugler* (aft cockpit) and *Eolis* (centre cockpit) but both required a fair amount of work and were discounted. It was a case of third time lucky though, when a scroll through the pages of '*Used Boats and Planes*' revealed a listing for an immaculate 1955 aft cockpit 6-tonner *Mavrodaphne* for sale in Chichester Harbour. Her purchase quickly followed and she was the perfect first boat, being easy to sail singlehanded and easy to maintain. She also fulfilled my desire of having an original and 'un-messed' with Hillyard.

Working in the marina industry was of course advantageous for meeting Hillyards with their owners. The Hargreaves on *Dorenda Ellen* were regular visitors at the marina and later they bought a house there. *Dorenda*'s original name was *Talis* and as chance would have it, *Talis II* a 1939 15-tonner was launched and recommissioned at the marina by owner Peter Cheek, before setting off global cruising.

Occasional local sailing was enjoyed in *Mavrodaphne*, which included attending my first Hillyard rallies. *Hannah*, along with a couple of other 9-tonners, were regular attendees. The thought of owning a 9-tonner one day had always appealed to me and it so happened that *Hannah*'s then owner John Barrett

---

[*]   Sister-ship to *Wendy Woo*, later owned by the author.

[†]   See Chapter 13.

was thinking of downsizing. I was given first refusal to buy her back.

Decision time came towards the end of 1999 and, following a phone call from him, it was with some trepidation that I agreed to buy her. I was acutely aware of the responsibility I was taking on to properly maintain *Hannah*, being not only larger but the very boat our family had grown up on. She fulfilled my requirements perfectly though. She was sound and remained totally original, right down to original bunk mattresses and her lovely two-cylinder Petter diesel engine (the standard fitment in the majority of 9-tonners produced from the late 1950s through to the late 1960s). I now found myself in the unenviable position of having two Hillyards to maintain and pay bills for! *Mavrodaphne* had to go and eventually found a new owner in the form of Mark Taylor, a shipwright at Hillyard's.

2001 saw me starting employment at Hythe Marina near Southampton and *Hannah* was soon moved to her new berth within the marina. I was very pleased to host some Hillyard meets at Hythe, which being a locked marina basin was ideal for manoeuvring without the added complication of the effect of tides. What's more, being only too well aware of the handling characteristics of our boats, the berthing allocation in the marina was left to me! How lucky was I, having Hillyards visiting my place of work!

Work and other commitments never saw *Hannah* venturing far afield, although some local cruising with my family was undertaken during the early years of my ownership. This generally comprised sailing in company with my brothers in their boats, and my parents as my crew on *Hannah*. A bit of a role reversal from the early days!

As time went by I began to have less time with which to enjoy *Hannah* and this led to me reluctantly putting her up for sale. In 2019 a new owner was found and whilst sad to see her go, we now had additional treasured memories from her second spell in our family. Just 9 months into her new ownership, she was severely damaged after breaking adrift from her mooring during Storm Dennis in February 2020. She was eventually re-covered ashore but now unlikely ever to put to sea again.

Although no longer the custodian of a Hillyard, I am thankful to continue with an active role in the Hillyard Owners Association, doing my bit to ensure these wonderful vessels are around for many more years to come.

Ken Pausey

I mention Ken Pausey, not only because I got to know him well, but because he was another man who was a typical Hillyard owner, even though he only owned one during his life. He exemplified almost better that anyone else how it is possible to maintain and keep in absolutely perfect condition, virtually single-handedly, a fifty-year-old wooden vessel, with limited means, whilst working full time running his own business. He was utterly committed to his family, his business colleagues and his boat and showed how this could be done.

He was born in 1926 in Fulham and he spent his early years in London. In his younger days he was a keen cyclist, involved in time trials, racing and longer events such as cycling trips to Paris. He kept this up all his life and he and Margaret, his wife, always carried two fold-up bikes on the boat. Ken and Margaret were married in 1957 and moved to a new house in Slough, from which they never moved. Ken qualified as an accountant and started his own firm, which one of his sons took over when Ken retired at age eighty-two. He always had boats, starting with one called *The Molley* when he met Margaret, then a Wayfarer dinghy and then, for eleven years, a Bermudan sloop called *Maid of Soay*.

Another *Maid* came into his life when in 1972 Ken became the second owner of an 11-ton Hillyard, built in 1968, called *Maid of Shannon*. She was the first of the hard chine bilge keeled transom sterned ketches designed by Dennis Cullingford of which a further ten were built. They were made to a high standard and *Maid of Shannon* was immaculate when Ken bought her and so she remained for the next forty years until Ken's death in 2012, after which she was sold.

Ken and Margaret sailed *Maid of Shannon* with their two boys from an early age, regularly cruising to the Channel Islands, Nor-

mandy and Brittany. They attended the Brest festivals on three occasions, meeting Michael Joyce in his sister ship, *Lina Arni,* at the
first one in 1992 (this prompted Ken to join the Hillyard Owners
Association). Wherever they went they were commended on the immaculate condition of their boat, particularly the always perfectly
varnished brightwork. The *Maid* was always wintered ashore un-
dercover in the shed at Wicormarine*, Chris Waddington's yard in
Portchester. Every Saturday during the winter, without fail, Ken
drove down from Slough for the day to work on her, with her going
back into the water at Easter. During Ken's long period of ownership,
he and the *Maid* attended numerous classic boat rallies both in the
UK and in France where he was habitually awarded prizes for the
best maintained boat.

In 2011 Ken, although still fit and active, was diagnosed with leu-
kamia and he died in November 2012. The *Maid,* now over fifty years
old, was sold on but remains in good hands, being well looked after
and a shining example of how a well-built wooden boat can look as
good as the day she was built provided she is given regular care and
attention.

Raymond Hey and family

Raymond and his family, with three Hillyards under their belts, are
another example of what it means to be a proper Hillyarder and
they demonstrated how the boats which Hillyard produced were
perfectly 'fit for purpose', doing everything that could be asked of
them, providing the means for ordinary people to gain satisfaction
and fulfilment.

This family made no long passages, undertook no ocean bashing,
visited no high or low latitudes, rounded no infamous Capes, but year
after year, quietly and with no fuss and bothering no-one, sailed low-
key voyages around our home waters in a sensible and seamanlike
manner, meeting all challenges and providing family and friends with
a sense of achievement and happiness, often hard to find elsewhere.
There follows a brief description of what this family achieved.

---

*   This is where I met Ken, as I kept a series of boats at Wicormarine during the
       1970s and 1980s.

Raymond Hey was born in 1924 in Halifax, far from the sea. As a child he spent time with relatives in Southampton, came to know the Hamble River, watched yachts and dinghies sailing by as well as seeing ships and even Empire flying boats in Southampton Water.

Later he moved to London and bought a Yachting Monthly 'Senior'* for family sailing on the Thames. He was a practical man; he fitted an inboard engine, acquired a road trailer, and sailed her in and around Poole Harbour. Wanting a vessel with sea-going potential he next bought a wooden clinker built Dauntless 22, which required some work. Soon Ray realised that winter refits would become an annual ritual. Ray attended navigation classes with a close friend who became his long-term sailing partner. In 1968 Ray found a mooring in Gosport in Portsmouth Harbour where he moored his boats for many years.

Ray learnt the ropes with the Dauntless; his first sail being a crossing of the Solent to Wootton Creek, a major adventure. In 1969, his first longer trip, he circumnavigated the Isle of Wight. Next, he headed west and made a slow trip (with little navigation equipment and in poor visibility) reaching Dartmouth. On the way home he anchored in Lulworth Cove next to a Hillyard 6-tonner. Leaving the next day he looked wistfully at the Hillyard thinking that he had found his next boat, not knowing that this would affect the rest of his life and that of his family.

Later that year Hey bought a Hillyard 6-tonner called *Eolis*, which had been built in 1947. She was 26ft long, drew 4ft 6in and had a 2-cylinder Stuart Turner petrol engine. With this proper seagoing vessel Ray could now dream of skippering his own yacht to France, which in those days was regarded as quite an adventure.

In 1970 he set off with two friends as crew. It took them over twenty-four hours to reach Cherbourg, much slowed by fighting the strong tides that run outside that harbour. They had a quicker trip back but were challenged throughout by lack of navigation equipment. It was quite normal in those days to set sail with nothing more than a compass and lead line and, maybe, a few flares—I have done so myself but

---

* The Yachting Monthly 'Senior' was a small 16-foot bilge keel sailing boat originally designed for home construction. She had a small cabin which could sleep two and an outboard motor. They were very popular in the 1950s and 1960s when money was short and boats were small.

we always got there in the end. The next year they set sail for France once more and again found they could make no progress against a foul tide off the Cherbourg entrance. His family then joined him and they sailed to Alderney. There they were faced by an imminent north-east gale and were advised by the harbourmaster to leave. They anchored as far inshore as they could get, found a little shelter and faced a scary night. Several yachts were torn from their moorings and smashed against the harbour wall.

The next year they headed west, visiting Yarmouth, Weymouth and Dartmouth, then Plymouth and Fowey. At the end of that season, Ray took *Eolis* to the yard in Littlehampton, her birthplace, for some much-needed work. Finding himself surrounded by other Hillyards, some part-built, Ray became convinced that these boats would fulfill his ambitions.

In 1973 *Eolis* made her longest voyage with Ray as skipper. They sailed from Gosport to Le Havre and Ouistreham and then returned via Brighton. On the outward trip they encountered a strong northerly wind with a heavy following sea and for the first time Ray appreciated the seagoing qualities of his yacht. Due to family commitments, from 1975 to 1978 *Eolis* was used for weekend and holiday breaks in the Solent and Poole. Ray soon joined the Hillyard Owners Association formed in 1977 and attended the first rally held at Cowes in 1978. By this time, Ray and his wife Audrey had two grown up daughters and they felt they needed a boat with more accommodation. He found a much neglected 9-tonner, called *Trooper*, on a mooring on the Hamble River, which he bought in the autumn of 1978. *Trooper* had been built in 1959, her original name being *Miss Marilyn*.

Much work was needed on the new boat and she was ashore at Moody's yard on Hamble River for the next eighteen months. In 1980 *Trooper* was sailed to her new home in Gosport when their daughter Liz produced a new boyfriend. He was Steve Tiffin, an experienced sailor and just perfect for the Heys. He soon became addicted to wooden boats and began to sail with them. In time Liz and Steve married and Steve is now Commodore of the Hillyard Owners Association. In August that year, Steve joined the family for a somewhat fraught trip to Cherbourg. *Trooper* suffered engine problems and filled the bilges with oil.

1981 saw *Trooper* in the Channel Islands, again suffering engine troubles. 1982 was a busy year, greeting the vessels returning from the Falklands war, seeing the return of the Tall Ships from their race in which Steve had taken part, and Ray deciding to give *Trooper* a new diesel engine. This was fitted the next year. With the new engine giving an added sense of security, *Trooper* in 1984 visited the Channel Islands and North Brittany. During the following years from a base in the Northney Marina in Chichester Harbour, many family trips, now including grandchildren, were undertaken. By 1988 it was clear that with increasing leaks, *Trooper* needed new decks. As Steve, then living in Buckinghamshire, would be involved with the work, it was decided to do the work near his home and *Trooper* was taken up the Thames to a boatyard at Eel Pie Island. The re-fit, as always, took longer than expected following which *Trooper* was happily sailed by the now extended family until 1994 when she was sold and a 13-tonner, *Ianthe*, was bought and which continues to be sailed by Steve and Liz Tiffin to this day.

Ray later acquired a motorboat and moved to Hayling Island where he could enjoy a view of the Isle of Wight. He died in 2017 and had said ' sailing, handling, owning and maintaining a Hillyard was a practical, emotional and not to say financial challenge at times but always worthwhile for the sense of achievement it gave and for all the happy times spent afloat with the family and friends.'

Steve and Liz Tiffin

Like his father-in-law Raymond Hey, Steve Tiffin's love of wooden boats and sailing predated his Hillyard ownership by many years. In the early 1960's on a family holiday near Pwllheli in North Wales he went for a sail on a wooden GP14. He was hooked. The following Christmas his father, after much pestering, took Steve to the London Boat Show at Earl's Court. It was here he saw a Mirror dinghy and decided he wanted one. His Dad didn't, but he said Steve could have one if he paid half of the cost! A year or so later, and after delivery of many newspapers, he put his cash on the table and his Dad was forced to match it. They bought a home-build kit, sail number 12747. It was built it in their garage and finished (to his mother's delight) in the Dining Room. This was the real start of Steve's sailing.

He learnt to sail not only in the dinghy but also on the Norfolk Broads sailing traditional wooden 27ft Broads cruisers (no engines) on organised school trips with the Green Wyvern Sailing Club, progressing through as cabin boy, crew, mate and finally skipper age seventeen. The club still thrives and continues to develop the sailors of the future, and the skills of sailing and boat maintenance learnt there have stood him in great stead ever since.

In 1979, whilst sailing on an Ocean 60 to Honfleur, Cherbourg and the Channel Islands, Steve first became aware of Hillyards, through Raymond's daughter Liz, now his wife. Steve was invited to sail on Raymond's 9 -tonner *Trooper* for a long weekend cross-channel trip. With little wind and an overworked and overheating engine it was a long trip there and even longer back, but he was taken by this sturdy, comfortable boat.

After getting married in 1982 (the day after the Falklands were invaded) Steve and Liz sailed *Trooper* regularly at weekends and on holiday but, with work commitments, they only ever managed two weeks at a time. This continued now with their young family with regular trips to the West Country, Normandy, the Channel Islands and Northern Brittany (the kids loved the beaches in Trebeurden). *Trooper* was also there to see the raising of the *Mary Rose* and the return of S.S. *Canberra* from the Falklands. After a major refit in 1988/89 on the River Thames, they sailed *Trooper* to Honfleur where both the boat and her crew were blessed by the Bishop of Rouen at the Pentecostal Festival. This was the first of many Festivals they would attend over the coming years in their Hillyards.

In 1994 they were storm-bound for several days in St Peter Port with both children and grandparents on board. With the poor weather and a number of visiting friends and neighbours all crammed into a small space celebrating Steve's birthday, his father-in-law suggested they needed a bigger boat. By the time Steve and Liz had sailed *Trooper* back home, Raymond had lined up four boats to view. *Ianthe*, a 12-tonner, was the first one they viewed and they completed the purchase in October, followed a week later by the sale of *Trooper*. They were *Ianthe*'s second owners—the first, Ken Monroe, a ship owner from Liverpool, had sailed her from North Wales to Southern Brittany and the Isles of Scilly with a season in Scotland.

For the next 15 years annual family holidays were taken on *Ianthe*, split between one half of the family taking the boat out to France and the other bringing the boat home. This gave everyone more time to spend exploring the French coast—whether it be east to St Vaast, Ouistream and Honfleur or west to St Malo, St Quai, Paimpol, Tregieur, Roscoff or round into the Rade de Brest. In between they attended many classic boat events both in the West Country and in Portsmouth (for the Festivals of the Sea held there in 1998, 2001 and 2005). They also went to many HOA rallies in Portsmouth, Southampton, Cowes and the West Country.

Steve and Liz both retired in 2009 and they decided to undertake a major refit of *Ianthe* to enable them to make longer trips in the confidence that the boat and equipment were up to scratch. This entailed a new engine and electrics, re-decking, new brightwork, updating instrumentation and swapping to a larger fully battened mainsail. At this stage Steve was approached by Michael Walden to take over the running of the Hillyard Owners Association in succession to him as Commodore. Liz also became involved as they brought in-house the editing/production of the newsletter and handbook, saving significant costs. Longer trips unfortunately still had to be put on hold with their four parents in deteriorating health.

They set themselves very ambitious targets each year based around classic sailing events, festivals and rallies, going to Paimpol in 2011, 2013 and 2019, Terre et Mer in Morlaix in 2013 and 2014, Douranenez in 2014 and 2018, Semaine du Golf in 2015, Binic in 2016 and 2018, Dahouet in 2019. They attended the Falmouth Classics rally most years from 2012 and were twice accepted for the huge Brest Festivals but engine problems stopped them in 2016, and the Covid-19 pandemic in 2020. On the back of these festivals they did much extensive cruising in Southern Brittany getting as far south as Ile de Noirmoitier. Since 2010 they have averaged over 1000 miles sailing most years, criss-crossing the channel between festivals.

Whilst *Ianthe* might not have done some of the longer trips achieved by other Hillyards, she has been extremely well used and loved by her owners. For her forty-fifth birthday in 2020 they were due to have been at the Southampton Boat Show representing the HOA but the show was cancelled due to that year's pandemic. Hopefully there will be another opportunity for this in the future so they can attract others to support Hillyard yachts, something they have been very successful at over the years.

David Stickland

Born in 1944 into a landlocked family in Winchester, David did not start sailing until 1982 when he was thirty-eight. His first marriage had just failed and a work colleague said to him, 'Dave, we're going sailing!' He was hooked straight away. He bought a one-third share in a 1973 25ft Spanish-built GRP yacht called *Vamos* which he and his three children sailed as often as they could. In due course the other two partners relinquished their shares and he became the sole owner.

In 1991 David remarried and his new wife, Carol, thought he should have a new boat. She had not sailed before but soon came to enjoy the pastime. One day in 1999 when Carol was on board *Vamos* alone with her grandson, she spotted a wooden boat for sale in the marina. On her return home she reported that she had seen a boat she had fallen in love with.

A few weeks later David and Carol became the new owners of a 1958 Hillyard 9-tonner called *Penny Plain*. The first person who had taken David sailing had issued him with a stern warning against buying a wooden boat and at that time he knew almost nothing about them. But he went ahead regardless. David and Carol had a daughter-in-law named Penny and they felt it unwise to continue the name so they came up with a new name by putting together the names of their two daughters, Natasha and Anna. They came up with *Tashana*. They did not believe in the superstition that it is bad luck to change a boat's name and in any event the boat already had two previous names, *Muffin Too* and *Felicity Jane*. *Vamos* was sold.

An early outing in *Tashana* was to the 2001 Festival of the Sea in Portsmouth where they discovered that they had an interest in traditional and classic boats. They joined the Hillyard Owners Association and enjoyed attending their rallies. They had some memorable sails in company with *Trimley Maid* (Michael Walden) and *Lady Ailsa* (Vincent van Walt) to rallies in the Solent, Poole, Fowey and beyond.

By this time David had been made redundant and was enjoying the luxury of a pension and more free time. They began making longer voyages to the West Country and across the Channel to classic boat events in particular. These included Falmouth Classics, Plymouth Classics, Paimpol, Brest, Douarnenez, Fowey Classics, Roscoff, Morlaix and even a memorable visit to the St Katharine Docks Classic Boat Festival.

Following their visit to the 2001 Festival of the Sea, the Sticklands realised that they really liked the hospitality, camaraderie and atmosphere of the great French traditional boat festivals. They became *habitués* at these events which have proliferated on the French side of *La Manche*. I asked David about why he spent so much of his time attending these events. He gave a clear and reasoned response highlighting how the French care for their fleet of heritage and classic boats in a far better way than we do in the UK, despite the years of our maritime history. He described how they use their festivals to help preserve their historic vessels and promote interest in them to the French population at large, who flock in their thousands to these events. He says that unless we in the United Kingdom start to do likewise, we are in danger of losing a large part of our maritime heritage. Here is what he said:

The French have a great respect for their historic ships, some of which are classed and supported as ancient monuments, and for their sailors who they treat as national heroes and heroines. Many French maritime towns have built replicas of the types of vessel which were built and sailed in their locality, funded by local and national support, with grants available of up to 75% of the cost.

Where in Britain, this great maritime nation, would thousands line the locks, docksides and cliff tops to watch classic vessels parade past? In recent years Falmouth Classics has come close to this, as has the more niche Fowey Classics, but the great British public do not appear to have the same enthusiasm for these events as do the French.

In 2011 we had our first taste of French hospitality in Paimpol at the Festival du Chant de Marin, followed in 2012 by our

first visit to Brest. It is said that up to a million visitors over the
week of the festival pay to visit the sight of the 2,000 vessels
on display. Can you imagine thousands of people paying good
money to look at classic boats and then to line the cliffs of the
Pointe de Pen-Hir on the Crozon peninsular to watch the parade of sail of hundreds of vessels of all shapes and sizes negotiate the Tas de Pois (Pile of Peas) on their way to the festival
in Douarnenez, which follows on immediately after Brest. This
we did for a second time in 2016, but sadly Covid 19 resulted
in the cancellation of the 2020 edition of this wonderful festival
which takes place only every four years[*].

However, Temps Fête in Douarnenez takes place every other year and we were able to renew our acquaintance with that
great sardine processing town again in 2014 and 2018. In 2013
the Baie de Morlaix hosted an interesting event which sadly
seems not to have been repeated called 'Entre Terre et Mer',
where farmers meet sailors. Starting in Roscoff we sailed via the
rock strewn but well-marked bay to Morlaix itself and moored
near the former Tobacco Factory on the quay, which was lined
with antique, but working, tractors and agricultural machinery.
Sadly, the channel to Morlaix is silting badly and is only marked
by withies. Even shallow-draught vessels can and do touch the
bottom. The same year, 2013, a further edition of Festival du
Chant de Marin took place in Paimpol, which we also visited.
We went there again in 2015 and hope to be there in 2021.

The French love their festivals and it is said it is possible
to visit a classic boat festival almost every summer weekend
somewhere in Brittany. Visitors with old boats which pass the
organisers' criteria pay no berthing fees (British marinas please
take note!) and receive hampers with local wine and food produce. The local Mayors realise that such hospitality reaps rich
rewards in hungry and thirsty sailors boosting the local economy. It is said that Paimpol's *pompiers* (firemen) are financed
from the proceeds of the sea shanty festival.

---

[*]   The first Brest festival was held in 1992 and was attended by many Hillyard-
       ers, including Frank Mulville, Michael Joyce and the author.

In many ways we have a far richer maritime heritage than the French but we seem incapable as a country of recognizing this or of making much effort to preserve it. Holland, Denmark, Sweden and Norway all do more than we do to look after their maritime heritage, which we are in danger of losing completely.

These sentiments are shared by the author and we may hope the recent initiative led by the Maritime Heritage Trust to designate certain harbours around our coasts as Heritage Harbours will do something to raise awareness of this country's rich but diminishing marine heritage.

*　　　　*　　　　*

Finally, what do other Hillyard people think of their boats, whether owners present or past?

One thing all owners seem to agree about is the superb sea-keeping characteristics of their Hillyard designed and built craft. 'Take you anywhere,' is a frequent comment by those who know. They also have plenty to say about their forgiving nature. 'There seems to be an in-built ability to look after you however much of a clown you may be,' wrote one grateful owner. Centre cockpits feel much safer in heavy weather, and the distinctive Hillyard canoe stern seems to part following seas in a reassuring way. After coping with huge waves in a Biscay storm, another described his 12-tonner as 'buoyant as a cork.' Yet another wrote about the sea-keeping abilities of his 12-tonner as 'superb—it never gave us an anxious moment.'

After a trip which took them from Poole to the West Indies and back, the then owner of the 9-tonner *Trimley Maid* described her as 'near ideal for a blue water cruise… handling 50-knot winds and 40-foot seas like the thoroughbred she undoubtedly is'. This owner, Michael Walden, used to wax lyrical about her sheer efficiency as a cruising yacht.

Many owners repeat the oft-quoted words about Hillyards, 'They might starve you to death, but they will never drown you!', which to them is high praise but to the many yachtsmen who do not 'get' Hillyards it is usually said with a derogatory sneer as a put down or maybe just as a joke.

What is more, wherever they go, owners seem able to smell out other Hillyard owners in the most outlandish places and to have their boats recognised as the classics they are. One owner was enjoying the beauty of an isolated anchorage in the West Indies when he became conscious of a swimmer ploughing round his boat in ever decreasing circles. Finally, with some exasperation, he called out and wondered if he could be of any help. The answer was that the swimmer was himself a Hillyard owner and was just admiring another of Hillyard's creations. Another 12-tonner spent many months in the yard in Littlehampton while the owner and his family fitted her out for a trip to Vancouver. When he eventually left, he was asked to let the yard know how the voyage went. In due course a letter and a photograph arrived showing the 12-tonner on a mooring in some faraway place with a boat moored on each side of her—both identical sister ships. One globe trotter summed it up when he reported 'the invariable and enthusiastic recognition of the Hillyard' in almost every anchorage or harbour they visited on a cruise which doubled the Atlantic. This was especially so when they were in the United States of America. For the Americans, Hillyards are the epitome of a small, traditional English cruising sailboat.

Of course, not all dreams of free and uninhibited cruising come to pass, even in a Hillyard. One intrepid skipper who set out to circle the globe in his 8-tonner only made it as far as Spain, probably Gibraltar, which has so often become the graveyard of people's dreams. A slow, wet and cold slog down the English Channel, followed by a rough crossing of the Bay of Biscay and an over-boisterous passage down the Portuguese coast, can too often put paid to all romantic dreams of trade winds, tropical islands and waving palm trees. From Spain this particular Hillyard owner called Dennis Cullingford that he had had enough and was giving the boat to charity. Sad as it may seem, Gibraltar is a very good place to find cheap abandoned boats!

Another Hillyard customer bought a second-hand one with the declared intention of extensive blue water cruising. Throughout the winter months the boat was stripped, repaired and repainted and fitted out with every conceivable thing it might need on ocean passages. Spring came and with-it departure day. With boat relaunched and moored to the pontoon, crammed with journalist friends and cameramen, busily clicking away, the skipper went aboard, started up the engine and cast off. Handkerchiefs waved and final words of encouragement were shouted across the widening gap, when it became apparent to the well-wishers that the boat was no longer moving. The cause—a rope wrapped around its propeller. The boat was hastily remoored and the excitement of the planned farewell dissipated whilst the crowd drifted away. They never had to say farewell again as the boat never left her moorings after that until she was sold. As can so often happen, the owner had forced himself into a corner having told all his friends about the voyage from which he could not escape. The fouled prop was his last, lucky and only hope of a way out.

There was yet another boat that did not move from the yard for many years. She was kept in commission and fully provisioned by her owner as a sort of floating bomb shelter/escape route in the event of a third world war. She lay on the slip for fourteen years and, for another three, hauled out under cover in one of the sheds. She was so unused that when she was eventually sold in 1996, she was like a museum piece and needed no more than a quick going over to make her ready for sea. During all the years he owned her, the owner made several visits each year to reassure himself that the boat was ready to put to sea, sitting aboard with a cup of coffee before catching the next train back to London. In these uncertain and fragile times, I am sure there are many other boat owners who regard their boats as an escape route for when things get too bad.

Other owners often speak of their recollection of and admiration for David Hillyard. There are many tales of his being 'difficult' but it was really more his being protective, and concerned to make sure buyers bought the right boat. It is true there were times when he refused to deal with a potential buyer, but usually because he did not think they were capable of handling one of his larger boats. A prime example of this was told by Jonathan Dodd, owner of a 12-tonner *Antipodes*, which was (eventually) built for his father in 1965.

In 1961 Jonathan's father, John, set about persuading Hillyard to build him a 12-tonner. In those days the order books were full and Hillyard only built boats of this size for people he thought could handle them. For some reason he was not happy about the Dodd family at all. In October 1963, after two years of visiting the yard and trying to get Hillyard to say yes, John Dodd, who was then aged forty, made one more visit this time with his family and mother in tow. She was then severely arthritic and in a wheelchair. She was much the same age as Hillyard, who hardly spoke to John but directed his conversation entirely at her. It went something like this:

'Mrs Dodd your son has been pestering me now for two years to build him a Hillyard. Do you really think he is capable of handling a vessel of this size?' John's mother replied: 'Mr Hillyard, sir, my son was a navigator during the war on an escort convoy destroyer and he has recently read up on his navigation and taken a medium frequency radio course. I think he ought to be able to, don't you?' Hillyard replied 'Jolly good, I'll build him one then. I really must go,' and turned round and walked away.

That was the last they saw of David Hillyard for he died the next month. Construction started in October the next year and *Antipodes* was launched in May 1964.

Postscript

Of the eight hundred pleasure boats built by Hillyard's (this number excludes the wartime vessels), some three hundred are believed to be still sailing today. The question to be asked is not why are there so few of the original boats still sailing, but how is it possible that there are still so many when so much of this country's maritime heritage has been destroyed. One interesting answer to this was put to me by John Lilley, yacht surveyor and member of a family of serial Hillyard owners. His answer is 'simplicity'. Whilst many people believe Hillyard cut corners (to keep costs down), John's riposte is that no corners were cut but that the boats were constructed simply and with good quality materials. They were built without any clever construction techniques, largely without the use of glues, and without the use of metal components for floors, knees, mast steps, or other structural parts. Such items may have led to a lighter and stiffer hull but once they began the inevitable process of decay or corrosion, the replacement of such items becomes time consuming, complicated and expensive.

It is also becoming clear that the glue used on boats built in the 1950s and 1960s, particularly resorcinol, has a limited life and many such yachts are showing degradation of their laminated parts. Many boats built in those eras were constructed with laminated stems, keels, sternposts, ribs and frames as well as deck beams, knees and floors. To replace these items is a very expensive operation. There are few such structures in Hillyards.

Hillyards with all wooden hulls, floors and knees and no structural metal parts are simpler, cheaper and easier to repair and maintain. Whilst maintaining an old wooden boat is never cheap, what this means is that much work in keeping Hillyards going can be, and often is, done by competent amateurs, and if professional assistance is needed this should not be too complicated. They were simple boats and no worse for that.

Despite all this and the enthusiasm and dedication of today's owners, preservation of the Hillyard fleet is going to face real challenges in the years ahead. Many of these boats, which range in age from one hundred years to a little under forty*, are still in remarkably good order. But as all wooden boat owners know, they all start to decay from the day they are launched. Whilst this decay can be delayed or postponed or even prevented by good and regular maintenance and lots of tender loving care, the time comes for all wooden boats when the actual replacement of planking, decks, frames and backbone can be put off no longer. The costs of this type of work can be large, often exceeding the value of the boat, and not many people can, or are willing to, undertake this. The comedian and broadcaster Griff Rhys Jones, who is a serial doer-upper of old, large, and wonderful wooden yachts, said recently, only half-jokingly, that maintaining old wooden boats is the only activity he knows where you can buy a specimen for £200,000, spend £2 million on doing it up, whereupon it is worth £200,000.

This is the conundrum facing Hillyard owners. They all want to preserve their boats and consider themselves guardians rather than owners, but they know that the 'market' considers Hillyards to be cheap boats. They too often get into a position where they find the cost of repairs exceeds the value of the boat with the repairs completed. At the time of writing there is a lovely looking little 6-tonner hauled out ashore and stored in the boatyard adjacent to the old Hillyard premises. The boat is for sale but it needs extensive structural work to its aft section. The cost of having this work carried out professionally will far exceed the value of the boat (even with the work completed). It is exceedingly unlikely therefore that the owner will find a buyer unless he can find someone who is prepared, and has the skills and space, to carry out the work himself at his own home. There are people like that but they are few and far between and meanwhile the boat concerned sits on a boatyard's concrete hard standing forlorn and forgotten whilst deteriorating further as each season passes.

Millions are spent every year by oligarchs, Silicon Valley tycoons, pop stars and the rich residents of Monaco on their mega- and super-yachts, which are traded between them for even more millions, but Hillyards are ordinary yachts for ordinary people and do not attract the sort of 'premium' value which often attaches to a Fife, a

---

*   The last Hillyard to be built was completed in 1982.

Mylne or a Herreshoff. The situation is akin to the fact that a fifty-year-old Ferrari might fetch several million pounds at an auction, whilst a fifty-year-old MG would fetch only some £15,000. Both look similar, perform much the same, cost much the same to build and seat only two people, but one has a premium value, the other does not.

Luckily there are people out there who are prepared to put their money into a wooden Hillyard on the basis that the 'true' cost of ownership can be spread over several years where the buying cost plus the annual maintenance cost will equate to what they would have spent over the same period had they bought and maintained a GRP vessel. They also appreciate the considerable satisfaction to be had just from the fact of ownership of a classic vessel, the attention it gets wherever it goes, and the pleasure to be had from looking after and sailing a piece of history.

Large and prestigious classic yachts trade at a considerable premium but this has not filtered down the chain to yachts of most Hillyard's size. Occasionally owners of small classic boats and yacht brokers dealing in them try to ramp up the level but this rarely works. Recently the owner of one of the 'small' Gauntlets built pre-World War II by the Berthon Boatyard tried to offer his fully restored 32ft wooden example at over £100,000 (a figure which probably equated to what had been spent on her) but it never worked and she never found a buyer at that price.

So what can be done? David Stickland in the previous chapter writes about how France and other continental countries are much better than we are in the United Kingdom at looking after, promoting and showing off their fleets of Classic and Heritage vessels. Not only are grants and loans more readily available there than here but it is common practice for Continental marinas to offer free or much reduced berthing charges to owners of classic vessels. Think what it would mean to the owner of a Hillyard 12-tonner, who can easily find himself paying out over £6,000 a year to berth in a Solent marina. This saving could easily pay for a year's maintenance.

Whilst organisations like the Maritime Heritage Trust, the National Historic Ships Register and the Old Gaffers Association do what they can (and do make small grants available) a much bigger effort is needed from them and organisations such as class associations, like the Hillyard Owners Association and the Harrison Butler Association, to promote the interests of historic, classic and heritage vessels in the harbours where they moor and visit. Local and National government needs to be made aware of the huge tourist and cultural benefit which can be obtained from the promotion and safeguarding of our rich maritime heritage. The recent initiative of the Maritime Heritage Trust to promote the designation of selected harbours around the coasts of Great Britain as Heritage Harbours is welcomed and only follows what has happened already in France, Germany and the Netherlands. The author is pleased to report that he has been largely responsible for his home port of Sandwich in Kent having been nominated as the fifth Heritage Harbour in the UK under this scheme.

A perfect example of what can be done is the establishment of the Scottish Fisheries Museum in the small sleepy harbour and town of Anstruther in Fife. There the museum took over a redundant boatyard which used to dominate the harbour (and is about the same size as the old Hillyard yard) and turned it into a living museum where visitors can see wooden boats being built and repaired together with displays explaining the history of the Scottish fishing industry. In the harbour are real working sailing craft including the 70ft *Reaper*, the largest remaining fishing lugger 'Fifie'. The museum and its exhibits have transformed the town which is one of the most visited places on Scotland's east coast. The same could be done in almost any small harbour on England's east or south coasts, even in David Hillyard's old shipyard in Littlehampton, which still remains almost intact, before the developers move in and destroy it forever. It is beholden on all of us to do whatever we can to preserve the remaining Hillyards before it is too late.

Finally, if this book has done nothing else, I hope it may have brought to the attention of the wider sailing population both here in the United Kingdom and elsewhere that Hillyards are not just boats to be joked about but are proper seagoing, safe and seaworthy boats, extremely well built out of first class materials, capable of going anywhere; they are a fleet of boats created by the fertile imagination of just one man, and that man was David Hillyard.

Appendices

Appendix 1

NON-HILLYARD HILLYARDS

David Hillyard used to claim that no boat came out of his yard which he had not designed. This is not strictly true, just almost true; in four cases, Hillyard is credited as joint designer with another. These are:

Beaver

A 28-tonner built in 1928. *Beaver* was a large expensive boat built for Major Younger, the Scottish brewer, who was meticulous, sparing no cost, in his requirements for the boat. R. E. Tupman is credited in Lloyd's as joint designer—'D. Hillyard and R. E. Tupman'.

Eaglet

A small 6-tonner built the next year, 1929 is also shown as being designed jointly with R. E. Tupman, but this time Shown in Lloyd's as—'R. E. Tupman and D. Hillyard'. We do not know who R. E. Tupman is or was. Could it be that the name Tupman is wrong and that it should be Todman? We know that Harry Todman was Hillyard's draughtsman in the early years and he would undoubtedly have had a part in the design of these two vessels.

D'Sel

A variant of Hillyard's 12-tonner but with a novel diesel/electric propulsion system built in 1931. Lloyd's shows an L. Clayton as joint designer, about whom we know nothing. It is, however, likely that Hillyard would have sought advice on the installation of the complicated power set-up and it could have been from Mr Clayton, hence the designation of joint designer.

Bonnie

A 10-tonner built in 1948. Mr G. L. Dalton, the first owner, is shown in Lloyd's Register as joint designer with David Hillyard. Many owners gave much input to the yard as to how their vessel was to be designed, shaped and fitted out. Lloyd's took information from owners and not the yards, and Mr Dalton claimed this credit for himself.

*   *   *

The following are a further four Hillyard-built vessels where the actual designer is not entirely clear:

Corona II

A 6-tonner built in 1923. The designer is shown in Lloyd's as a Mr G.E. Cohen. The first owner of the boat was a Mr F.G. Cohen. This is a mystery but related to the next boat.

Corona III

A 12-tonner built in 1939 for a Mr H.E. Cohen (were these three Cohen's all related?). The designer is shown as Engineer Rear-Admiral Turner. Admiral Turner, although not a yacht designer, was greatly interested in the design of yacht hulls and was well known in the mid-1930s for promoting his 'metacentric shelf' theory of hull balance* . He wrote many papers on the subject. It is considered unlikely that Admiral Turner would have designed this boat and I do not know of any boats which he actually designed. Hillyard was aware of the Admiral's theory through his friendship with Dr Harrison Butler, who was an advocate for Admiral Turner's ideas, but Hillyard, being a practical man, probably thought them bunkum (as many others did!). I cannot think of any reason why the Rear Admiral is cited as designer. I can only surmise that the 'Cohens', the first owners of both *Corona II* and *Corona III* and the designer of number *II* , might have been disciples of the Rear Admiral and incorporated his ideas in the vessels.

Solace

This vessel, built in 1929 and referred to in detail earlier was origi-

---

*   Basically a theory of how to design a yacht's hull so that its balance remained the same at all angles of heel. It was dismissed by many as fanciful but did have some adherents, noticeably Dr Harrison Butler, a well-known amateur designer of that time. (Naval Architecture and Engineering. *Nature* 140, 597 (1937). https://doi.org/10.1038/140597a0).

nally designed by an American, believed to be John Alden. The original owner took the plans to Hillyard and asked him to build the boat according to those plans. Hillyard demurred at first but eventually agreed to do so without acknowledging the original designer, by altering much of the underwater profile so that he could claim, if challenged, not to have breached Mr Alden's copyright in the design. It is unlikely he would have succeeded in a Court of law! Interestingly, the boat is shown in all annual entries in Lloyd's Register of Yachts (published each year until 1980) as having no designer at all.

D'Sel II

A 39-tonner built by Hillyard's in 1939. All editions of Lloyd's Register show the designer as W. McC. Meek & Co. Ltd. This is incorrect. The boat was designed by Hillyard, but William McC. Meek was asked by the original owner to design the interior layout of what was a very large and complicated boat. McC. Meek was a well-known yacht designer in the 1930s working for Brookes Marine in Lowestoft and responsible for many fast motor yachts and other 'superyachts' of their day. (Incidentally, McC. Meek was the same man who suggested to Arthur Ransome that he should buy *Nancy Blackett*.)

* * *

This leaves three boats which Hillyard built but does not seem to have designed.

Soma

This boat was indeed built by Hillyard's in 1939 but the original design was by Maurice Griffiths, a prolific yacht designer and Editor of *Yachting Monthly* for many years. She was designed for amateur building and an amateur did start her, but finding it too difficult asked Hillyard to complete her, which he did. She was a particularly 'boxy' hard chine barge-type yacht and Hillyard was probably pleased not to have had anything to do with its design.

Lady Betty

This is a mystery. Built in 1932, this 27ft 6-ton sloop, later called *Lady Betty Too* and *Blue Seas*, is stated by Lloyd's as having been designed by Fred Shepherd. I consider this to be unlikely. Shepherd was one of the best-regarded naval architects of that era who designed very few yachts, if any, of less than 35ft[*] and always insisted on supervising their construction (something Hillyard would have baulked at). He was best known for mid-size cruising yachts together with some very much larger ones. One answer might lie in the fact that in 1926 Shepherd co-founded a yacht building business on the Hamble River called Frederick Shepherd and Morgan which was not a conspicuous success and closed down in 1929. During this period, he might have designed *Lady Betty* but never got round to building her when his yard closed. The prospective owner would then have been left with a set of plans but no builder. Might he have taken these plans to Hillyard and asked him to build her? I can think of no better solution.

Zero

This is a complete mystery. Built in 1925, this boat, a 14-tonner, is shown in Lloyd's as having been designed by Clive Mort. We have no information on Mr Mort or about the boat and we do not know if she is still afloat. Her name was later changed to *Mea Mater* and then to *Riduna III*. Who was Clive Mort?

*   *   *

Finally, according to Lloyd's Register, there is one boat which Hillyard designed but did not build.

Day Dawn

A 13-tonner, she was built in Trondheim in Norway in 1938. The circumstances that led to her being built in Norway are entirely unknown, including whether she was built with the designer's permission. Maybe the plans were 'lifted' or pirated from the yard without Hillyard's consent. This has often happened, the best-known offender being a Spanish yard which in the 1950s and 1960s built several boats to pirated designs from the famous New York design office of Sparkman & Stevens without their permission.

---

[*]   As related in Chapter 15, Shepherd designed Arthur Ransome's 35ft 6in yacht *Selina King*.

Appendix 2

AN APPRENTICE'S STORY

by Chris Barnes

Chris Barnes was an apprentice at Hillyard's from 1961 to 1968 and he wrote this vivid and engaging account of his time at the yard, which was originally published in *The Hillyarder*, the newsletter of the Hillyard Owners Association, in 2014.

*　　　*　　　*

Wishing to give a good account of myself I attended the interview promptly at the address provided—the David Hillyard Shipyard in Littlehampton. I found myself squeezed into a small cramped office, littered with a muddled profusion of papers, specifications and drawings, most protruding from haphazard shelving around the walls. There was nowhere for me to sit. A brief and cursory interview was conducted by the owner's nephew, Dennis Cullingford, a shy and hesitant man probably in his mid-thirties, who appeared ill at ease.

Toward the end of the interview a thin, stooped elderly man shuffled into the office. Sunken watery pale blue eyes could just be discerned beneath the shadow of a wide flat cap from which odd tufts of white hair protruded. His down-turned mouth was partially disguised by a white, droopy, unkempt moustache. He wore a long dark threadbare overcoat with a grubby white silk scarf around his neck, thick grey flannel trousers, liberally coated with sawdust, and half covered heavily scuffed boots. From beneath his cap he looked me up and down, grunted then nodded to Dennis Cullingford before shuffling out of the office again. Unknown to me at the time, David Hillyard had just given his assent to my employment.

I was told to be at work punctually at 8.00 a.m. each morning starting the next week. I was told I would be on one month's trial after which, if successful, I would be taken on as an apprentice for a five-year term.

Arriving at the shipyard on the Monday morning, highly conscious of my awkwardness and not knowing where to go or whom to approach, I found the office where my interview had been conducted and waited there. After what seemed like an eternity of being scrutinised by the men arriving for work, a short, tubby and bespectacled middle aged man who had ridden in on an ancient motorbike introduced himself as Tom Jeffers, foreman of the 'Bottom Shop'. I extended my hand by way of introduction but was ignored; he merely requested that I follow him.

Pointing to the old canvas cricket bag I was carrying, containing my pitiful collection of second hand tools I had managed to scrape together, he showed me my allocated space between large well stocked toolboxes, which made my limited assortment look even more than pathetic.

The 'Bottom Shop', where I was to spend the next five years learning my trade, was a spacious dilapidated building with tall half-glazed sliding doors adjacent to and on the same level as the Rope Walk, the access road to the yard which ran parallel with the river. The concrete floor was smooth and shiny with many years' wear; heavy wooden beams criss-crossed the building supporting a high-pitched corrugated iron roof. On one side of the workshop and attached to those beams were the frames and the carcase of a partially planked boat. On the other side a fully planked and decked boat complete with cabin top sat in a wheeled cradle. Around the walls were a haphazard arrangement of work benches supporting long lengths of odd-shaped timber planking. Everything was covered with a liberal coating of sawdust including Tom Jeffers, who wore a collar and tie, an old tweed sports jacket and dusty trousers. The other men all wore bib and brace overalls, open neck shirts and flat caps.

Tom Jeffers, or Mr Jeffers as he liked to be called, introduced me to Ron, a short well-built and hard-bitten man, in his mid-thirties. He had a cigarette permanently lodged in the corner of his mouth. This fascinated me in that it remained in place while he spoke and while he worked. When finished, it was immediately replaced by another one. He was an accomplished master shipwright and boatbuilder, experienced and skilful. He was friendly with a good sense of humour and had a gift for teaching and passing on his well-honed skills to the apprentices, or 'boys' as we were called. Ron led by example and never expected any of us to do a job that he could not do to perfection himself. Whilst I did not realise it at the time, I could not have received a better grounding in what was to become my trade.

One of the more notable theories that Ron taught us was what we apprentices later called the 'Law of Diminishing Strength'. Whilst we found this quite amusing at the time, it does have a great deal of validity and was a theory I have applied to all practical building work I have done since. It was a lesson well learnt. Applied to boat building the theory simply said that if in any doubt about what size a timber component should be, allow approximately an extra 10 to 15 per cent in dimension. This provides a sufficient margin of error, or as Ron explained, if part of the component rotted away sufficient component strength would be left.

The work was physically hard and demanded stamina, agility and a great deal of strength. Being unable to rise to the occasion was not an option. I was taught not only to have pride in my work but also pride in the stamina and strength required to accomplish that work. What is today referred to as the 'work ethic' was in those days instilled in the individual as a matter of course.

1960's Britain was an entirely different place with contrasting values from those of today. Manufacturing industry generated a large proportion of the country's wealth and was the main contributor to the economy. Therefore, manual workers who had served an apprenticeship and were skilled in a particular trade received far more recognition and respect than is the case today.

Week after week of exacting hard physical work can only realistically be maintained on a regular basis if there are occasionally brief periods of relaxation; an apprentice's safety valve if you will. This took the form of workshop banter which invariably developed into horse play which could last upwards of an hour or more and usually commenced with a wood off-cut projectile being aimed at an unwary apprentice who would then retaliate. The ensuing chase with the exchange of missiles was conducted across the main support beams high up in the roof of the workshop and required agility and balance at precarious heights in order to score a decisive blow resulting in a cessation of 'hostilities'. By today's health and safety standards such horse play would be unthinkable and, at the very least, a dismissible offence.

During my apprenticeship I came to recognise what a rich variety of characters worked in the shipyard. I learnt to cut through their thick Sussex dialect, grasp their idiosyncrasies, understand their euphemisms, appreciate their ribald and often black humour, and become conversant with the wide assortment of expletives, all of which were a complete revelation to me. In my time at Hillyard's I learnt my trade, yes, but what I did not realise at the time was that it gave me a totally different perspective on life, a life far removed from that which I had been brought up to understand, which in many ways prepared me for my life at a lower level than was originally envisaged for me.

I worked under Ron's tutelage for the duration of my apprenticeship and for some time afterwards but, thankfully, I never emulated his chain smoking or his ability to retain a 'fag' in the corner of his mouth. Whilst Ron was a skilled tradesman, his lack of a proper education often resulted in him picking up words the meaning of which he did not understand. Not wanting to embarrass him, we had to turn away when he came up with a real howler and creep away into a corner, stifling our laughter. We referred to him as Ron 'Malaprop'. He never did understand the joke and no one was foolhardy enough to try to explain it to him.

Apart from Tom Jeffers and Ron, two other men plus three apprentices including myself worked in the 'Bottom Shop' building '9- tonners' which were carvel built with mahogany or iroko planking on oak backbone and frames, spruce stringers and gunnels and softwood decking. The completed boats were 30ft long and were double-enders, like the majority of Hillyards, with a Bermudan rig.

There were always two boats being built at any one time. Ron, myself and two other apprentices, a rather dim individual called Steve and Mike who had a very high opinion of himself, were employed on building these boats. We built from laying the keel,

assembling the stem and sternpost, fitting 'floors', planking, timbering, caulking, fitting gunnels, stringers, deck beams and decks.
With the shell of the boat completed, it was lifted onto a wheeled
cradle and hauled to the other side of the 'shop'. There engine and
shaft were installed, interior joinery fitted and the deck was completed with all fittings.

In those days whilst there were temporary frames and patterns
for the various component parts each boat was really built by 'eye.'
In other words, the hull shape was determined by the lay-up of the
planking which was 'eyed' in by those building the hull. Achieving
a good 'eye' was very much a part of my apprenticeship. Each boat
shape was dependent on the eye of the person building the hull;
therefore, no two boats were the same. There was a high demand
for these boats and always a full order book. In all the years I was
employed there was always more than enough work.

*   *   *

The shipyard covered a large area sited along the west bank of the River Arun, opposite the town and below a swing bridge which in those
days was part of the old A259 South Coast Road. A new bridge was
subsequently built much later above the old swing bridge to handle
the increased level of traffic. The old bridge, prior to being demol-
ished, was relegated to foot traffic only and closed to vehicles.

All the yard buildings were of timber construction with corrugated iron roofs and painted in admiralty grey; they were
continually under repair. In addition to the 'Bottom Shop', the
buildings comprised the wood mill, spar shop, engineers' shop,
riggers shop, paint shop, chandlers store, engineers store, timber
store and then the 'Top Shop', a large dilapidated building which
accommodated up to four boats under construction. This was
adjacent to the river, with slipways running from the building
down into the water.

12-tonners and 14-tonners were built in the 'Top Shop' under
the control of a particularly belligerent foreman called Bert, who
struck terror into his apprentices, ruling them with a very firm
hand and a very loud voice; quite unlike Tom Jeffers who was meek
and mild by comparison.

The congested main slipway in which our 9-tonners were launched was the central part of the whole yard around which most activity took place. It accommodated vessels in various stages of finishing and those awaiting sea trials or to be handed over to their new owners. A further building area open to all weathers with only a roof was located at the top of the slipway where single chine 5-tonners were built.

The yard 'canteen' was situated between the timber store and spar shop and located in a brick built air-raid shelter constructed during World War II for the safety of those building wartime landing craft. The canteen was ruled over by a large fierce-looking but benign man called George Mant, or Mr Mant to the apprentices. There was a large pot-bellied stove at one end of the building which in winter was continuously fed by George with timber offcuts he had salvaged from around the yard. Shipwrights sat nearest the stove end and apprentices in descending order of seniority down towards the open end of the building. In winter, the glowing red-hot stove required a large volume of air for combustion and it created and drew in a tremendous draught of cold air through the narrow open entrance where the hapless apprentices had to sit.

The working day was eight and a half hours, with strict ten-minute-only tea breaks morning and afternoon and a half-hour for lunch. Tea was brewed in a large urn with loose tea leaves tied in a muslin cloth and steeped in the urn for fifteen minutes prior to tea breaks. Only with permission from George were apprentices allowed to approach the shipwrights' end of the canteen and the glowing stove to toast their sandwiches. On occasions and much to the dislike of the assembled company a cultured and very well spoken 'gentleman of the road', a well-known local tramp, who liked to be known as Mr Coles but whom we named 'Old Coley,' would visit for a free cup of tea, which George always provided him.

The daily canteen banter was usually directed at one or other of the assembled company who had disgraced himself, either by incompetence in the workshop or, more amusingly, by some social indiscretion, usually concerning a local woman of easy virtue, or in the case of the apprentices, some local time good time girl.

In those days it was not uncommon for the more affluent boat owners to employ a full-time skipper who would live aboard the boat and carry out maintenance work in the winter. Deprived of a normal family life, a lone skipper could usually be found in the canteen where there was warmth, company and conversation. During the summer months the larger vessels which visited the harbour and used Hillyard's moorings would often carry skippers resplendent in brass-buttoned jackets with gold braided cuffs, wearing black peaked yachting caps with white tops. Such a person wandering into the canteen during a tea break would inevitably provoke the comment 'Ay up—the 31's in. Hold very tight please'. This referred to the number 31 bus that ran from Brighton to Portsmouth via Littlehampton: the bus driver's and conductor's uniforms, especially their hats, being remarkably like those of the yacht skippers.

*　　　　*　　　　*

The Engineer's shop was a dirty, murky and hostile place. There was a permanent oil slick on the floor made up of spent engine lubricants, iron filings and drillings together with machine slurry and a liberal collection of fag ends included in a slithery melange. This glutinous mix was sufficiently viscous to cling to your boots thus preventing an easy or hasty exit, the viscosity bearing a remarkable similarity to some of the floors and tabletops in Littlehampton's pubs at that time. This workshop was only to be entered with a degree of caution and trepidation. The engineer, also a blacksmith, was a large heavy-set man; a broad shouldered and black hearted individual with an unpredictable temper and with whom it was unwise to argue. His engineering apprentices, a surly collection of boys, cowered in his presence.

In addition to fitting engines in the boats, he was responsible for making the many heavy metal fastenings and fittings used in the boats. His forge, which had an enormous antediluvian electric blower mounted beside it, had a selection of just three fan speeds marked S, F and FF, slow, fast and …, the latter being of Anglo-Saxon derivation. This same man, when something went awry, was known to throw a tantrum and propel whatever metal missile was to hand, usually a hammer, around his workshop. In his defence, when in a good temper and in the pub, he could be an extremely likeable individual and was always very generous to the apprentices.

By comparison, the Wood Mill foreman was a quiet even-tempered man, tall and lean with gaunt hollow cheeks laced with a complex network of red thread veins. He wore a wide flat tweed cap, a pair of heavy blue serge trousers held up with string and complete with cycle clips, an ex-army battledress jacket, heavy black army boots and a three-foot wide apron made from a canvas off-cut tied around his waist with a large rope. Invariably covered in sawdust and wood chips, he continually muttered expletives to himself whilst working, but otherwise seldom spoke to anyone. Just his presence was sufficient to discourage anyone from entering his domain until they had his silent nodded assent as he peered over the top of battered thick-lensed spectacles.

The Wood Mill was, by today's standards, a highly dangerous place, powered by a huge electric motor driving a wide unguarded flapping canvas belt connected to a wobbly rotating shaft running along the length of the ceiling. This shaft in turn drove several wheels from which further rotating belts led back down to various powered machines spread around the mill. To cut planking from a three-foot diameter log on the circular saw, there was one man pulling with a rope and tackle at the leading end and two men pushing at the other end, as the log was dragged through the saw.

Screaming under the severe load the friction on the saw produced blue smoke and slowed it to half speed while the belts slipped and screeched before the log was withdrawn allowing the saw to resume full speed. The log was then fed in repeatedly until the cut was completed. The sawn planks would then be fed into a thicknesser with the same dramatic results, at times halting the belts and ultimately the electric motor under the extreme loads exerted. The expression on the Mill foreman's face during these operations was a study in contorted concentration as to how long he thought he could get away without burning out the electric motor. I witnessed three horrific occasions there, two when a finger was severed and once when the fingertips of one hand were lost whilst being accidently drawn across the overhand planer.

The dark and seemingly deserted Riggers' Shop always appeared a quiet and mysterious place, seemingly devoid of any hint of activity until your eyes became accustomed to the dim light which revealed the outline of an almost motionless figure, blending into the surroundings, stooped over his work bench methodically splicing the end of a length of heavy rigging wire.

Regardless of the season, rigger Bob Button's appearance never changed, looking as if he had slept in the same clothes. He was an ancient and decrepit looking man always in a grubby reefer jacket and battered seaman's cap, with an ever-smouldering pipe hanging from his bewhiskered mouth. Bob, who had no apprentice, worked alone and had no conversation; the best you could expect in answer to a question was a disinterested grunt.

Across the alleyway and opposite the Bottom Shop, was the Spar Shop where, as the name implies, the masts and spars were made, the denizens of which provided unparalleled entertainment, inhabited as it was by the two unwitting boatyard comedians.

Unquestionably the most immoral and debauched of all the employees were those in the Paint Shop, the worst of whom was their foreman Bill, a man in his late fifties and in poor health. He was a widower and was fond of relating his shameless and unnatural marital practices in an effort to shock you.

The Paint Shop was in a loft above the Engineers' Shop, accessed by narrow external wooden steps, and was the only place in the yard which boasted a sink with hot water. It was here that everyone 'washed up' at the end of the working day. A boatyard working environment is a grimy one and hands are often contaminated with paints, varnishes and adhesives necessitating removal with solvent and a thorough hand and face wash with soap before leaving the yard.

In the 1960s little or no importance was attached to worker's washing facilities so employees were obliged to use whatever was to hand. Prior to washing your hands with soap and water, paint and varnish had to be removed either by turpentine or, much quicker, by slurping over them a liberal quantity of acetone from a forty-five-gallon drum. Tilting this produced a wave inside of sufficient velocity to slurp out a measure to be caught in ones hands to instantly clean badly soiled hands. The fact that it drained all the oil from your skin at the same time was irrelevant to us.

The chandlery store was in a loft above the canteen accessed by steep exterior wooden steps. This store contained all the galvanised steel, copper, brass and gunmetal fixtures, fittings and fastenings, the value of which would have been considerable. The store had no door, let alone a lock and key, but was never taken advantage of by employees nor indeed was it ever burgled by outsiders. I mention this only because today such a store would have to be manned and totally secure with a detailed record of incoming stock and outgoing requisitions. In the 1960s we were trusted to just take what was required for a job. The chandlery store's greatest benefit to us apprentices was as a place to hide and to skive, it being full of nooks and crannies and ideal places of concealment.

As apprentices we were of course expected to become totally conversant with all boatbuilding practice and techniques. We also obtained a good working knowledge and understanding of all the other trades mentioned above. After the first year we had to attend technical college on a day-release basis to learn boat design and building theory, in order to sit and hopefully pass the City & Guilds examination. Although the college was in an adjacent town, just a bike ride away for me, I disliked being closeted in a classroom. A large part of the course included mathematics and technical drawing when it was as much as I could do to stay awake. I have always preferred to learn 'on the job' but I managed to pass the examinations in time to complete my apprenticeship.

*   *   *

Below I set out how we went about building the '9-Tonners'.

One of the more onerous duties for apprentices to carry out was the threading of keel bolts. This was done with a threading machine which, with great effort and the aid of a large turning handle and liberal quantities of used engine oil, cut an inch long 'whitworth' thread on either end of an inch-and-a-half-diameter galvanised mild steel rod, which first had been cut to length. Once cut and threaded, oakum grommets were fashioned to fit. These were liberally coated with black varnish and fitted on either end of the bolt.

A one-and-a-half-ton iron keel was manhandled into the Bottom Shop. Each man using an iron shod wooden lever or 'pry'
together with steel rollers to move the iron keel. Then using a
rocking motion, with one or more apprentices as a counterbal-
ance, the iron keel was gradually lifted on its side onto two-feet
high wooden blocks. A twelve-inch section oak keel, also on its
side, was then lifted onto the wooden blocks and bolted to it using
the keel bolts.

Then roughly sawn three-section stem and sternposts were fitted and bolted together and then bolted to the wood keel. These
were fashioned into shape using an adze and drawknife and then
finished with a smoothing plane and spokeshave. This assembly
formed the backbone of the boat.

A rebate was cut into the length of the wood keel, stem and
sternpost on both sides to receive the planking before the whole
assembly was lifted upright, levelled and secured to the workshop
roof beams. Temporary frames were then fitted over the wooden
keel and secured in place before the garboard and bottom three
planks were fitted around the frames and into the previously cut
rebate. The top four planks forming the gunnel strakes were then
fitted around the frames with the ends of each secured into the
rebate.

Temporary stringers were fitted around the frames at equal
spacings matching the shape of the hull, against which successive
planks would be wedged to facilitate a tight fit against the adjacent planking. Building was from the bottom up and from the top
down until a predetermined gap was left which was closed by the
'shutter' strake, precisely measured then fitted in by means of a
heavy hammer, wedging it against the existing top and bottom
strakes and making for a tight fit.

Once the top and bottom four strakes were complete, four-
inch wide oak transverse 'floors' were fitted at intervals along the
wooden keel, high enough to cover the garboard and bottom three
strakes. Heavy copper nails were driven through the planks and
into the floors. Temporary beams were fitted across the gunnel to
hold the assembly in place-whilst the next operation, 'timbering'
was carried out.

Timbering was the process of fitting oak 'timbers', each one by one and a half inches in section and long enough to bend inside the hull from the keel to the gunnels, at nine-inch intervals along the length of the backbone. To facilitate the bending of these timbers, they had to be steamed/boiled to make them pliable enough to fit to the contours of the hull. They were immersed in the kiln, a large water-trough heated by a rudimentary boiler. After being cooked for approximately four hours, individual timbers were 'run' by apprentices from the kiln to the boat, a distance of about one hundred yards, so they could be fitted before they cooled. Once a timber was *in situ* it was temporarily fixed in position. This frenetic operation took most of a day and was accompanied by the men inside the hull fitting and fixing the timbers shouting and verbally abusing the exhausted apprentices for not running the timbers fast enough or their not being hot enough to bend. The fitted timbers were then copper fastened through the top four and bottom four strakes, prior to the fitting and fixing the subsequent planking and the shutter strake.

The planking operation consisted of the cutting to shape in the Mill individual mahogany planks, each approximately one-inch by six-inches. These were then brought into the workshop to be finished by eye and a caulking seam was cut on the top outside edge, forming a wedge-shaped slot when the plank was fitted against the bottom of an adjacent square edged plank. This facilitated caulking when the build was complete. Each strake was then fitted in position, nail holes drilled and countersunk and the plank fastened into place with copper nails driven through into the individual vertical oak timbers.

With the hull planking complete and the shutter fitted it was time for caulking. Apprentices were tasked with spinning the many balls of caulking cotton required, not too tight or too loose.

If found to be incorrect the likelihood was the ball would be thrown with great force at the unfortunate apprentice along with a succession of curses. The spun cotton was caulked in shallow loops along the caulking seam before being hammered tight and hard into the seam. This was a laborious job using a selection of special caulking irons and a heavy long handled hardwood mallet.

An experienced 'caulker' could tell by the sound the mallet made when the cotton had been driven in correctly. To caulk a whole hull usually took two days for two men to complete.

The hull now had to be fully secured by 'clenching' the exposed ends of the copper nails protruding through the timbers. A 'rove', a small copper concave washer, was fitted over the copper nail end with a steel rove punch. The nail end was cut off leaving approximately one quarter of an inch of the copper nail protruding. Using the ball part of a ball pein hammer, the exposed nail end was then 'clenched' by being hit with fast and successive blows to draw up the nail tight into the nail hole. The excess soft copper was then flattened with the flat part of the hammer. To stop the copper nail from being forced back out of the plank on the outside, a 'dolly', a heavy piece of pig iron with a pin protruding from one end, was placed on the nail head, held there by a luckless apprentice pushing his whole body weight against it. This was no mean feat given the shape of the hull and the contorted posture that had to be adopted, especially when clenching the underside of the hull.

This operation would last two or three days. As may be imagined, with two or three 'clenchers' inside the hull and their 'dolly hangers' on the outside, the noise of the hammering was pretty intolerable. The apprentices were invariably exposed to cussing and invective hurled if they lost track of which nail they were supposed to be on, did not hold on tight enough or, as sometimes happened to keep an apprentice awake, the clencher would deliver a really heavy hammer blow designed to knock him off the nail or off his stance.

'Finishing' the hull required various tools to fashion the irregular planked shape of the hull into a smoothly contoured and symmetrical surface. A great deal of trouble was taken over this before the 'stopping' and priming process could be carried out. The thousands of nail holes and the caulked seams had to be stopped with linseed oil putty, which was a relaxing job allowing conversation and banter between the apprentices, whose job this was. When the stopping was dry a coat of primer was applied to the whole hull.

To complete the hull, heavy internal spruce stringers and gunnels were fitted, oak deck beams were constructed and fitted, shroud plates bolted in place and a tongue and groove softwood deck constructed, finished and overlaid with canvas.

In order to make space for the next keel to be laid the hull was now moved from its initial position across the workshop and turned through 90 degrees with the sternpost facing the workshop door ready for fitting out. This was done by manpower alone, using wood blocks and iron shod wooden levers. The boat was lifted from its two-foot high blocks by rocking and levering onto a succession of higher blocks until it was high enough for the cradle to be wheeled underneath. The hull was then lowered onto this and made fast.

'Fitting out' involved building and fitting the cockpit, the cabin tops, tabernacle and deck fittings, rubbing strakes, foot rails and stanchion sockets, plus all interior furniture including the galley and 'heads' complete with inlet and outlet valves. Engine beds and the engine were fitted as were the water and fuel tanks, the rudder mechanism, sacrificial anodes and any other equipment as per the owner's individual specification. A 'boot top' was cut in for the waterline and the initial hull painting undertaken. The cockpit, cabin tops, rubbing strakes, footrail and the mast and boom received initial coats of varnish. With fitting out complete the hull was moved out of the workshop on to the slipway, ready for launching.

With the workshop doors open, and any passing traffic halted, the boat was wheeled out into Rope Walk, turned ninety degrees along Rope Walk and then a further ninety degrees into a narrow alleyway where with the aid of manpower and blocks and tackles the boat was hauled up the alleyway, guided by men with levers on either side. At the top of the alleyway a further turn was made then after some twenty-five yards there was a final ninety degree turn which found the boat parallel with the slipway to await the final hull painting and anti-fouling.

At high tide the boat was floated off the cradle and moored securely in the slipway for lifting in the mast. This operation needed as many hands as possible to manhandle the mast onto the boat and secure its foot in the tabernacle. Then with the aid of a hoist and additional manpower the mast was lifted to the vertical and the shrouds and stays were fitted.

Owners, prior to taking final delivery, usually made some gesture to the men and apprentices who had built his boat. One memorable owner who visited the yard on a regular basis to check the build progress had a chain of bakery retail outlets and on every visit provided a large selection of cakes, buns and pastries. When his boat was completed an extra-large consignment of 'goodies' was laid on for us and was much appreciated.

*   *   *

Whilst work in the Bottom Shop was physically hard there were occasional relaxing diversions. Often during the summer months, repair work afloat was required at the various moorings along the river. On a hot day it was possible to slip over the side for a swim when no one was watching. Masts sometimes had to be lowered and removed from a boat moored on the opposite side of the river at the town quay. This necessitated transferring the mast across the old swing bridge. Being single carriageway, it was controlled by traffic lights and with a two wheeled cart taking the weight of the mast and three or four of us to push we were obliged to run it across as fast as possible in the face of the honking queue of impatient traffic behind. Work sometimes had to be carried out on boats moored in one of the mud berths that belonged to the yard further along Rope Walk. There they sat safely in the mud at low water. Work below the water line, usually the lot of an unlucky apprentice, could only be accessed by a makeshift platform laid on the mud which invariably gently sank into the mud.

During the early years of my apprenticeship David Hillyard died and the yard was shut for the day to enable the workforce to attend the funeral. Predictably it was a cold and exceeding wet day with a howling wind as we all stood around the grave trying to look suitably grief stricken. This was difficult since only very few of us had ever been addressed by him, let alone had a conversation with him. In the pub afterwards the conversation was limited to the cost and quality of the timber used for his coffin.

Some will recall the Big Freeze in the bitter winter of 1962/63, the coldest in living memory. The snow lasted from Boxing Day until well into March. On parts of the coast the sea froze over and in Littlehampton the river froze right across. To emphasize how cold our working conditions were that year, we cut a large block of ice from the slipway, bored a hole and suspended it from a beam in the workshop, where it didn't melt until the end of March.

I must refer to one more character who was employed in the yard as a general labourer. Stan was ancient, well into his sixties. He was short and bent in a permanent stoop and wore an oversize bib and brace overalls and a greasy flat cap. A permanent 'fag' protruded from the corner of his always smiling and unshaven mouth. He had clearly had a hard life but with his natural good humour he would regale anyone who would listen with a wealth of tall stories.

When timbering, it was Stan who fired the kiln boiler, kept it red hot and the water almost at boiling point. It was he who gave us apprentices who were running timbers a kindly word when he knew we were being verbally abused. Stan always 'officiated' when the yard cesspit was being emptied. He and the tanker driver could be seen peering into the manhole keeping a check on the extraction process, whilst happily eating their lunchtime sandwiches.

*   *   *

I was at Hillyard's from 1961 to about 1967/8 when I left to pick up additional experience with the then new GRP or Fibreglass construction. Realising after a year or so that my skills were wasted on 'plastic boats', I returned to the fold with time at Watercraft in Shoreham, Burne's Shipyard in Bosham, and at yards in Itchenor and Dell Quay. I spent eighteen months self-employed as a jobbing boatbuilder all around Chichester harbour, before finally fetching up at Camper & Nicholson in Gosport, where I spent a year working on a 1920's J class yacht named the *Allie Blanche*. I left the trade after that because the wages were so low and I went on to 'seek my fortune' in other areas.

Now pushing seventy years of age, I have written about my time at Hillyard's, how I learnt my trade, the conditions under which we worked and above all about the marvellous characters employed in the yard at that time. I am glad that the Hillyard Owners are keeping these boats afloat and pleased that amongst them there are a good few 9-tonners on which I worked.

ACKNOWLEDGEMENTS

First and foremost, I must thank Dr John Balchin for allowing me free use of his original work, without which it would have been almost impossible to write this book today. His research, undertaken nearly twenty years ago, has proved invaluable; much important information would have been lost forever without Dr Balchin's efforts.

My thanks go to Dick Wynne of Lodestar Books for making the book happen, and to the officers and members, past and present, of the Hillyard Owners Association for their help in its writing; for their enthusiasm throughout the project; and for putting up with my persistent requests for information, photographs or copies of documents and papers from the Hillyard archives. In particular, I must thank the Commodore, Steve Tiffin and his wife, Liz, who uncomplainingly took on the unenviable task of scanning the whole of Dr Balchin's original book, much old Hillyard sales literature, and almost every Hillyard newsletter from 1978 onwards. Thanks also to David Stickland, Keith Tullett, Doug Coulson, Guy Smith, Steve Long, and yacht surveyor John Lilley, who seems to know the full history, and structural condition, of virtually every Hillyard ever built! And, of course, to Professor Ted Evans for conveying to me his encyclopaedic knowledge of Arthur Ransome's involvement with Hillyards. Thanks to Chris Barnes for his permission to reproduce his tale of his time at the Hillyard yard, 'An Apprentice's Story'.

All thanks to the Association of Yachting Historians (of which organisation I am a member) for their marvellous work in digitizing every single edition of Lloyd's Register of Yachts from 1878 to 1980, whose contents are now instantly retrievable from a tiny and elegant memory stick. This has been a wonderful and essential research tool in writing this book.

I must also thank John Lambton and Nicholas Charman for their knowledge of the later years of the shipyard, Peter and Richard Gregson of Wooden Ships, David Dillistone for reading my text and pointing out various nautical howlers, Bob Brinton who has the unnerving ability to recall the names of a large number of Hillyards from many old and indistinct photos, Steve and Antony Parish of Ramsgate Marine, Robert Holden, Joost Meulenbroek and others at the Nevil Shute Norway Foundation for information on *Runagate*, the Association of Dunkirk Little Ships, the Royal Cruising Club, Anne Hammick and John Maddox of the Ocean Cruising Club, the staff at the Littlehampton Museum, Simon Winter, Clare Allcard, Bob Comlay, Chris Waddington, Henrietta Barnes, Katy Stickland (*Yachting Monthly*), and Mark Ansell of SPC Design & Print in Sandwich (for retrieving Dr Balchin's original manuscript from an old DVD in an obsolete format).

Finally, my thanks, as always, to my wife Josephine, who since I started writing books has had to become an expert researcher, editor and proofreader, which duties she carries out with unfailing enthusiasm.

BIBLIOGRAPHY

Barton, Humphrey, *Atlantic Adventurers*, Adlard Coles, 1953

Brann, Christopher, *The Little Ships of Dunkirk*, Collectors Books, 1989

Brice, M.H., *WW2 Landing Craft*, ISO Publications, 1989

Butler, Nicholas, *The Story of Wivenhoe*, Quentin Press, 1985

Chambers, Roland, *The Last Englishman*, Faber and Faber, 2009

Chapelle, Howard, *Boatbuilding*, W W Norton, 1941

Clark, Victor, *On the Wind of a Dream*, Hutchinson, 1960

Clark, Victor, *Triumph and Disaster*, Parapress, 1994

Coles, Adlard, *Close Hauled*, Seeley, 1926

Drummond , Maldwin, *The Riddle*, Nautical Publishing Co., 1985

Dumas, Vito, *Alone through the Roaring Forties*, Adlard Coles, 1960

Elleray, D. Robert, *Littlehampton, a Pictorial History*, Phillimore Press, 1991

Finnis, Bill, *The Passage Maker's Manual*, Waterline Books, 1993

Graham, R.D., *Rough Passage*, Granada Publishing, 1984

Griffiths, Maurice, *Post War Yachting*, Hutchinson, 1946

Griffiths, Maurice, *Little Ships and Shoal Waters*, Conway Maritime Press, 1972

Griffiths, Maurice, *Sixty Years a Yacht Designer*, Conway Maritime Press, 1988

Hammett, Brian, (Ed) *Racundra's Third Cruise*, Fernhurst Books 2002

Harrison Butler, T., *Cruising Yachts*, Lodestar Books, 2015.

Heaton, Peter, *Cruising*, Nicholas Kaye, 1958

Hiscock, Eric, *Cruising Under Sail*, Oxford University Press, 1950

Hiscock, Eris, *Voyaging Under Sail*, Oxford University Press, 1959

Jones, Iris, *Wartime Littlehampton*, Arun District Council, 1989

Jurd K.H.C., *Yacht Construction*, Adlard Coles, 1977

Kemp, Dixon, *A Manual of Yacht and Boat Sailing*, Horace Cox, 1891

Lambert, J. & Ross, A., *Allied Coastal Forces of World War II*,
    Conway Maritime Press, 1990

Leather, John, *Albert Strange*, Lodestar Books, 2015

Leather, John, *The Northseamen*, Terence Dalton, 1971

Leather, Margaret, *Saltwater Village*, Terence Dalton, 1977

Lee, Adrian & Philpott, Ruby, *Laurent Giles: An Evolution of Yacht Design*,
    Nautical Publishing Co., 1990

Lenton, H.T. & Coledge, J.J., *Warships of World War II*, Ian Allen, 1973

Lloyds Register Group, *The Complete Lloyd's Register of Yachts*,
    The Association of Yachting Historians, 2016

Mulville, Frank, *Terschelling Sands*, Adlard Coles, 1987

Mulville, Frank, *In Granma's Wake*, Seafarer Books, 1970

Mulville, Frank, *Schooner Integrity*, Seafarer Books, 1979

Mulville, Frank, *Dear Dolphin*, Ashford Buchan & Enright, 1991

Mulville, Frank, *Rescue and Recovery*, Seafarer Books, 1997

Ransome, Arthur, *Racundra's First Cruise*, Jonathan Cape, 1948

Ransome, Arthur, *We Didn't Mean to Go to Sea*, Jonathan Cape, 1983

Robinson, K, Lt. Col., *Islands of Blue Water*, Adlard Coles, 1968

Robinson, K, Lt. Col., *Islands Ahead*, Robert Hale, 1972

Rushworth-Lund, A., *By Way of the Golden Isles*, Chapman & Hall, 1972

Scott Hughes, John, *Macpherson's Voyages*, Methuen & Co, 1944

Sharp, Nigel, *Troubled Waters – Leisure Boating and the Second World War*,
    Amberley Publishing, 2015

Shute, Nevil, *Marazan*, Cassell, 1926

Shute Nevil, *Stephen Morris & Pilotage*, William Heinemann, 1961

Shute, Nevil, *Slide Rule*, William Heinemann, 1954

Shue, Nevil, *The Seafarers*, Paper Tiger, 2002

Shute, Nevil, *Trustee from the Tool Room*, Vintage Classics, 2009

Shute, Nevil, *What Happened to the Corbetts*, Pan Macmillan, 1970

Wardale, Roger, *Arthur Ransome under Sail*, Sigma Leisure, 2010

Watts, C.J., *Practical Yacht Construction*, Adlard Coles, 1957

Watts, W.J.L., *Little Ship Charters*, Published by the author, 1930

Whitaker, Ray, *Two and a Half Ton Dream*, Herbert Jenkins, 1959

Willis, Peter, *Good Little Ship*, Lodestar Books, 2017

Winter, L.B., *We Who Adventure*, Oxford University Press, 1956

Winter, L.B., *Nor They Understand*, The Jacandra Press (Brisbane), 1966

In addition to UK magazines for the cruising sailor
    (*Classic Boat, Yachting Monthly, Yachting World, Practical Boat Owner*):

The Marine Quarterly

The Yachtsman (no longer published)

The Hillyarder, the journal of the Hillyard Owners Association

Flying Fish, the journal of the Ocean Cruising Club

The Littlehampton Gazette

INDEX